REA

S0-BKV-612

S
GUIDE TO
EDUCATIONAL

THE PARENT'S GUIDE TO EDUCATIONAL SOFTWARE

A handbook to help you choose the best computer software for your child—preschool through high school. Reviews software in all major subjects—reading, writing, reasoning, and math—for all popular personal computers.

Marion Blank, Ph.D.

Laura Berlin, Ph.D.

A Tempus Book

PUBLISHED BY
Tempus Books of Microsoft Press
A Division of Microsoft Corporation
One Microsoft Way
Redmond, Washington 98052-6399

Library of Congress Cataloging-in-Publication Data

Blank, Marion.
    The parent's guide to educational software / Marion Blank, Laura
Berlin.
        p.   cm.
    Includes bibliographical references and index.
    ISBN 1-55615-317-1
    1. Education--United States--Computer programs--Reviews.
I. Berlin, Laura J.   II. Title.
LB1028.68.B58   1991
016.3713'345360296--dc20   91-21723
                                                                   CIP

Printed and bound in the United States of America.

1 2 3 4 5 6 7 8 9   RDRD   3 2 1 0 9

Distributed to the book trade in Canada by Macmillan of Canada, a division of
Canada Publishing Corporation.

Distributed to the book trade outside the United States and Canada by Penguin
Books Ltd.

Penguin Books Ltd., Harmondsworth, Middlesex, England
Penguin Books Australia Ltd., Ringwood, Victoria, Australia
Penguin Books N.Z. Ltd., 182-190 Wairau Road, Auckland 10, New Zealand

British Cataloging-in-Publication Data available.

Tempus® is a registered trademark and the Tempus Books logo is a trademark of
Microsoft Corporation. Tempus Books is an imprint of Microsoft Press.

Apple®, Apple IIGS®, and Macintosh® are registered trademarks of Apple Computer,
Inc. Commodore® is a registered trademark of Commodore Business Machines, Inc.
IBM® and PS/2® are registered trademarks of International Business Machines
Corporation. Microsoft® is a registered trademark and Microsoft QuickBasic™ is a
trademark of Microsoft Corporation. Tandy® is a registered trademark of Tandy
Corporation.

Acquisitions Editor: Dean Holmes
Developmental Editor: Erin O'Connor
Project Editor: Mary Ann Jones

To our fathers,
Morris D. Hersch and Howard B. Corwin,
men who led us always to see the excitement of new ideas
and so helped make this book possible.

CONTENTS

ABOUT THE AUTHORS

Marion Blank is an educational psychologist who earned a Ph.D. at Cambridge University in England. She has over 30 years' experience in developing language and learning programs for school-age children. Well known for her innovative work in linking assessment and treatment programs for children with academic difficulties, she currently serves as a consultant to over a dozen school districts in New York, New Jersey, and Connecticut as well as to Laureate Learning Systems, a company that designs educational software for individuals with learning disabilities. She lectures extensively, both in the United States and overseas, and has served as a consultant to government bureaus in the United States, Great Britain, The Netherlands, Australia, and Israel. The Software Publishers Association named *The Sentence Master,* a software program she designed for students with reading problems, the Best Special Needs Program of 1990.

Laura Berlin is a developmental psychologist who obtained a Ph.D. from the Albert Einstein College of Medicine at Yeshiva University in New York. She is licensed as a school psychologist and has over 20 years' clinical and research experience with both normal and learning-disabled children. With Marion Blank and Susan Rose, she developed the Preschool Language Assessment Instrument, a test of language abilities that is widely used in schools throughout the United States and other English-speaking countries.

Both authors are parents of children growing up in the new Information Age and so have a personal as well as a professional perspective on their subject.

ACKNOWLEDGMENTS

We are grateful to the following institutions, which helped us carry out our work: the Apple Lab and the Curriculum Lab of Central Connecticut State University, New Britain, Connecticut; the H.P. Kopplemann, Inc., Educational Resource Center, Hartford, Connecticut; Network for Action in Microcomputer Education, Wayne, New Jersey; and the Teachers College Library of Columbia University, New York. We also deeply appreciate the many colleagues who gave us their advice and support: Debra Beckman, Jay Cowen, John Cowen, Michael Costa, Dona Ostrander, Geoffrey Pickard, John Riccio, Rosemary Seitel, Missy Schweitzer, Alberta Tabak, and Jeanette Warner.

INTRODUCTION

Let us declare that—during the decade of the nineties—our goal will be to have all parents become full partners in the education of their children.

—Ernest L. Boyer, President
Carnegie Foundation for the
Advancement of Teaching

Most parents are deeply interested in their children's educations. That is almost certainly the reason you picked up this book. You want to give your child every advantage possible—an ambitious goal that includes guiding your child to the best in toys, books, TV programs and movies, sports, and other activities.

The responsibilities are substantial, but in most areas you have a big advantage: your own life experience. Through this experience, you've developed invaluable, near-intuitive guidelines that help you lead your child with knowledge and skill.

A NEW AREA

In one area, however, you can't rely on the "tried and true." Computer-based education is new! You probably had little or no experience in your own childhood with computer technology, and you're likely to feel at a loss when you try to determine how your child can best take advantage of it. At the same time, you recognize the learning potential computers offer, and you probably either own a home computer or are planning to buy one. According to U.S. government statistics, the number of computers in homes is soaring. At the start of the 1980s, there were fewer than one million, but by the end of the decade, the number had grown to over 20 million.

For the most part, your child probably uses the computer for playing games. It's easy to understand why. Computer games are phenomenally attractive, and many of them are instructive as well. But the computer can do far more than entertain. By selecting the right range of programs, you can regularly and consistently bring much of the school curriculum to your child's fingertips—an opportunity that represents a dramatic change from what you could do in the past.

A NEW KIND OF INVOLVEMENT

Concerned parents have always tried to stay abreast of their children's schooling. They have long been active in organizations such as the PTA and in urging schools to offer the best to their children, but they have rarely been able to affect the teaching itself. Traditionally, instruction in "the three R's" was the near-exclusive province of the schools, and it took extraordinary effort for a parent to influence the teaching of the basic skills.

We can no longer afford to exclude parents from taking an active part in their children's school learning. Education in the United States is in serious trouble. Every time you pick up a newspaper or listen to the news, you're likely to encounter another story about the decline in educational achievement in our country. No one knows exactly what is responsible for this crisis. Government is blamed, schools are blamed, TV is blamed, our values and life-styles are blamed. In all the turmoil, one fact remains: *Children who succeed in school have parents who are committed to their education and who play an active role in guiding their learning.*

Becoming an active participant in your child's education doesn't mean that you must develop an adversarial relationship with his or her school. It is far more useful to think in terms of a partnership in which you support and extend your child's school curriculum. Educational software offers you a splendid opportunity to do just that.

The Educational Potential of the Computer

Thousands of software programs cover the skills and subjects your child is learning in school. When you choose the best of these programs, you have not only a teacher in your home but the designs of the best teachers. One good teacher's influence is no longer limited to the immediate classroom; it can now reach the great numbers of children who have access to computers. By making the right software choices, you can become an effective facilitator of your child's education.

Sorting out the right choices, however, is not easy. Currently you can choose from over 10,000 programs, covering almost every subject imaginable. And, as always, excellence is rare. If you're like most parents, you probably don't see this array of options as a pool of resources but as a mire of confusion. How do you even begin to identify "the best"? This book will help you get started.

Our goal is to provide you, as parent and educator, with a guide to what is currently best in educational software. To that end, we describe and rate over 200 top programs, many of which have won awards for excellence from major rating agencies in the United States.

The Guidelines for the Selections

In arriving at our final selections, we developed a set of guidelines that helped us focus on appropriate programs.

Quality. Quality, of course, was a first concern. We evaluated both the educational content and the software design of each program, and we devote an entire chapter to the criteria we used.

But we needed to distinguish further because your child will be using the software at home, not at school. The differences between the two settings are important.

Attractiveness. Schools have the power to get children to use a program even when the software might be less than appealing. At home, this approach simply won't work. Children—like adults—won't use their free time to work on projects that don't interest them. All the programs we describe in this book have proved attractive to children, as well as educational.

Scope. Some educational programs are designed to allow children to practice a small, restricted range of skills. Despite their narrow aims, these programs can be productive in a school setting because children usually use the programs there for only short periods. But narrowly focused programs are not good choices for your child's home use. He or she has to be able to use a program on a regular basis and still find it challenging. Our software selections include only programs varied and extensive enough that your child can use them over and over without quickly tiring of them.

Still, you're likely to find that some of the programs we suggest are ones your child already uses in school. This shouldn't pose a problem. Because computer time in school is limited, your child will rarely have a chance to practice for long on the school's software. Furthermore, many of the programs teach skills that require a great deal of practice. Repetition with these programs is all to the good.

Cost. The expense of building a software library isn't astronomical, but when you're buying a wide range of programs, the costs can add up. Therefore, we selected only programs priced under $100; most of them cost under $50. Our goal is to allow you to build up a good library at reasonable expense.

Appropriateness for learning-disabled children. Finally, as you are probably aware from the media coverage, a relatively large segment of our children—somewhere between 10 and 15 percent—have learning disabilities. These are children of normal intelligence who have difficulties in one or more specific learning areas such as visual processing, language, and organizational skills. Many of the programs we selected are useful to children with these sorts of disabilities. The software reviews indicate when this is the case. (It is beyond the scope of this book to review programs for children who have severe learning handicaps. Appendix A, however, suggests books and other resources that provide information for parents of these children.)

HOW THE BOOK IS ORGANIZED

A list of good programs is not, by itself, sufficient. Many parents are understandably unfamiliar with the educational role of the computer and the educational demands of the classroom. This book speaks to these overriding concerns as well. Our goal is to provide you with the information you need to feel comfortable in guiding your child through the world of educational software.

Chapter 1 presents a framework for understanding the educational uses of the computer. The framework will help you judge the teaching goals of the programs you'll be selecting for your child.

Chapter 2 describes some of the major curricular demands your child encounters in school and provides an overview of what schools expect your child to accomplish from preschool to about sixth grade. We chose to focus on the elementary grades because it is during this period in your child's development that he or she most needs your guidance. By the time your child is about 12 years of age, he or she will probably know which programs are most useful and will make choices independently.

Chapter 3 describes the criteria we used for judging the quality of the software programs. These criteria serve as the basis for the reviews you'll find in Chapter 4. We hope these criteria will also help you later, as you make your own selections from the welter of educational programs.

Chapter 4 provides a full review of each program we selected. Every program we review is of high quality, but even so, a particular program might not be appropriate for your child. The review helps you make this decision by detailing the curriculum area the program addresses, the kinds of skills and activities it requires of your child, and the features it has that will affect how you and your child use it. If your child is very young or has reading problems, for example, long text passages in a program will require that you be available to guide him or her — at least in the initial sessions. Knowing about such requirements will help you plan how to use the program. Of course, each review also provides important purchasing details — the program's publisher, the price, and the kind of computer and other equipment you need to run the program.

Chapter 5 suggests how you might set up an educational computer center in your home and talks about the ways in which you can help your child as he or she works with the programs. The chapter discusses such topics as the best place to put the computer, how to establish a routine, and how you can participate with your child in using the software.

Appendix A is an annotated list of suggested readings, and Appendix B is a directory of the names and addresses of the software publishers whose programs are reviewed in this book.

HOW TO USE THE BOOK

Books, by their nature, present information in sequence. But you needn't confine yourself to reading this book from cover to cover. As we wrote, we anticipated a variety of approaches to using the book. Each chapter builds on the previous chapter, but each chapter can also stand alone. Thus, although you might want to read the book straight through, you might also choose to focus on particular sections and simply scan others. We hope you'll see this book as a basic reference source you can consult in whatever way best suits your needs.

1 THAT MOST VERSATILE OF MACHINES

[The computer] can take on a thousand forms
and can serve a thousand functions, it can appeal
to a thousand tastes.

—Seymour Papert,
designer of Logo Math

Educational software is probably unfamiliar territory to you. Over time, this will change, and you'll become as comfortable in selecting software programs for your child as you are in selecting toys and books. In the meantime, we'll help you chart a course through this new terrain.

THE EDUCATIONAL ROLES OF THE COMPUTER

In his book *The Computer in the School* (Teachers College Press, New York, 1980), Robert Taylor identifies three major educational functions of the computer: tutor, tool, and tutee. These functions provide a useful framework for analyzing different types of software and for determining how your child can benefit from a program.

The computer as tutor is the computer in the role of teacher. In this role, the machine either teaches your child a new skill or strengthens a skill he or she has begun to acquire.

The computer as tool is the computer as an instrument. It helps your child carry out certain tasks. When serving in this role, the computer—much like a typewriter or calculator—helps your child accomplish a task he or she already knows how to do.

The computer as tutee is the machine in the role of student. Your child becomes the teacher who programs, or "teaches," the computer. The machine, if properly "taught," then uses the information for further interaction with your child.

Each of these uses of the computer is valuable to your child. You'll find programs that serve each function in Chapter 4. But right now, let's look more closely at the three functions and at the types of learning best served by each.

The Computer as Tutor

Anyone who has felt the excitement of conquering a new skill can testify that learning is fun. A baby learning to walk, a kindergartner learning to write, an adult learning to ski—these are only a few examples of experiences in which learning is a real joy.

Voluntary Learning vs. Imposed Learning

The enjoyment of learning, however, depends a great deal on whether the learning is voluntary. When you decide for yourself that you want to master a new subject of skill, learning is usually fun. But when learning is imposed, you're likely to feel more pain than gain. Then, because your goals are not self-initiated, learning can be boring.

Unfortunately, some imposed learning can't be avoided, and this is especially true of educating children. After all, you can't count on your child's having an innate desire to learn arithmetic tables or spelling lists. Thus, schools are in the unpleasant position of being the major institution for imposed learning in our society.

Imposed learning is unappealing not only because it is other-directed but also because much of it consists of mastering inherently

---

VOLUNTARY EQUALS DESIRABLE

In *The Adventures of Tom Sawyer,* Mark Twain's classic tale, Tom has to whitewash a fence. Naturally, he hates the job, but he convinces the children who are watching him that it's great fun. Soon they are vying with each other to have a turn with the brush. If, like Tom, they had been required to do the work, they would have resisted. But because they want to do it, whitewashing the fence is not a chore but a great opportunity.

boring details: punctuation rules, history dates, columns of addition and subtraction, and the like. Almost everybody—even a highly motivated student—finds some segments of the school day uninteresting.

The Need for Repetition

According to an old adage, "Practice makes perfect." And for many skills, repetition *is* essential for mastery. If your child is to learn such skills as spelling, grammar, and counting well enough for them to be useful, he or she has to practice them over and over again.

So learning some skills has a second disadvantage. Not only does the learning involve tedious details, it also requires lots of practice. The boring learning that no child would elect to do is precisely the learning that must be practiced over and over, at least for awhile. The practice is necessary so that your child can reach the point at which he or she can perform the skill without conscious thought or control. This unthinking but capable execution of a skill is called *automaticity*.

Automaticity is the antithesis of thought, and, as a result, the skills learned through drill and practice are not accorded a high position in the hierarchy of mental talents. We are much more likely to value skills such as reasoning. Nevertheless, because automaticity is vital to everyday competence, it offers your child a double advantage: Once automated, the skill is ready to be used at a moment's notice. At the same time, it demands almost no attention, so your child is free to think about more important, or more satisfying, matters.

Transforming the Boredom

Drill and practice is one learning activity in which the computer can effect its magic. As you've probably already seen, your child views the computer as a source of fun-filled games. When drill-and-practice activities are embedded within motivating game formats, these activities are transformed. The seemingly endless practice goes on as it must, but its unattractive aspects recede into the background because your child is focusing on finding hidden information, getting a high score, and responding as quickly as possible. If he or she notices the practice at all, it is only as an activity necessary for getting the game to work. Even the most tedious tasks become fun when the program designers have done their job well.

Drill-and-practice activities are no more fun for the teacher than they are for your child. A teacher needs almost inhuman patience to keep presenting the same tasks without showing signs of boredom or annoyance. For the computer, of course, inhuman patience is a given. Computers can offer the endless repetition learners need without showing the least sign of of these negative reactions. They always provide supportive, upbeat responses, such as the one in Figure 1-1. They couldn't yawn or snap at your child if they "wanted" to.

Most drill-and-practice programs simply strengthen or reinforce a skill your child has begun to acquire in the classroom. Others, however, not only offer practice but also teach one or more skills from scratch. This is an important distinction, and the reviews in Chapter 4 indicate whether a drill-and-practice program teaches as well as offers practice.

If your child spends a great deal of time with these programs, don't be concerned. In general, the more practice, the better. The more time your child spends on these activities, the greater the likelihood of smooth mastery.

In summary, the computer as tutor is the computer teaching or reinforcing skills best learned through drill and practice. Interacting with the computer when it is serving as a tutor is generally easy. Your child needs to know little about the inner workings of the programs.

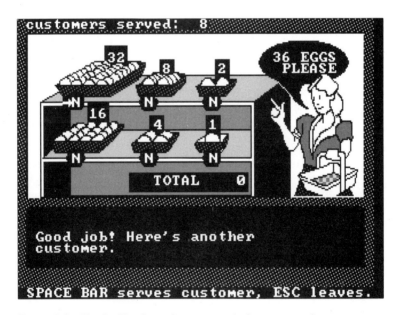

Figure 1-1. *The feedback on the screen reinforces a previous success as the program presents a new problem.*

They are designed to accommodate him or her. Tots, even at 2 or 3, can handle these kinds of programs.

The Computer as Tool

The computer as tutor overcomes the boredom that characterizes many educational tasks. The computer as tool solves quite a different problem—that of relevance.

Parents and others frequently complain to schools that their teaching is not relevant, that schools require children to learn too many skills and facts that appear to have little or no meaning in their daily lives.

The Problem of Relevance

Relevance in education is a fairly new concern. Until the last century, most teaching took place directly in the work setting. Learning was based on the apprenticeship system, a system of "learning while doing" in which youngsters worked next to the masters who trained them. The "pupils" could easily relate the skills they were learning to the skills they would need when they reached adulthood. The issue of relevance was irrelevant. It never came up.

The introduction of public education dramatically changed the situation. Schools teach skills years before they are actually going to be used in adult life. A child must take a relatively long view to be willing to learn subjects that might not be useful for years to come. Delay of this sort is not particularly compatible with childhood in general, and it is even less compatible with the "now" life-style of modern America.

One reason schools haven't been able to put learning in real-life contexts is that the available technology has limited their options. One clear example is in the teaching of writing, a multistage process that requires a variety of skills. For many years, the only tools schools could offer children were paper and pencils. With these tools, writing is certainly possible, but it is not easy to complete all the stages and create a finished product. In addition, children's encounters with books, magazines, and newspapers tell them what "real" writing looks like; no matter how hard they try, their efforts with paper and pencil don't produce a resemblance.

Word processing programs eliminate many of these obstacles. Seymour Papert, an expert in the use of computers in education, describes the change in his book *Mindstorms* (Basic Books, New York,

1980). Papert captures both the problems besetting students before the advent of word processing and the profound changes that have resulted from the introduction of word processing technology.

> *Writing means making a rough draft and refining it over a considerable period of time. [The image of writing] includes the expectation of an "unacceptable" first draft that will develop with successive editing into presentable form. But I would not be able to afford this image if I were a third grader. The physical act of writing would be slow and laborious....For most children rewriting a text is so laborious that the first draft is the final copy, and the skill of rereading with a critical eye is never acquired. This changes dramatically when children have access to computers capable of manipulating text. The first draft is composed at the keyboard. Corrections are made easily. The current copy is always neat and tidy....Even more dramatic changes are seen when the child has physical handicaps that make writing by hand more than usually difficult or even impossible....The computer as writing instrument offers children an opportunity to become more like adults, indeed like advanced professionals, in their relationship to their intellectual products and to themselves.*

Abundant evidence points to the positive effects of word processing on children's writing, even at the earliest stages. One study of the primary grades notes that children using a word processing program are far more willing to continue working on a piece when, without a word processor, they might have given up. Their compositions become longer and more detailed, and they understand that their efforts can be refined and polished over time. There is also a major change in their attitude towards writing. They are thrilled with the appearance of the finished products. As children become more skilled, they can explore desktop publishing, with which they can create professional-looking publications, such as newspapers with banners and illustrations.

Using a computer as a tool for word processing is very different from using one for drill and practice. As a tool, the computer allows your child to carry out a full-fledged, meaningful activity. The computer's power is so great that many educational leaders are once again talking of education as a process of learning while doing. The computer has the potential to restore the relevance that the apprenticeship system provided.

Extending the Uses

Proficiency in using the computer as a tool is what educators mean when they speak of "computer literacy." A computer-literate person is one who is skilled in using the computer as an instrument for carrying out a wide range of tasks. Indeed, using the computer as a tool works for almost any creative enterprise that might interest your child. There are programs now that allow children to compose music and create graphics. Others allow them to create crossword puzzles. Still others let children use databases to seek and retrieve information in a variety of areas. Your child can pursue almost any activity that lends itself to computer technology.

The computer as tool doesn't eliminate the work your child must do. But by taking over some of the more tedious activities, such as handwriting, and by easing other tasks, such as making corrections, the computer frees your child for the more intellectual, more creative, and more meaningful aspects of the tasks he or she undertakes.

Almost certainly, this development will transform the curriculum. Helping your child to become adept in using the computer as a tool is one of the best ways to prepare him or her for the changes in store—not only in school, but throughout life.

The Computer as Tutee

The computer, in its tutor and tool functions, can deal with the problems of boredom and relevance. In its role as tutee, it has the power to address another problem—one it has helped to create: vast quantities of data, which can result in information overload.

The Need for Focus

In this age of information, the key to success is not to produce or retrieve more information, but to be able to sift out what is important or relevant and reason about it more astutely. From an intellectual point of view, controlling and shaping information is demanding. From a motivational point of view, it isn't. When the computer is functioning as a tutee, it gives your child access to an intellectual genie that will do his or her bidding—a highly compelling prospect!

Model building. You can see the process at work in simulation adventure games. In these games, your child has to create a model, or plan, that will enable him or her to meet whatever challenge the program presents. For example, a program might ask your child to plan a trip through the unexplored territory of the American West in the 1800s, re-creating experiences like those the pioneers faced.

Your child can handle this sort of program effectively only by integrating a range of skills: recalling facts, doing research, predicting consequences, ordering priorities, and so on. He or she might have to anticipate obstacles, such as weather and terrain, and analyze the best use of money, supplies, and other available resources. After juggling these factors and weighing alternative plans, he or she must then choose the best approach. But each decision your child makes can affect the direction the game takes, and thus the plan will evolve as the game progresses.

Essentially, the computer as tutee presents your child with a situation in which the content is created as the interaction proceeds. Your child leaves behind the narrow black-and-white world of single correct answers and encounters a range of options as different patterns emerge, depending on the information that your child chooses to offer, or teach, the computer.

Programming. As he or she becomes more adept at using the computer in its role as tutee, your child might become interested in programming. Programming requires learning one or more languages, such as Logo, Pascal, or Basic, that are meaningful to the computer. After acquiring this direct means of communication with the computer, your child can do more than simply interact with an established program; he or she can instruct the computer itself by writing programs that will perform specific tasks. For example, your child might program the computer to create a game or track sports statistics.

A Wide-Open Field

The use of the computer as tutee is one of the most exciting—and controversial—aspects of education. Exactly what constitutes thinking, reasoning, and problem-solving skills and precisely what role the computer can play in fostering them are widely debated.

Fortunately, the debate needn't delay your child's progress. The computer as tutee gives your child the freedom to "play around" with ideas. Because this experience is so appealing, he or she is likely to be attracted to a wide variety of programs that serve this function, and most of what you can offer is likely to be useful. If your child indicates an interest in a particular sphere, you have every reason to cater to it. Indulging your child's intellectual curiosity can only produce the best of results.

THE NEXT STEP

As you've seen, the different roles of the computer lend themselves to different aspects of the curriculum. The tutor function fits with drill-and-practice needs in nearly all subjects; the tool function facilitates writing and other processes, such as information gathering and organizing; and the tutee function supports higher-level skills, such as reasoning and problem solving. But to get the most out of educational software, you need to know more about the specifics of the curriculum your child faces in school. In the next chapter, we'll explore these demands.

2 THE SCHOOL CURRICULUM

*The powers not delegated to the United States
by the Constitution, nor prohibited by it to the
States, are reserved to the States respectively.*

—Article 10
United States Constitution

You're probably wondering why a chapter on the school curriculum opens with a quotation from the Constitution. It might seem far afield, but Article 10 is central to what your child is studying in the classroom.

Article 10 grants states the right to act in all matters except those the Constitution specifically reserves to the federal government or forbids the states. One such matter is education. Thanks to Article 10, each of the 50 states can, and does, operate its own independent educational system.

If you've moved around the country at all, you have experienced firsthand the various school practices, standards, and options offered by different states. Because of Article 10

- Some states mandate kindergarten programs, and others do not.

- Some states require standardized achievement tests at various grades, and others do not.

- Some states teach the metric system of measurement, and others do not.

- Some states demand that children learn a foreign language beginning in the first grade, and others do not.

In contrast to many other countries, the United States does not require a standardized set of subjects for the entire nation. In brief, there is no single school curriculum. There is, however, a core set of skills that even the most vehement supporters of diversity agree are vital. These skills are the ones deemed essential to functioning in a modern, literate society.

THE FOUR R'S OF LEARNING

Howard Gardner, a Harvard University–based psychologist and an advocate of diversity, referred to this core set of skills when he acknowledged that "the basic literacies of reading, writing, and calculating [ought to] constitute a primary agenda of the elementary grades."

This agenda is, of course, the familiar "three R's"—reading, writing, and arithmetic. (In the Age of Future Shock, it is comforting to find that some things do not change.) This three-R agenda serves as the framework for the software selections in Chapter 4.

However, the programs reviewed in Chapter 4 go beyond the three R's in one major area: higher-level thinking skills. Parents have long been calling for schools to provide more than the basics. They want schools to teach the three R's, but they also want them to teach the skills that will help children become independent and creative thinkers.

Many schools have responded to the call for higher-level skills by incorporating thinking and problem-solving programs into the existing curriculum. As we head into the twenty-first century, then, the core school curriculum is made up of four, rather than three, R's: reading, writing, arithmetic, and *reasoning*. Consequently, our software selections encompass reasoning skills as well as the basics.

In this chapter, we'll describe key phases of learning in the four R's. Our goal is to help you understand the skills the school requires your child to learn in the four major curriculum areas and to point out the ways in which educational software can enhance your child's achievements in the classroom.

Along with the discussion of each curriculum area, you'll find a chart summarizing the skills in that area. For example, in the section on reading, the chart lists skills such as *rhyming words* and *blending clusters of letters into sounds*. These are the skills that the school expects your child to master. Each review in Chapter 4 contains a Curriculum Areas section that describes, in phrases such as these, the specific skills the program covers. This information will help you determine whether the program might be useful to your child.

We suggest you use this chapter as a reference source that you can consult at different points for help in selecting the software that best fits your child's needs at the moment. You might find it most useful to start with the curriculum area that is of greatest immediate interest to you and your child and read about the other areas as the need arises.

THE FIRST R: READING

It's almost impossible to overstate the importance of effective reading. Reading is the key to academic success in all other areas of the school curriculum. As your child moves through the grades, he or she must learn more and more material by means of reading. Even the number-based world of mathematics relies heavily on word problems—problems that your child must be able to read in order to solve. The ability to read with speed and comprehension is essential if your child is to progress not only in English but in all the other key subjects—social studies, science, and math.

Perhaps you are among the parents and educators who worry that the computer will cause a decline in literacy. Although it is almost certain that literacy will take on different meanings as the information revolution proceeds, change of this sort is not unusual. Technology clearly has powerful effects on our language, on our methods of communication, and on our way of life. For example, after the telephone was introduced, the personal letter was doomed. But change should not necessarily be equated with loss.

The computer age hasn't altered the need for skills in reading. Although what our children read and how they read might change, literacy will continue to play a central role in their lives. If anything, the coming age is one in which the demand for literacy will be intensified.

A Complex, Evolving Process

If your child is well prepared in reading, he or she will adapt to any changes the future holds in store. The key to his or her success is to establish as strong a reading base as possible. This takes time. Like most complex skills, reading skill develops slowly over the course of your child's schooling. Reading begins well before your child ever sees a classroom. In everyday life, your child has a range of experiences that foster reading skills—experiences such as listening to bedtime stories; noticing signs on shops, which then become familiar markers; or seeing written notes posted on a refrigerator. Through these experiences, your child develops readiness skills that are important first steps in the process of becoming literate.

After your child is in school, he or she learns to read in three major stages:

- In the first stage, sometimes called *cracking the code,* your child learns to associate letters with words and to see how letters form words.

- In the second stage, your child consolidates what he or she has learned and becomes adept at using the skills.

- In the third stage, your child makes a major transition. Instead of learning to read, your child reads to learn.

The Initial Stage

Each of the three stages can be broken down into two overarching processes that your child has to master: *decoding,* in which your child translates the visual cues of letters and spaces into words; and *comprehension,* in which your child combines the words and understands their meaning.

Decoding: Learning About Print

In the initial stage, which takes place in kindergarten and first grade, the focus is on decoding. The teacher puts great effort into teaching the conventions, or rules, of written language.

For a start, your child must learn the letters of the alphabet and the sounds that the letters represent. You'll often see this referred to as *sound-symbol correspondence.*

Software programs offer definite advantages in helping your child link letters with sounds and words. Because paper and pencil are silent, your child can fill reams of paper with letters without realizing that the letters create words—words that he or she already knows in spoken language. The computer, with its ability to synthesize speech, is ideal for helping your child understand the relationship between letters and their sounds and words, and an increasing number of reading programs take advantage of this capability.

Your child encounters other obstacles in the decoding process. As a skilled reader, you probably take the process for granted and have stopped noticing the unique demands that reading places on our way of interpreting the visual world. But your child must "relearn" some of the earliest and most fundamental visual skills he or she has developed, such as recognizing objects. In learning to recognize objects, your child also learns not to be distracted by changes in an object's direction or position. A cup remains a cup whether it is turned to the right or the left, or whether it is upside down or right side up. Indeed, everyday experiences have taught your child that such changes are not only inconsequential, they are irrelevant, and he or she is not led astray by them.

What your child has learned about the everyday visual world, however, must be put aside when he or she approaches the world of print. In identifying letters and words, your child can no longer ignore direction. On the printed page, depending on how it is placed, a letter can be a *b*, a *d*, a *p*, or a *q*. What was previously unimportant is now critical.

The issue becomes even more complex when your child has to deal with words, not simply letters. In word pairs such as *o-n* and *n-o*, *p-a-t* and *t-a-p*, *n-o-w* and *w-o-n*, each pair shares identical elements. To your child's way of thinking, that should make them the same. But with words, of course, the sequence of the letters matters.

When your child fails to take note of this newly important difference, he or she is likely to read or write a word in reverse. One frequent example is a child's decoding the word *was* as *saw*.

Reversals have received a great deal of attention in the press as signs of potential reading problems. Nevertheless, occasional misperceptions of this sort are not signs of abnormal learning. They are simply an indication that your child is interpreting print in the same way he or she has learned to interpret concrete objects. Quite reasonably, your child is applying the "tried and true" until he or she realizes that new methods are called for.

Your child encounters similar complications with respect to spacing. In ordinary experience, the distance between objects rarely affects how they are identified. A chair and a table can be close or far apart; they remain the objects they always were. But look what happens with words. *Top it* is not at all the same as *to pit*. A simple difference in spacing changes not only the sounds of the words but their meaning as well.

Good early reading programs address decoding problems by making your child sensitive to the visual rules about direction, sequence, and spacing that govern written language and by providing practice in applying the "new" rules to the world of print. Many decoding programs start at the prekindergarten level, so your child can use them by the time he or she is 3 to 4 years old. The majority, however, are designed for use when your child is in kindergarten and first grade.

Comprehension: Relying on the Spoken Word

Your child's limited decoding abilities mean that at the start of the process, he or she will work with text that has very simple messages. The following is an example:

> *Tab is a sad cat.*
> *Tab has a pal.*
> *His pal is Mac.*
> *Mac is a rat.*
>
> — B. W. Makar, *Primary Phonics*
> (Educators Publishing Service,
> Cambridge, Massachusetts, 1977)

It's easy to see why beginning texts are like this. At this stage, your child could not decode more complex written language. On the other hand, your child has been a sophisticated speaker for a long time—long before he or she has had to decipher language in print. Thus, in early reading, there is a split between decoding and comprehension. The language your child first learns to decode is far simpler than the language he or she actually uses and understands.

Although the split is unavoidable, you should not let it impede your child's progress in acquiring further language skills. A rich language base is critical to his or her eventual proficiency in reading. If your child has good spoken-language skills, he or she is likely to read well. Consequently, you need to continue encouraging your child's progress in understanding and using language.

The texts your child is learning to decode won't be of much help in that effort. The near–baby-talk language your child is learning to decode can't provide messages that challenge his or her comprehension of language. You must rely on means other than school primers. Principally, your child needs to speak with and listen to adults.

One of the most enjoyable ways to accomplish this is through story-telling. Computer programs offer interactive fiction in which you read to your child while you sit together at the computer. In one type of interactive program, the two of you work together to complete a quest. At points of choice, the selections you make together determine how the story will proceed. And the computer's graphics and animation capabilities are ideal for extending your child's interest in stories. This type of activity doesn't replace reading to your child from books; it is simply an attractive and motivating extension of book reading.

The Second Stage

As your child advances into the second and third grades, he or she is expected to make continued progress in the two major areas of decoding and comprehension.

Decoding: Analyzing the Makeup of Words

In decoding, your child moves from slow, painstaking efforts at word identification to reading with ease and speed. As the decoding burden eases, your child is ready to face some of the complications of written English. At this stage, your child must learn that individual words have parts that can be dissected and analyzed. He or she learns about the conventions of the language, among them the silent *e* rule (in words such as *tape* and *cane*), the spelling and pronunciation of double vowels

---

GHOTI = FISH ?

George Bernard Shaw once highlighted the difficulties of written English by pointing out that the "illogical" spelling and pronunciation conventions of English could allow the word *fish* to be spelled *ghoti*. The "f" could be pronounced like the *gh* in *enough*, the "i" like the *o* in *women*, and the "sh" like the *ti* in *nation*.

Shaw overstated the case. The letter-sound combinations he proposed never actually occur in the ways he used them. For instance, *gh* at the beginning of a syllable is never pronounced as "f." Still, the example does point out the complexity of English-language conventions.

(in words such as *rain, coat,* and *meet*), the sounds of consonant clusters (in words such as *street, press,* and *choose*), and the makeup of compound words (such as *broomstick* and *toothbrush*). Learning about these conventions is often referred to as *word analysis.*

The computer can help your child at this stage too. Word-game programs provide an enjoyable way for your child to expand his or her command of word-analysis skills. One of many productive activities involves crossword puzzles. Traditional crossword puzzles improve word-analysis skills such as using synonyms and abbreviations. A software crossword puzzle taps a greater range of skills because it allows your child not only to complete preset puzzles but also to create puzzles from scratch.

In learning to analyze words, your child will benefit from a variety of activities that support and extend word analysis. You're likely to see study skills such as alphabetizing and, concurrently, using a dictionary assigned as part of your child's homework. In these supporting activities, too, you will find a range of software programs that will strengthen your child's learning.

Comprehension: Closing the Gap

In the second stage of reading, the split between decoding and comprehension starts to narrow. Your child can now read text that is complex and interesting. The following is typical of the meaningful messages your child might encounter in the second stage.

> *It is a good night to be inside. But the lookout must watch for danger. He is high above the ship in the crow's nest. He stares into the darkness.*
>
> *Suddenly the lookout sees a dark shape. It is a mountain of ice! And the Titanic is heading right into it!*
>
> — Judy Donnelly, "The Titanic Lost ...
> and Found," *Step into Reading*
> (Random House, New York, 1987)

This text is challenging enough to further your child's comprehension skills. And it is also interactive in that it calls for active processing from your child. As your child reads this kind of text, questions such as "How could that have happened?" and "What is going to happen next?"

should come to mind. Every good reading program attempts to engage your child in becoming an imaginative, interactive reader.

The computer, with its power to individualize text, is ideal for training your child to be an interactive reader. As a story moves along, the program can provide additional information and ask questions which meet your child's interests and responses. The text that follows can reflect your child's responses. The computer can then offer feedback that can steadily guide and correct your child's comprehension. Figure 2-1 shows an example.

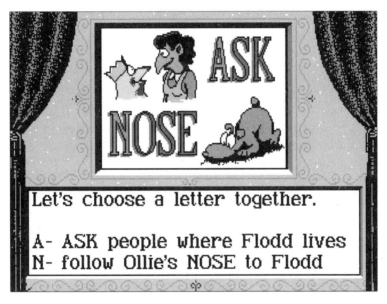

Figure 2-1. *The computer can individualize text and respond to your child's interests.*

The Third Stage

By the end of the first two stages, your child has completed the task of learning to read. At about fourth grade, your child's reading takes on a new character.

Decoding: Handling More Complex Words

In the third stage, the emphasis in decoding is on enlarging your child's vocabulary so that he or she becomes adept at using longer and less familiar words. Your child can read words such as *location* rather than *place, examine* rather than *look at,* and *admire* rather than *like.*

Many of these less common words come from Latin, a language that makes abundant use of prefixes and suffixes. Your child might have to complete exercises using prefixes such as *un-* (as in *unable*) and *dis-* (as in *disable*) and suffixes such as *-tion* (as in *attention*) and *-ly* (as in *decently*). Your child's decoding at this stage extends word-analysis skills, in contrast to the early decoding, which focused more on the visual components of reading.

Comprehension: Mastering a New Language

Your child's comprehension activities also become far more complex in the third stage of reading. The teacher expects him or her to use reading to get new information and new ideas. Your child starts to learn about other countries and cultures, about the laws of the universe, and about current events. Science, social studies, and literature come to the fore. Reading is no longer an end in itself; now your child reads to learn.

At this point, the relationship between your child's speaking and reading skills undergoes a remarkable turnaround. Until now, your child's spoken language has been more complex than the printed text he or she has been reading. Now the language that your child must read is more complex than the language he or she speaks. The following text is typical of the kind of language your child is expected to deal with:

> *Building a new life in a wilderness is a job for strong and heroic people. The Puritans of the Massachusetts colony had to surmount unbelievable difficulties in order to stay alive. Their first years, of course, were spent in setting up houses and clearing enough ground to plant crops.*
>
> *In order to clear a space of land for farming it was necessary to plan for years ahead, and the work required a strong back and a strong faith. The trees were cut down by hand with an axe in such a manner that they would all fall inward upon one another.*
>
> — Shirley Jackson, *The Witchcraft of Salem Village* (Landmark Books, Random House, New York, 1984)

People simply don't speak this way. Books do, and have to if they are to convey complex messages. You might think of the kind of text your child reads at this stage as almost a language unto itself.

Many kinds of text. Not only is the language of reading to learn complex, it is also varied. Different kinds of text are appropriate for different subjects and purposes, as you know from your own experience in reading newspapers, business letters, instructions, reports, novels, history books, science articles, and so on.

You might encounter many descriptive labels for different kinds of text—such as narrative, fiction, nonfiction, poetry, exposition. But the most useful distinction to keep in mind is that between *fictional* and *nonfictional* text. Your child should have as wide a range of experience as possible with each of these two major forms. To help you choose software that will provide experience in both forms, the reviews in Chapter 4 indicate which of these two categories applies to the program in question.

Cultural literacy. The term *cultural literacy,* coined by E.D. Hirsh, refers to the knowledge your child gains from higher-level reading. Everyday experiences with spoken language, such as conversations, movies, and TV, are fun and even informative. But they are not the experiences that lead your child to know the history of the pioneers, the development of our government, and the discoveries of famous scientists. Reading is your child's chief entry into these areas of knowledge. And as with any complex skill, your child can become competent in higher-level reading only by doing lots of it.

Computer programs, because they are so attractive and absorbing, can help motivate your child to spend time reading. Educational researchers David Lancy and Bernard Hayes set up a special summer workshop in which students from fifth through ninth grade used educational software. They found that the students became so engrossed at the computer that even those "who had expressed little or average interest in reading spent as much as 3 hours a day for 4 weeks involved in reading activities as they interacted with their programs."

It is well worthwhile to encourage and support your child in higher-level reading. The payoff—both in school and throughout life—is huge. Figure 2-2, on the following page, lists the major reading skills that software programs can help your child master.

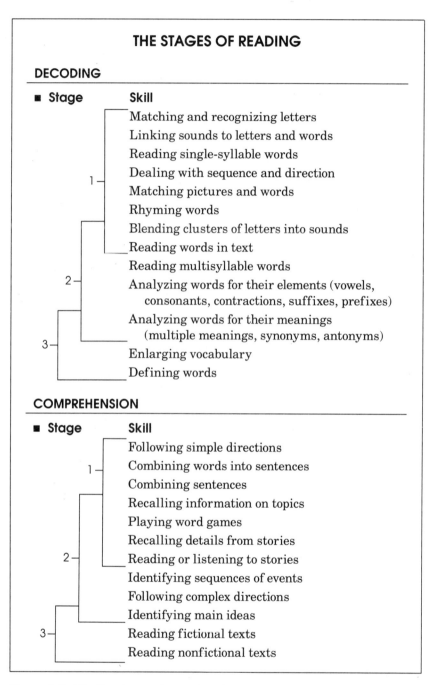

Figure 2-2. *The brackets indicate that the three stages overlap one another as your child progresses in reading.*

THE SECOND R: WRITING

Literacy entails not only reading but writing as well. The two processes are intertwined, and you'll often find that a single program combines both reading and writing skills. Nevertheless, the two processes are far from similar. Most of us find reading to be far easier than writing.

Part of the difficulty stems from the minimal practice most of us have had with the process of writing. In the early 1980s, many educators and parents were concerned by studies conducted at Stanford University revealing that elementary and high school students were rarely, if ever, asked to write texts longer than one paragraph. Even in English classes, writing activities typically did not take up more than 10 percent of the teaching time. And teachers rarely required students to edit; usually, they asked for only one draft. These findings have led to dramatic and continuing change in writing curricula throughout the United States. Almost every school has experienced an explosion in the demand for writing instruction, and computers play a major role.

Mechanical Skills and Process Skills

Writing, like reading, is divided into two major skill areas. One concerns the *mechanics of writing,* which involve skills such as spelling and grammar; the other concerns the *process of writing,* which includes skills such as planning, reporting, and fantasizing—skills that allow your child to create a meaningful story or text.

For many years, teachers in the early grades emphasized mechanical skills at the expense of process skills. The thinking was that no child could write a substantial message without at least a modicum of skill in handwriting, spelling, and grammar. This thinking no longer holds. Your child does not have to develop a core of mechanical skills before he or she begins the more interesting processes of composition. His or her writing skill can benefit from opportunities to describe ideas and events which the teacher can then record. Thus, your child's development in both the mechanics and the process of writing is likely to be given attention from the outset.

The Writing Process

In the earliest grades, the school will engage your child in the process of composing by encouraging him or her to talk or write about topics that are personally meaningful. This might involve creating stories about subjects that intrigue your child, or it might involve keeping a journal of important events in his or her personal life.

In the early stages, the teacher usually puts as few obstacles as possible in the way. Often your child will be allowed to spell in whatever way the words emerge. For example, *u* might appear for *you*, *y* for *why*, *wun* for *one*, and *kleks* for *clicks*. "Invented" spellings are part of normal development, and the freedom to bypass conventional spelling at the beginning helps the writing to flow.

The computer is particularly effective in overcoming inhibitions your child might have about writing. Its word processing capability, for instance, allows even a young child to become an active writer. For example, your kindergartner or first grader might look at a picture on the screen and then choose from a range of supplied phrases or sentences in order to construct a story about the picture. Figure 2-3 shows an example of such a program. The format frees your child from the stressful demands of mechanics and permits him or her to devote energy to the thinking processes of writing, to creating the story itself.

Figure 2-3. *A word processing program for a very young child allows him or her to explore ideas and think about sequence.*

Writing Compositions over Time

With writing established as a regular activity, your child is ready to move on to more complex compositions. Your child will learn that each significant piece of writing changes over time. Depending on where your child is in the process, his or her writing might take the form of notes, an outline, a draft, a revision, or a final, edited composition.

Without a computer, it is difficult for a child to understand this process of composition, let alone to engage in all the stages that produce polished writing. It simply requires more time and effort than he or she can spare. In addition, the appearance of the final handwritten product never approximates those of the printed publications a child thinks of as "real." This perception discourages the child about his or her own writing.

Word processing programs have remedied these problems. With this tool, children not only devote more time to writing and revising, but they do so much more willingly. They can make needed revisions or explore new ideas without having to start over from scratch. And they characteristically report that the clear, neat drafts allow them to edit more easily and think more clearly about a theme.

Your child might be in one of the many schools that encourage the writing process through the use of word processors. His or her school might be demanding major writing assignments that your child must carry out over the course of several weeks or even months. Without these sorts of assignments, your child probably won't choose to do a lot of writing at home. Nevertheless, through your home computer, you can help develop your child's writing skills in several areas.

Elements of the writing process. You can support your child's writing by providing programs that teach key stages of the writing process. The following are some examples of skills that software can develop or reinforce:

- Constructing stories. A program offers a range of cues and choices that allow your child to develop and complete different stories.

- Generating outlines. A program asks questions about particular topics, and these help your child construct an outline.

- Recognizing the way in which sentences and paragraphs build on one another. A program presents jumbled sentences for your child to put in proper sequence.

- Editing text. A program offers your child texts that need to be revised for better clarity and organization.

- Taking notes. A program presents key information that your child must identify and record in order to successfully complete an "assignment," such as determining the best route to a particular destination.

Keyboarding. Although keyboarding is a mechanical skill, it supports the process skills so closely, we want to mention it here.

Even with word processing in its curriculum, your child's school might not require him or her to become proficient at touch typing and related keyboarding skills. In the first and second grades, your child doesn't need sophisticated keyboarding skills. The "hunt-and-peck" method is more than sufficient because he or she must do only a limited amount of writing, and pressing keys on a keyboard will still be easier than writing by hand.

By about third grade, however, the typing process itself becomes important. Your child's writing goals are more ambitious, and limited keyboard skills become an impediment. Even if your child's school doesn't teach keyboarding, you can offer your child an effective tutorial program that does.

The Mechanical Skills

Your child is likely to find the writing process demanding but pleasantly challenging. Most children take great pleasure in developing an attractive, well-designed composition that expresses a set of interesting ideas. But writing, like reading, also requires your child to master a group of more routine skills. These skills involve knowing how to construct sentences, how to spell words correctly, and how to use punctuation. These mechanics of writing are ultimately essential for your child to write with precision and clarity.

The mechanics of writing are more exacting than the mechanics of reading. Because they are more demanding, your child may be less willing to practice them. But practice is essential because your child's mastery of the mechanics must become automatic.

The need for automaticity brings us back to the issue of drill and practice. As we pointed out in Chapter 1, the computer is an ideal medium for this type of teaching. The computer is a patient, nonjudg-

THE MECHANICS: DECODING VS. SPELLING

Decoding and spelling seem to be mirror images of one another. In decoding, your child must translate letters into words; in spelling, he or she must translate words into letters.

But decoding is far less exacting. Suppose your child incompletely scans a word so that he or she "sees" *elephant* as *el_pha_t*. Even with the gaps, your child can probably decode the word. No such leeway is possible with spelling. Even a single misplaced letter is enough to make the whole word incorrect.

mental teacher that can provide the repeated drills in a pleasant way. And, as your child becomes more advanced, meaningful games can further enhance the mechanical skills he or she acquires. Word-completion problems, for example, are an excellent way of teaching spelling and vocabulary, as shown in Figure 2-4.

Figure 2-5, on the following page, summarizes the major writing skills that software programs can help your child master.

```
THE WIND IN THE WILLOWS  K. Grahame(1)
When they got home, the Rat made a
bright fire in the parlour, and planted
the Mole in an arm-chair in front of
it, having fetch█d -o-n -
d-e-s-n--g-w- a-d -l-p-e-s -o- h-m,
-n- t-l- h-m -i-e- s-o-i-s -i-l
-u-p-r-i-e. -e-y -h-i-l-n- s-o-i-s
-h-y -e-e, -o-, t- a- e-r-h--w-l-i-g
-n-m-l -i-e -o-e.
```

Figure 2-4. *Word-completion programs exercise your child's vocabulary and spelling skills. In this example, the game is set at the most difficult level.*

WRITING SKILLS

THE PROCESS

- Creating simple written messages
- Applying supplied messages to visual materials (captions, labels)
- Completing fictional texts
- Completing nonfictional texts
- Creating messages for visual materials
- Creating fictional texts
- Creating nonfictional texts
- Editing texts
- Using organizational strategies (taking notes, outlining)

THE MECHANICS

- Spelling single-syllable words
- Using elements of a word processing program
- Spelling multisyllable words
- Constructing phrases and sentences
- Analyzing sentences for grammar
- Using punctuation and capitalization
- Using study skills (alphabetizing, dictionary skills, index skills)
- Keyboarding
- Using a word processing program
- Proofreading

Figure 2-5. *Today mechanical skills are not necessarily taught before process skills.*

THE THIRD R: ARITHMETIC

Mathematics generates a level of anxiety and tension unmatched by any other subject in the curriculum. Despite the strong negative feelings that mathematics can evoke, your child must master core arithmetic skills. He or she needs to attain a basic level of proficiency in everyday arithmetic—for example, in such skills as calculation, measurement, and using the decimal system. Mastery of these skills has been described as *numeracy,* a term that is an obvious parallel to *literacy.* Just as we don't question the value of literacy, we shouldn't question the value of numeracy.

Achieving the Goal of Numeracy

As with literacy, your child has learned and used a range of readiness skills in numeracy well before he or she ever meets a teacher. The school systematically shapes and extends these skills through its teaching of five major areas: numeration, mathematical concepts, fundamental operations, application, and measurement.

Numeration

This skill area allows your child to answer the question "How many?" Your child generally takes the first steps in this area by matching, in which—using one-to-one correspondence—he or she fits one set of items to another. For example, your child might place a cherry on each cupcake in a set of cupcakes or hand out a balloon to each doll in a group of dolls.

Matching gradually develops into counting, a process in which your child uses numbers, either as words (*eight*) or as symbols (*8*), to determine the number of items in a cluster. After your child masters the basic digits 0 through 9, he or she moves on to learning about the place values and columns of the decimal counting system. For example, your child comes to understand that *2001* is not the same as *1002,* even though the digits in the two sets of numbers are identical.

Mathematical Concepts

Like every area of knowledge, numeracy entails a vocabulary and set of concepts that your child must master. Your child has to understand terms such as *bigger than, smaller than, equal to, the same as, group, series, multiply by, take away,* and *total.*

Math concepts encountered in the later years of school—in advanced algebra, trigonometry, and calculus—can seem discouragingly complex. But the math concepts of the early school years usually evoke a very different reaction. Your child is likely to be stimulated by many mathematical ideas. You have probably seen this firsthand in your child's fascination with birthdays and the concept of being a year older. Few things in a child's life can compete with the power of changing numbers and what they mean.

MATH CONCEPTS CAN BE INTRIGUING

Children sense that math holds a key to unlocking the mysteries of time and space. Their desire to understand can keep them challenged as few other things can. One 5-year-old was greatly disconcerted when he first encountered the word *infinity*. The explanation of the concept contradicted everything in his experience. Finally, he thought he had grasped it, and he went to his mother in triumph: "Imagine I had all the pennies in the world. Then I added one more. Is that infinity?"

Good schools want to keep this curiosity alive by encouraging your child to explore and "play with" mathematical ideas. Curriculum developers generally agree that your child should have as broad an understanding of mathematical concepts as possible before he or she moves on to mathematical operations, such as formal addition and subtraction.

Fundamental Operations

A basic component of numeracy is calculation. Calculation, in turn, requires your child to be adept at the four basic mathematical operations of addition, subtraction, multiplication, and division. In acquiring calculation skills, your child faces two major sets of demands.

First he or she has to learn both the symbols for the various mathematical operations ($+$, $-$, $\times$, $\div$) and the different horizontal and vertical formats in which problems can be presented:

$3 \times 5 =$

vs.

$$\begin{array}{r} 3 \\ \times\,5 \\ \hline \end{array}$$

Second, your child must memorize the arithmetic tables. With memorization, he or she can smoothly solve any problem without having to count to arrive at an answer. In other words, he or she achieves a certain degree of automaticity.

Application

In applying mathematics, your child must be able to solve word problems. These problems call upon a combination of skills. Your child has to understand both the concepts in a particular problem and the appropriate operation or operations that will solve it. The links between concepts and operations are often more complex than they appear. For example, consider the following word problems:

Amy had 8 balloons and gave 4 away. How many did she have left?

Amy had 8 balloons and David had 4 balloons. How many more balloons did Amy have than David?

If you draw both problems, you will quickly see that they represent markedly different concepts. The first, a take-away problem, would look something like this:

The second, a comparison problem, would look something like this:

Even though take-away and comparison are different concepts, your child must solve both problems by using the same operation: subtraction. The solution to both problems takes the form

$$8 - 4 = x$$

Measurement

Skill with measuring allows your child to answer the question "How much?" Measurement concepts are more complicated than those of numeration. Your child must become familiar with the traditional and seemingly arbitrary ways in which we use measurement.

Your child has to learn that liquids, at least in the United States, are measured in ounces, pints, quarts, and gallons, whereas lengths are measured in inches, feet, yards, and miles. To measure temperature, your child must become familiar with two scales involving degrees. And to measure time, your child must use seconds, minutes, hours, weeks, and years.

In learning measurement, your child must also learn the process of conversion, in which the unit of measurement changes but the total measure remains unchanged. For example, your child must understand that 3 feet equal 1 yard, 60 seconds equal 1 minute, and 2 pints equal 1 quart.

Figure 2-6 lists the major arithmetic skills that software programs can help your child master.

Encouraging Numeracy

You might find that your child truly loves arithmetic. But even if this is not the case, he or she can accomplish a great deal if you provide software programs that offer appealing opportunities to practice.

Many arithmetic skills lend themselves to everyday tasks such as shopping, cooking, and planning a party. Your child will find drill-and-practice activities in simulation games to be appealing and relevant.

In addition, your child will be encouraged by the way in which problems are presented on the computer screen. Unlike printed worksheets, which display confusing clusters of problems, the monitor presents one problem at a time. Your child can focus on the problem at hand and is not dismayed by seeing, all at once, a seemingly endless series.

ARITHMETIC SKILLS

NUMERATION

- Matching objects to objects
- Matching numbers to objects
- Counting objects
- Counting sequentially

CONCEPTS

- Understanding spatial concepts
- Recognizing signs and terms for mathematical operations
- Understanding relational concepts
- Understanding equations

FUNDAMENTAL OPERATIONS

- Operating with addition
    horizontal formats
    vertical formats
- Operating with subtraction
    horizontal formats
    vertical formats
- Operating with multiplication
    horizontal formats
    vertical formats
- Operating with division
    short division
    long division
- Applying operations to decimals, fractions, percentages, negative numbers, and equations

APPLICATIONS

- Analyzing word problems
    single operations
    multiple operations
- Creating or using visual representations (maps, grids, graphs)
- Using estimation
- Applying measurement to simulated real-life situations

Figure 2-6. *Mastery of core arithmetic skills results* *(continued)* *in numeracy.*

Figure 2-6. *continued*

MEASUREMENT

- Using units of time
- Using units of weight
- Using units of liquids
- Using units of length
- Using units of temperature
- Using units of money

Arithmetic, like reading, can be taught in a manner in which each discrete skill is presented by itself. It can also be taught in a more integrated way, in which your child must combine a number of different skills. Some of the best software programs teach this way. For example, a program might have your child work in a series of different stores. In one store, he or she serves as the cashier, giving change to the customers. If you or your child adjusts the level of difficulty, the program might request your child to give the change in the fewest number of coins possible. After working as a cashier, your child might move on to other shops, in which he or she is responsible for cutting lengths of material, measuring cans of paint, or packing bags to weigh specific amounts. As you can see, in a program of this sort, your child has to integrate a range of skills including using operations, solving word problems, and using measurement.

In selecting arithmetic programs for your child, keep in mind that math skills do not develop along a single path. Skill areas of numeracy are more like parallel strands within which each specific skill develops somewhat differently over time. For example, your child's school might emphasize spatial concepts in kindergarten and first grade with activities such as learning the names of shapes. These spatial concepts might then not play a major role in your child's education until several grades later, when they reemerge in geometry courses. Consequently, the most productive approach is to find out how the major areas of math study fit into your child's curriculum and then provide programs that match his or her grade level in each category.

THE FOURTH R: REASONING

The charter of schools is to teach the three R's, the basic skills. Indeed, how well students have mastered the skills and content of the major disciplines is the basis on which schools are evaluated. But educators and parents also want students to become independent, creative thinkers. Reasoning skills are critical to the development of a well-trained population—a population able to cope with change, which Christopher Dede, writing in *Educational Leadership*, characterized as one that is skilled in "creativity, flexibility, decision making, complex pattern recognition, information evaluation/synthesis, and holistic thinking."

A Difficult Process to Define

Although there is widespread agreement about the goal of teaching higher-level thinking skills, little agreement exists about what skills, exactly, constitute a proper curriculum in reasoning. Consequently, educators and professional groups have developed various sets of guidelines that often focus on different skills or describe them in different ways. Curiously, the lack of precise definition does not seem to be a hindrance—probably because reasoning skills are not taught as a separate discipline but are applied to the various subjects of the existing curriculum. A reciprocal, almost symbiotic, relationship results: Teachers must use the content of the basic subject areas in order to teach reasoning, and the application of reasoning skills to particular subjects reinforces and extends content knowledge in those subjects.

In the absence of a precisely defined set of required skills, then, we'll describe characteristics that should be common to all reasoning problems. These can serve as guidelines to help you extend the work your child might be doing in school.

The Problem Must Have Concrete Content

An outline for a reasoning curriculum would include an array of terms that make reasoning seem remote and abstract, such as *classifying, deducing, inferring, hypothesizing,* and *monitoring.* These are the reasoning processes that the school wants your child to learn. But reasoning skills cannot be learned in the abstract. Each skill can be practiced only when it is applied to an actual problem. We can reason only when there is something to reason about.

All the major subject areas taught in school—language, mathematics, literature, social science, art, music, and physical science—can offer productive content for the application of thinking skills. Software programs are now increasingly available in all these areas.

The problems your child must solve might be current ones, such as the problem of pollution. But the problems don't have to be new. Your child is likely to be intrigued by grappling with problems others have faced. For example, he or she might find it challenging to take on the role of an explorer traveling through the uncharted West of nineteenth-century America. This type of simulation, which you'll encounter in many software programs, serves multiple purposes. Not only does it exercise reasoning skills, it helps your child learn history and geography and allows him or her to see the world through someone else's eyes.

The Problem Must Be Interesting

A set curriculum is a powerful motivator. It establishes definite goals that your child knows he or she must meet, even when the subject matter might not be particularly appealing. Failure to meet the goals leads to negative consequences such as low grades and low self-esteem.

But reasoning currently has no set curriculum. Consequently, the principal motivation your child has for working on reasoning problems is the interest they hold for him or her. Problems must capture your child's imagination and desire for a solution. Software programs that teach reasoning won't be effective unless they're fun, and they won't be fun if you force your child to work with them. Consequently, your best strategy is to offer your child reasoning programs that he or she finds inherently interesting. Fortunately, this strategy shouldn't result in a major limitation. Something in the human mind makes us love solving a problem—even for no purpose other than the pleasure of its solution. This in itself is likely to broaden your child's definition of "interesting."

Your child is also likely to be attracted to reasoning programs because in many of them, he or she is placed in the position of guiding or programming the computer. Your child becomes the tutor, and the computer is the tutee. It does what your child tells it to do, but the directions have to make sense, or the computer won't perform well. Your child gets the reward of controlling the computer only if he or she learns the power and limitations of the program.

For many of us, reasoning is tightly linked to language. And indeed, many of the best reasoning programs do call upon verbal skills. But these programs are by no means restricted to language. Spatial concepts, for example, offer a rich arena for nonverbal reasoning.

For example, one program capitalizes on this area through a game in which your child fills an area at the bottom of the screen with pieces of varying shapes that float down from the top, as shown in Figure 2-7. The goal is to fill the area in such a way that the pieces fit together with as little empty space between them as possible. Working against the clock, your child must use a variety of reasoning processes, including predicting how the pieces will fit and determining how they might be rotated so as to achieve the best fit.

Figure 2-7. *Your child must apply reasoning skills to his or her knowledge of spatial concepts in order to play this game.*

The Problem Must Allow Alternative Approaches

Many of the problems in the basic three-R subjects—in arithmetic, spelling, and punctuation, for example—require your child to home in on a single correct answer. There is nothing wrong with this; that's what's called for.

Problems in reasoning are different. In order to exercise reasoning skills, your child needs to work on problems in which he or she can explore several routes to the solutions. As in the real world, where events are unpredictable, he or she must deal with the unexpected. Assuming the role of a cross-continent explorer, for instance, your child might chart a route using a particular pass. Then he or she might suddenly discover that an early heavy snowfall has closed the pass. The change in conditions requires a change in plans, and he or she must come up with an alternative.

This type of simulation forces your child into the important process of *decision making*. In this process, your child has to determine a course of action by calling on such thinking skills as

- Memory—recalling other possible routes

- Comparing and contrasting—weighing the merits of alternative routes

- Recognizing cause and effect—projecting the consequences of selecting alternative routes

- Synthesizing parts into a whole—combining factors such as time, resources, and obstacles to determine whether a new plan is feasible

- Monitoring—determining whether the new plan is working

Figure 2-8 lists the major reasoning processes that software programs can help your child master.

REASONING SKILLS

GATHERING INFORMATION

- Recalling relevant information
- Seeking information in reference and available sources
- Taking notes

ANALYZING INFORMATION

- Distinguishing relevant cues from nonrelevant cues
- Comparing facts and categories
- Organizing or sequencing details
- Recognizing patterns

Figure 2-8. *Reasoning skills can be applied to any subject area.* *(continued)*

Figure 2-8. *continued*

DEVELOPING HYPOTHESES

- Making inferences and deductions
- Formulating rules and generalizations
- Eliminating alternatives
- Determining cause and effect

PLANNING STRATEGIES

- Making decisions
- Selecting relevant information to create a plan of action
- Formulating solutions
- Managing resources

SOFTWARE AND YOUR CHILD'S CURRICULUM

In choosing educational software for your child, you need to know how well the programs fit the curriculum he or she is studying in school. But that information alone will not enable you to make good choices. You need to know how to evaluate the software itself. With thousands of educational programs available, you must be selective about the ones you offer your child. In the next chapter, we outline the features and characteristics you should be looking for in evaluating the quality of a software program.

3 WHAT MAKES A GOOD PROGRAM

Bodily exercise, when compulsory, does no harm to the body; but knowledge which is acquired under compulsion obtains no hold on the mind.

—Plato
The Republic

The curriculum skills your child has to learn are vital, but as we pointed out Chapter 1, they come at a price. Acquiring them is compulsory. Plato almost certainly overstated the case in saying that imposed knowledge has *no* "hold on the mind." After all, we were able to conquer our ABCs even though they were imposed by the curriculum. But Plato's 2000-year-old message is still one we can't afford to dismiss.

Compulsory learning is far from ideal. It is likely to cause problems in two major areas. One concerns the *motivation* your child feels in situations that are thrust upon him or her; the other concerns the *understanding* he or she gleans in those situations.

The motivational aspect of learning can be compared to the packaging of a product. An attractive package or container on a supermarket shelf grabs your attention and invites you to take a closer look. After the box is in your hands, however, your attention shifts to the contents. Then you're concerned with whether the product inside the package is what you need. Analogously, an effective educational program is one that offers the content in a way that will help your child best understand the skills he or she must master.

The success of any educational program rests with how well it handles the issues of motivation and comprehension. In the next chapter, we review programs that do manage these problems effectively.

Here we want to clarify the criteria we use for judging the motivational and design features of a program. We'll discuss the motivational features first and then go on to consider the design features that foster understanding. Our aim in talking about these criteria is twofold. First we want to introduce you to terms that describe these criteria throughout the reviews in Chapter 4—terms such as *rewards, feedback,* and *game format.* Second, we want to help you set up a framework for judging educational software on your own.

TRANSFORMING COMPULSORY LEARNING: MAKING IT APPEALING

Educators of every philosophy agree that learning requires motivation. If your child is motivated and involved in the learning process, the chances of his or her learning successfully are much greater. Motivation is a given when your child takes the initiative because he or she wants to master a particular skill. But you can't count on motivation when learning is imposed on your child. Imposed learning can be successful only when it is transformed so that it has the appeal of self-directed learning.

On this score, software programs can offer major advantages over most other school materials. Their built-in capabilities give them the power to

- Capture attention

- Offer play opportunities

- Provide interaction

Through these capabilities, software programs can change your child's feelings about imposed learning. Imposed learning can take on many of the qualities of self-initiated learning.

The Power to Capture Attention

Certain experiences have a near-universal appeal. Just by themselves, they are a "turn-on." For example, no one has to tell people at a fireworks display to pay attention. They are riveted by the lights, the sounds, and the changing patterns. Educational software can bring these attention-getting properties to the learning process. In sharp contrast to the lifeless sheets of paper that have, for many years, been the stock-in-trade of schools, educational software embeds learning in captivating formats with cartoon characters, bright colors, sounds, voices, and animation.

This advantage is invaluable but not free of pitfalls. Entertainment is beguiling; if it becomes paramount, your child can be mesmerized by the "light-and-sound show" and be unable to focus on learning. The entertaining aspects of software should grab your child's attention, but they should not override the educational content. We excluded one program from our reviews, for example, that had appealing graphics and animation. Unfortunately, a child could leave the main body of the program at any point and concentrate simply on having the characters move and talk. When you're selecting programs on your own, keep in mind that a program needs to be attractive without going overboard on stimulation.

The Power to Offer Play Opportunities

Once your child's attention is engaged, it must be sustained. Learning is not instantly accomplished, and your child has to keep working with the same material for a reasonable length of time if he or she is to learn. Again, the computer has a built-in advantage because good programs can embed material in a variety of play formats that will keep your child's attention focused on the task at hand.

The attraction of play comes in part from the *rewards,* or *positive reinforcements,* that can be built into educational programs. The rewards can take many forms. For example, in some programs, your child might have to complete a certain number of problems in order to reach a goal, such as launching a spaceship. Other programs might offer your child an individualized printed certificate that attests to his or her level of accomplishment in the program. Still others might set up a competition in which your child works to outsmart another player—with the computer always available to serve as the other player should the need arise.

But play can offer much more than concrete rewards. Play encompasses a broad array of game formats, ranging from the intellectual challenge of solving a problem to the exhilaration of defeating a terrible monster, and from the fun of manipulating parts to invent a new machine to the fantasy of living in a different world. Play allows your child to feel the excitement of every important emotion but to do so under conditions that are safe and under his or her control. Through play, your child can fulfill his or her wildest dreams.

Well-designed play is considerably more demanding than mere entertainment. As a result, it represents an important phase in the learning process. Think of the effort your child puts into building a Lego model, acting out scenes with dolls, or competing with friends at a board game. Both children and adults are willing to work hard at play because of the pleasure it offers.

Educational software can incorporate many of the major components of play into programs. In so doing, it moves another step closer to transforming your child's feelings about imposed learning. But again, you need to be on the lookout for some pitfalls.

One source of difficulty is that play is so captivating. It can entice your child to do more than he or she should. If a program demands too much in terms of either speed or complexity, your child will feel inadequate. You need to protect your child from this outcome by ensuring that a program's level of challenge is appropriate for him or her.

On the other hand, your child might find that even well-designed programs become boring when played over and over again. You can guard against this limitation by selecting programs that give your child a variety of play experiences. A program might, for instance, allow you or your child to increase the challenge level as your child's skill at the task improves.

The Power to Provide Interaction

Among the attractions of the computer is its ability to interact and provide us with many of the key elements we expect in communication. When effectively programmed, it responds to every message we send. It seems to be listening to us. Because it's so good at grabbing our attention, we listen to it.

Close Encounters of a One-to-One Kind

The computer offers not only interaction, but the opportunity for one-to-one interaction. A one-to-one relationship with an experienced teacher is the most effective dynamic for learning. It gives the teacher an opportunity to respond in a supportive, on-target way to each effort a student makes. That's why, when we are serious about acquiring a new skill, we hire a tutor or an instructor. Whether we're learning to drive a car, speak a foreign language, or take the SATs, nothing is as efficient as one-to-one interaction.

Schoolwork, of course, is not usually done in a one-to-one environment. It takes place either in the classroom, where your child works as a member of a group, or in the home, where he or she works alone on school assignments. Both settings have their uses. In the group, your child learns to interact in situations in which he or she is not the center of attention; in the home, your child learns to work without steady support from others. But neither setting offers the advantages of one-to-one instruction.

Software programs can embody the ideal of the one-to-one instruction. The software can talk directly to your child, and it can respond to the actions your child takes. Your child's every effort is important because the computer treats it as important. The steady accommodation between the program and your child can make compulsory learning feel much like self-initiated learning.

But here, too, you must view the potential advantage with a critical eye. In one-to-one situations, every action and reaction are important. Teacher and student must adjust to each other, and the adjustment must be smooth, or the results will be anything but productive. The best software programs are designed to accomplish one-to-one interaction effectively. A good program allows your child to adjust it according to his or her needs. Your child can give instructions that set the skill level (from simple to more complex), the response time (the time allotted to come up with an answer), and the pace of the program (the speed with which the material is presented).

Ease of use is essential. Your child can give instructions and responses only if the program is easy to use. If the messages needed to run a program are too complex or in some other way inappropriate, your child will get no benefit from the interaction. A key feature of any program is its menu (the list of the software's contents that your child sees at the start of a program). Menus should be easy to read or interpret, and instructions should be clear and simple. Figure 3-1 on the following page shows an example of an appropriate menu.

As your child interacts with the software, he or she should also be able to move around in the program without great difficulty. This means being able to go back to the menu or scroll to different places in

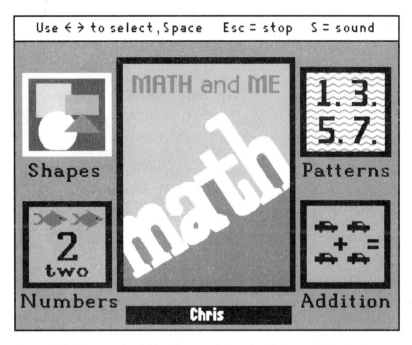

Figure 3-1. *Menus should be clear and simple. This one offers both text and icons.*

the program easily. It means, as well, that your child should be able to escape from any part of the program whenever he or she chooses to do so. All the programs we review meet these qualifications.

Of course, if your child is very young or if a program is very complex, the instructions—no matter how well designed—might exceed his or her ability. The program might still be a good one for you to choose, however. You'll simply need to work with your child during the first few sessions, until he or she becomes familiar with the demands of the program. When doing this might be an appropriate strategy, the reviews will say so.

TRANSFORMING COMPULSORY LEARNING: MAKING THE CONTENT MEANINGFUL

Appealing graphics, challenging games, and an interactive format go a long way toward creating effective motivation for learning. They set the stage, but are not, by themselves, sufficient. They do not deal with the central issue of school learning: the teaching of the actual skills.

Cartoonist Bud Blake captured the problem in one of his drawings. Two children are talking on their way home from school. One child says, "Today in school, the teacher explained all about inflation." The second child, his curiosity piqued, asks, "Well, what is inflation?" To this the first child replies, "All I said was she explained it. I didn't say I understood it."

This child's confusion flags the other major disadvantage of compulsory learning: the gap that can exist between the level of the learner and the level of what he or she must learn. When you elect to learn a skill, you have clear goals. You know where you want to go, and you know whether you're making progress. If necessary, the instructor can restructure the teaching based on the feedback you provide. In contrast, when learning is compulsory, you don't have all these advantages—at least in the beginning. Because the goals are imposed, you're not sure what the ultimate objective is, and it's more difficult to know whether you're making progress. It might even be difficult to give appropriate feedback. The result is that lots of well-intentioned teaching can result in little or no understanding. Closing this critical gap depends on how well the instructor, whether teacher or software program, presents an unfamiliar subject to the learner.

Conquering the New and Unknown

No matter how useful any learning will eventually be, at the outset, it represents unfamiliar territory. Dealing with the new and unknown is not easy; we inevitably feel vulnerable and sometimes even distressed. Your child faces this challenge throughout his or her development. The school curriculum, after all, is made up of new skills that your child is expected to learn from scratch.

The end point of learning is wonderful, but the path to that point is often far from smooth. A good software program is one that helps your child traverse that path in the best possible way. In order to determine how well a program will help a child to deal with the unknown and unfamiliar, we consider the following:

- The program's coherence of focus

- The program's response to your child's errors

- The program's level of difficulty

The Program Should Have a Coherent Focus

In a good program, the parts fit neatly into a unified whole; in a poor program, the segments are simply a collection of parts that lacks coherent organization.

Imagine, for example, a program that is designed to teach your child how to use latitude and longitude readings. This is a reasonable, curriculum-based goal that, when mastered, will allow your child to locate different places around the world on either a three-dimensional globe or a two-dimensional map.

A coherent program teaching this goal might be a game in which your child plays the hero who, armed with latitude and longitude information, must find and rescue other children from evil aliens who have imprisoned them at various points around the world. Your child would have to call on a variety of cognitive processes, including researching information, making notes on the information, and planning strategies for the most effective use of time. These processes would add to the attraction and meaning of the task. Some supporting information might be supplied by the program itself, through graphs and flowcharts that highlight important points for your child. The longitude and latitude focus unifies all the cognitive processes that your child must call upon.

Another program might call on a wide variety of cognitive processes but have no meaningful focus to tie the processes together. In some programs for young children, segments have different subjects. For example, one segment might deal with shapes, another with letter recognition, and still another with numbers. In such a program, any single segment might be fine, but your child doesn't get the insight that he or she would get from working with information that has an integrated, coherent focus.

You'll see most of the discussion about a program's focus in the section of each review called *The Program*.

The Program Should Provide Feedback About Errors

Making mistakes is an important part of the learning process. When you don't know how to do something, you make a lot of mistakes until you do. Errors come in every possible variety. You go too fast, you go too slow, you leave out an essential step, you put in something that doesn't belong. Even after things have moved smoothly for a while, an error can interrupt the flow and you might have to start all over again.

Errors are unavoidable, but they can be useful. Each error has the potential to provide your child with a bit more information about what he or she is doing and about what he or she needs to change in order to reach a goal. Mistakes, if properly handled, can be signposts along the road, telling your child how to continue the journey.

Profiting from error happens only if your child receives information about the mistake. Such information is called *feedback*.

The feedback your child receives in most classroom situations is quite different from the feedback he or she receives from the computer. In the classroom, your child's mistakes in front of the group can embarrass him or her. Feedback your child gets on corrected homework assignments is more private; but often, by the time your child receives the feedback, the issue is closed, and your child has moved on. Delayed feedback offers no direct opportunity for change.

Good computer feedback is immediate, nonjudgmental information that your child can use to improve his or her performance at the moment. The computer does what a good teacher can do in a one-to-one situation: It responds reasonably and patiently to incorrect answers, telling your child what is wrong and, at times, why.

You'll find variants and mixtures of three types of feedback in educational software programs:

- *Confirmation feedback* tells your child whether an answer is correct or incorrect. Little figures might nod their heads to indicate "yes" and shake their heads to indicate "no," or the computer might beep one way for a correct answer and another way for an incorrect answer. When a program offers confirmation feedback, your child will usually have no trouble interpreting it. The strong visual and audio capabilities of the computer make the information unequivocal.

- *Correct-response feedback* tells your child, if he or she gives the wrong answer, what the correct answer is, usually by highlighting the correct choice. Most programs don't offer correct-response feedback until your child has made at least two errors on the same item. After telling your child the correct response, the program is likely to offer your child another chance with the same item or a similar item. That

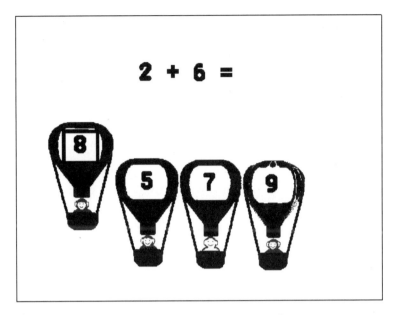

Figure 3-2. *Correct-response feedback indicates the correct answer.*

chance might occur immediately, or it might come up later in the program. Figure 3-2 shows an example of this kind of feedback.

- *Explanatory feedback* is particularly appropriate in programs that involve reasoning. Explanatory feedback does not focus on the correct response but rather on the steps your child has to take in order to reach a correct solution. If your child has failed to apply an appropriate rule, for example, the program might bring up the rule or show instances of the rule's application, thereby setting your child on the path to the correct answer. Figure 3-3 shows an example.

The Program Should Be at the Right Level

Even a focused program will be of little or no use if it's too difficult for your child (or not difficult enough). The title bar of each software review shows the age and grade range for which the program is appropriate. A section called *Abilities Needed* tells you the skills your child will need in order to use the program. For example, a program might require your child to have third-grade reading skills if he or she is going to use it independently. This section also indicates whether the program

Figure 3-3. *Explanatory feedback offers clues to the correct answer.*

is appropriate for children with learning disabilities and, if so, what cautions you might need to exercise in using the program.

Record keeping is helpful. Programs that have record-keeping capabilities can also help you determine the suitability of a program for your child. At the end of a session, a program with a record-keeping feature will summarize what your child has done. Over time, you can use the summaries to evaluate the program's appropriateness.

Don't expect perfect performance, particularly at the start, when your child is learning a new skill. As time goes on, though, the results in general should show a high level of success—scores in the 80 percent range or better. At this level of performance, your child's experience is predominantly one of success. If your child's performance is consistently low, the program is probably too difficult for him or her at the moment, and you might want to put it aside for awhile.

As your child attains mastery, the potential problem is not that the program will be too difficult but that it will be too easy. A good program can expand its offerings. Some of the best programs are open-ended—that is, you can alter what they ask of your child as his or her skill develops.

MASTERY: THE MOST POWERFUL MOTIVATOR

Imposed learning can definitely handicap the learning process, but it doesn't have to sidetrack it in any permanent way. When educational programs are attractively packaged and well designed to help your child deal with the new and unknown, they can transform imposed learning into an enormously effective process.

And the good news is that once your child is on the right path, he or she will experience a snowball effect. The more your child succeeds at learning, the more he or she will want to learn. At that point, it does not matter if the process began through compulsion. The power and rewards of learning take over. You've probably seen for yourself the intense pride and pleasure your child takes in completing a task successfully.

In her book *Children's Minds* (W.W. Norton and Company, New York, 1978), Margaret Donaldson speaks of the "fundamental human urge to be effective, competent and independent, to understand the world and to act with skill." And it's true, few things in life can compete with the confidence and satisfaction we get from success—from knowing that we *can do*. Mastery is the most powerful motivator.

Thus, the more skilled your child becomes, the more committed he or she will be to learning. Good educational software now offers you the chance to help your child reach this goal in ways that were never before possible. In the next chapter, we review some of the finest programs available for your selection.

4 THE SOFTWARE SELECTIONS

An education is... a set of tools, equipment with which to accomplish whatever one needs or wants to do.

—Marvin Grosswirth and Abbie Salny,
MENSA Genius Quiz Book 2

In this chapter, we review the programs we've selected. The reviews themselves, which begin on page 78, are arranged in alphabetic order by program title. Note, however, that titles beginning with the word *The* are alphabetized under the letter of the first significant word. Thus, you will find *The Dinosaur Discovery Kit,* for example, under *D,* not *T.*

Immediately preceding the reviews, on pages 59–77, you'll find four summary charts, which list all the programs by curriculum area and age/grade level. The summary charts will allow you to easily identify the programs that are most relevant to your child; we'll say more about them later.

WHAT YOU'LL FIND IN THE SOFTWARE REVIEWS

The reviews give you an overview of each program so that you'll be able to judge if it is one that will be useful for your child. Each review is organized in five parts: Identifying Information (given in the title bar), Hardware, Abilities Needed, Curriculum Areas, and The Program.

The sections are designed to present information in such a way that you can easily find what you need.

Identifying Information

Each review begins with a title bar that contains the name of the program, its publisher, the year of publication, the retail price, and the age range and the corresponding grade levels for which the program is appropriate.

The ages we recommend might vary somewhat from those suggested by the program's publisher. Our basic goal is to enable your child to work independently with a program whenever possible. Thus, we are more conservative than the publishers in recommending appropriate age ranges. For example, a publisher might recommend a reading program as suitable for second graders. However, if your child is to work independently with the program, he or she might need third-grade skills. In that case, we would recommend the program as appropriate for third grade and higher. You, of course, are the best judge of your child's abilities, and you should make the final determination about the suitability of a program.

Hardware

This section lists the makes and models of computers the program can run on and the amount of memory needed to run the program. (Memory is the computer's capacity to store data; it is usually expressed in kilobytes [KB] or megabytes [MB]. The greater the number, the more memory is needed to run the program. For instance, a program requiring 64 KB of memory uses less memory than one requiring 128 KB.) This section also lists other hardware that is either essential or recommended. The size of the disk drive needed for a program always appears under essential needs. Many programs use various peripherals (devices that plug into the computer). These peripherals include

- Monitor—a black-and-white or color output device that displays the software program and user input on the screen
- Printer—an output device that prints text or images on paper
- Mouse—a hand-size "box" that is moved on a pad or a desktop in order to control actions on the screen

- Joystick—a gearshiftlike stick that is manipulated in order to control actions on the screen

- Koala Pad—a digitizing device used to enter a graphic image into a computer

- Color Graphics Card—a printed circuit board often required to operate programs on the IBM PC and compatible computers

We'll tell you whether any peripherals are essential or recommended. In some instances, we've classified elements as essential that the publisher states are highly recommended. For example, although a program might run with a black-and-white monitor, a color monitor might have such a major effect on the program's usefulness that we state it to be essential, even though technically, it is only recommended. If no peripherals are listed, the program runs solely with the keyboard.

PROGRAMS WITH MULTIPLE VERSIONS

In some cases, a program is available in more than one version— for example, in a talking version and a nontalking version. The alternative versions often have hardware requirements that differ from those listed in the Hardware section, and you need to know them in order to determine whether you can use the alternative version on your computer. When another version of a program exists, the title, price, and hardware requirements (if they are different) appear in a sidebar called "Alternative Versions." Other sections of the main review, however, apply to the alternative version as well as to the "original" version. The titles of alternative versions of a program appear, in alphabetic order, in the summary chart for the appropriate curriculum area.

In general, you'll find the talking version of a program particularly useful when your child's reading skills are still limited. Hearing, rather than reading, the instructions allows your child to work independently and enjoy a range of programs that would otherwise require your steady involvement.

Abilities Needed

In this section, we discuss the abilities or skill levels your child needs in order to use the program. For example, a reasoning program might require that your child read at the second-grade level. This information will help you determine whether the program is appropriate for your child and to what extent your own involvement is required.

Selections for a Child with a Learning Disability

We also indicate, in this section, whether the program is appropriate for the learning-disabled child. The chief criteria that led us *not* to recommend a program as appropriate are demands for speed and the presence of long, complex directions. In making selections for a learning-disabled child, you can generally assume that the child should be 1 to 2 years older than the ages recommended in the title bar of the review. This suggestion is only a loose guideline; you can modify it depending on your child's skills.

In addition, we let you know whether the program might be problematic for a learning-disabled child who has difficulties in particular skill areas. The following categories cover the main areas that might adversely affect a child's performance:

- Visual-spatial skills, such as those needed to analyze maps and complete visual patterns

- Language skills, such as those needed to deal with complicated instructions and long segments of reading

- Memory skills, such as those required for memorizing lists of information

- Timing skills, such as those required for working under tight time constraints

- Organization skills, such as those required for planning and note taking

If we caution you about these skill areas, it doesn't mean that your child cannot use the program. It does mean that the program might cause special problems and that you will need to see how well your child works with the program before allowing him or her to use it on a regular basis.

Curriculum Areas

This section outlines the specific curriculum area or areas that the program covers—specifically, reading, writing, arithmetic, or reasoning. Under each curriculum area, we describe the program's subject matter using the terms and phrases you encountered in Chapter 2. For example, you might see a program described in this manner:

Writing

- *The Process*—completing fictional texts, editing texts
- *The Mechanics*—analyzing sentences for grammar

The Program

This section tells you whether the program functions as a tutor, tool, or tutee; describes its special virtues and features; and assesses how well it does the job it sets out to do. You'll find information about

- The program's game, or "mission," and how it works
- The kinds of rewards, feedback, and help the program offers your child, including how it handles your child's errors
- Whether you or your child can customize the program
- Whether the program lets you or your child keep a record of his or her work

---

PROGRAMS IN A SERIES

When we review a program that is part of a series, you'll see the word *Series* in the title bar of the review. At the end of the review, following the ▼ symbol, we provide short descriptions of the other programs in the series. Because the basic format remains the same from one program to another in a series, the full review tells you what to expect in the other programs. Generally, the only difference is content. For example, in a math series, one program might cover basic math operations such as addition and subtraction with whole numbers, whereas another might cover addition and subtraction with decimals, fractions, and percentages. The titles of all programs in a series appear, in alphabetic order, in the summary chart for the appropriate curriculum area.

HOW TO USE THE SUMMARY CHARTS

You can use the following summary charts to identify programs that might be of immediate interest to your child. Then you can turn directly to the reviews of those programs without having to search or read through other reviews that are not relevant at this time. Simply find the section of the chart that covers the curriculum area you are interested in and run your finger down the age/grade column that is appropriate for your child. A dot in that column indicates that the program listed at the left is suitable for your child's level. Other dots on the same line indicate other curriculum areas that the program covers.

Titles within each curriculum area are listed alphabetically. If you are looking for a specific title, simply look in the appropriate part of the alphabetic listing in the Programs column to see whether the program is reviewed in this book.

SUMMARY OF PROGRAMS BY CURRICULUM AREA

READING PROGRAMS

PROGRAMS	OTHER SKILLS COVERED			AGES AND GRADES							
	Writing	Arithmetic	Reasoning	2–4 / PreK	5 / K	6 / 1	7 / 2	8 / 3	9 / 4	10 / 5	11+ / 6+
1-2-3 Sequence Me	●			●	●	●					
Ace Detective (*See* Ace Explorer)	●							●	●		●
Ace Explorer	●							●	●	●	●
Ace Reporter (*See* Ace Explorer)	●							●	●	●	●
Alphabet Circus	●			●	●	●					
Beamer	●										
Chariots, Cougars, and Kings			●					●	●	●	
Colors and Shapes		●		●							
Crossword Magic	●	●	●					●	●	●	●
Crossword Magic Puzzle Disks (*See* Crossword Magic)	●	●	●					●	●	●	●
Dinosaurs		●	●	●	●						

(continued)

READING PROGRAMS

PROGRAMS	OTHER SKILLS COVERED			AGES AND GRADES							
	Writing	Arithmetic	Reasoning	2–4 / PreK	5 / K	6 / 1	7 / 2	8 / 3	9 / 4	10 / 5	11+ / 6+
Donald's Alphabet Chase (*See* Arithmetic—Goofy's Railway Express)				●	●						
Easy as ABC				●	●	●					
European Nations and Locations (*See* States and Traits)		●							●	●	●
First Letter Fun				●	●	●					
First Letters and Words				●	●	●					
Fun from A to Z	●			●	●	●					
Hide 'N Sequence	●							●	●	●	●
McGee				●							
McGee Visits Katie's Farm (*See* McGee)				●							
Memory Castle	●										
Mickey's ABC's: A Day at the Fair				●	●						
Mickey's Colors and Shapes: The Dazzling Magic Show (*See* Mickey's ABC's: A Day at the Fair)		●		●	●						

(continued)

Mickey's Crossword Puzzle Maker

Microzine: Premier Issue

Microzine: The Series
(See Microzine: Premier Issue)

M-ss-ng L-nks: Classics Old and New
(See M-ss-ng L-nks: Young People's Literature)

M-ss-ng L-nks: English Editor
(See M-ss-ng L-nks: Young People's Literature)

M-ss-ng L-nks: Micro-Encyclopedia
(See M-ss-ng L-nks: Young People's Literature)

M-ss-ng L-nks: Science Disk
(See M-ss-ng L-nks: Young People's Literature)

M-ss-ng L-nks: Young People's Literature

Muppets on Stage

Muppetville

Muppet Word Book

Paint with Words

READING PROGRAMS

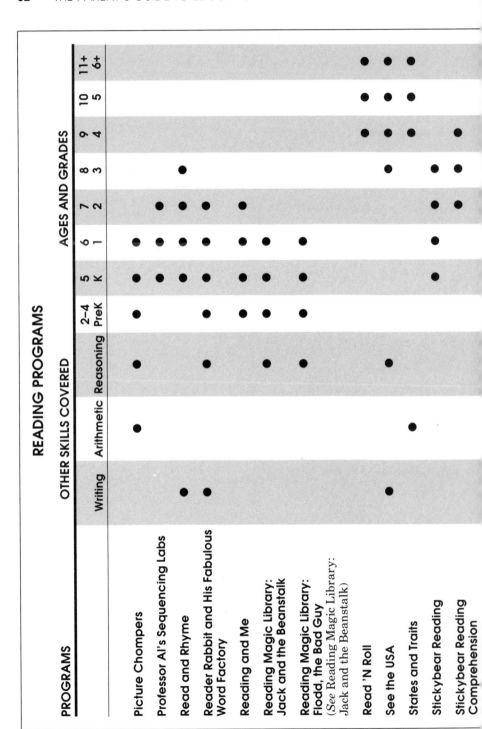

PROGRAMS	OTHER SKILLS COVERED			AGES AND GRADES							
	Writing	Arithmetic	Reasoning	2–4 / PreK	5 / K	6 / 1	7 / 2	8 / 3	9 / 4	10 / 5	11+ / 6+
Picture Chompers		●	●	●	●	●					
Professor Al's Sequencing Labs					●	●					
Read and Rhyme	●		●		●	●	●	●			
Reader Rabbit and His Fabulous Word Factory	●			●	●	●	●				
Reading and Me			●	●	●	●	●				
Reading Magic Library: Jack and the Beanstalk				●	●	●					
Reading Magic Library: Flodd, the Bad Guy (*See* Reading Magic Library: Jack and the Beanstalk)			●	●	●	●	●				
Read 'N Roll	●		●					●	●	●	●
See the USA									●	●	●
States and Traits		●							●	●	●
Stickybear Reading					●	●	●	●			
Stickybear Reading Comprehension							●	●	●		

Super Story Tree

Talking Reader Rabbit
(*See* Reader Rabbit and His Fabulous Word Factory)

Talking Reading and Me
(*See* Reading and Me)

Those Amazing Reading Machines: I

Those Amazing Reading Machines: II
(*See* Those Amazing Reading Machines: I)

Those Amazing Reading Machines: III
(*See* Those Amazing Reading Machines: I)

Those Amazing Reading Machines: IV
(*See* Those Amazing Reading Machines: I)

Tic Tac Show

Word Attack
(*See* Word Attack Plus!)

Word Attack Plus!

Word Munchers

WRITING PROGRAMS

PROGRAMS	OTHER SKILLS COVERED			AGES AND GRADES							
	Reading	Arithmetic	Reasoning	2-4 / PreK	5 / K	6 / 1	7 / 2	8 / 3	9 / 4	10 / 5	11+ / 6+
Author! Author!									•	•	•
Bank Street Beginner's Filer	•		•				•	•	•	•	•
Bank Street School Filer (See Bank Street Beginner's Filer)	•		•							•	•
Bank Street Story Book	•								•	•	•
Bank Street Writer Plus								•	•	•	•
Bannermania							•	•	•	•	•
Be a Writer! (See I Can Write!)	•							•			
Children's Writing and Publishing Center									•	•	•
Create with Garfield!									•	•	•
Create with Garfield! Deluxe Edition (See Create with Garfield!)									•	•	•
The Dinosaur Discovery Kit	•			•	•	•	•	•			
Friendly Filer	•								•	•	•
The Grammar Examiner			•							•	•

(continued)

Grammar Gremlins

Grammar Toy Shop

I Can Write!

Kidswriter
(*See* Kidswriter Golden Edition)

Kidswriter Golden Edition

KIDTALK

Magic Slate II:20
(*See* Muppet Slate)

Magic Slate II:40
(*See* Muppet Slate)

Magic Slate II:80
(*See* Muppet Slate)

Magic Spells

Mavis Beacon Teaches Typing

Microtype: The Wonderful World of PAWS

Muppet Slate

Mystery Sentences

The New Print Shop

The New Print Shop Companion
(*See* The New Print Shop)

WRITING PROGRAMS

PROGRAMS	OTHER SKILLS COVERED			AGES AND GRADES							
	Reading	Arithmetic	Reasoning	2–4 PreK	5 K	6 1	7 2	8 3	9 4	10 5	11+ 6+
The New Print Shop Graphics Library (*See* The New Print Shop)	●					●	●	●	●	●	●
Once upon a Time						●	●	●	●	●	●
The Print Shop (*See* The New Print Shop)		●				●	●	●	●	●	●
Punctuation Put-On	●							●	●	●	●
Remember!						●		●	●		●
Snoopy Writer	●					●	●	●	●		
Spellicopter	●					●	●	●	●	●	●
Spell It! (*See* Spell It Plus!)									●	●	
Spell It Plus!	●										
Super Spellicopter (*See* Spellicopter)								●	●	●	
Switchboard			●				●	●	●	●	●
Talking Once upon a Time (*See* Once upon a Time)	●					●	●	●	●	●	●

Teddy Bear-rels of Fun

Text Tiger

Type to Learn

Writer Rabbit

ARITHMETIC PROGRAMS

PROGRAMS	OTHER SKILLS COVERED			AGES AND GRADES							
	Reading	Writing	Reasoning	2–4 PreK	5 K	6 1	7 2	8 3	9 4	10 5	11+ 6+
Addition Logician (*See* Circus Math)											
Alge-Blaster!								●			
Alge-Blaster! Plus! (*See* Alge-Blaster!)											●
Algebra Shop (*See* Math Shop)											●
Arithmetic Critters					●	●	●				
The Boars' Store			●				●	●	●		●
The Boars Tell Time					●	●	●				

(continued)

ARITHMETIC PROGRAMS

PROGRAMS	OTHER SKILLS COVERED			AGES AND GRADES							
	Reading	Writing	Reasoning	2–4 PreK	5 K	6 1	7 2	8 3	9 4	10 5	11+ 6+
Circus Math							●	●			
Clock Works							●	●			
Comparison Kitchen				●	●	●					
Conservation and Counting (*See* Reading—Colors and Shapes)				●	●						
Conquering Decimals (+, −) (*See* Decimal Concepts)									●	●	●
Conquering Decimals (x, ÷) (*See* Decimal Concepts)										●	●
Conquering Fractions (+, −) (*See* Decimal Concepts)									●	●	●
Conquering Fractions (x, ÷) (*See* Decimal Concepts)										●	●
Conquering Percents (*See* Decimal Concepts)										●	●
Conquering Ratios and Proportions (*See* Decimal Concepts)									●	●	●
Conquering Whole Numbers (*See* Decimal Concepts)								●	●	●	●

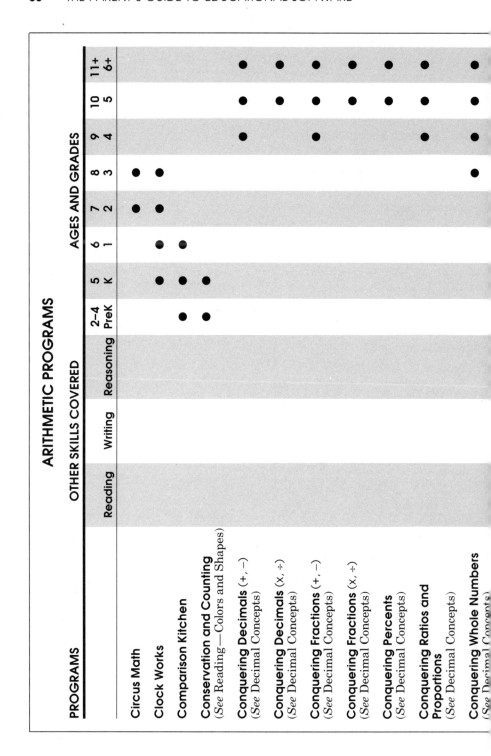

Coordinate Math

Counting Critters

Decimal Concepts

Digitosaurus

Early Addition
(*See* Circus Math)

Easy Graph

Easy Graph II
(*See* Easy Graph)

Estimation: Quick Solve I

Estimation: Quick Solve II
(*See* Estimation: Quick Solve I)

Fish Scales

Fraction Concepts
(*See* Decimal Concepts)

Fraction Munchers
(*See* Number Munchers)

Fraction Practice Unlimited
(*See* Decimal Concepts)

Get to the Point

Goofy's Railway Express

How the West Was One +
Three x Four

(*continued*)

ARITHMETIC PROGRAMS

PROGRAMS	OTHER SKILLS COVERED			AGES AND GRADES							
	Reading	Writing	Reasoning	2–4 PreK	5 K	6 1	7 2	8 3	9 4	10 5	11+ 6+
Jumping Math Flash							●	●	●		
The Magic Cash Register						●	●	●	●	●	●
Math and Me				●	●	●					
Math Blaster Plus!			●			●	●	●	●	●	●
Math Blaster Mystery			●				●	●	●	●	●
Math Maze			●			●	●		●	●	●
Math Rabbit					●	●	●	●	●		
Math Shop						●	●	●	●	●	●
Math Shop Jr. (See Math Shop)											
MATHTALK							●	●	●	●	●
MATHTALK FRACTIONS (See MATHTALK)								●	●	●	●
Measure Works (See Clock Works)				●	●						
Mickey's 123's: The Big Surprise Party (See Reading—Mickey's ABC's: A Day at the Fair)				●	●						

(continued)

Mickey's Runaway Zoo
(*See* Goofy's Railway Express)

More Teasers from Tobbs: Decimals and Fractions
(*See* Teasers by Tobbs with Whole Numbers)

Multiplication Puzzles
(*See* Circus Math)

New Math Blaster Plus!
(*See* Math Blaster Plus!)

Number Farm

Number Munchers

Ollie and Seymour

Path Tactics

The Playroom

Power Drill

Quotient Quest
(*See* Circus Math)

Sailing Through Story Problems

Space Subtraction
(*See* Circus Math)

Speedway Math

Stickybear Math

ARITHMETIC PROGRAMS

PROGRAMS	OTHER SKILLS COVERED			AGES AND GRADES							
	Reading	Writing	Reasoning	2-4 / PreK	5 / K	6 / 1	7 / 2	8 / 3	9 / 4	10 / 5	11+ / 6+
Stickybear Math 2 (*See* Stickybear Math)							●	●	●	●	●
Stickybear Word Problems	●						●	●	●	●	
Subtraction Puzzles (*See* Circus Math)								●			
Talking Math and Me (*See* Math and Me)				●	●	●					
Talking Math Rabbit (*See* Math Rabbit)			●	●	●	●					
Talking Money					●	●	●	●	●		
Teasers by Tobbs with Integers (*See* Teasers by Tobbs with Whole Numbers)			●				●	●	●	●	●
Teasers by Tobbs with Whole Numbers			●				●		●	●	●
Tobbs Learns Algebra (*See* Teasers by Tobbs with Whole Numbers)			●								●
Wild West Math: Level 3								●			

Wild West Math: Level 4
(*See* Wild West Math: Level 3)

Wild West Math: Level 5
(*See* Wild West Math: Level 3)

REASONING PROGRAMS

PROGRAMS	OTHER SKILLS COVERED			AGES AND GRADES							
	Reading	Writing	Arithmetic	2–4 PreK	5 K	6 1	7 2	8 3	9 4	10 5	11+ 6+
Animal Photo Fun		•		•	•	•					
Ant Farm	•		•					•	•	•	•
Backyard Birds (*See* Mystery Objects)											
The Berenstain Bears: JigSaw! Jr. (*See* JigSaw!)											
Blazing Paddles		•	•	•	•	•	•	•	•	•	•
Blockout			•		•	•	•	•	•	•	•
Code Quest	•								•	•	•
ColorMe		•		•	•	•	•	•	•	•	

(*continued*)

REASONING PROGRAMS

PROGRAMS	OTHER SKILLS COVERED			AGES AND GRADES							
	Reading	Writing	Arithmetic	2–4 / PreK	5 / K	6 / 1	7 / 2	8 / 3	9 / 4	10 / 5	11+ / 6+
Designasaurus	●	●			●	●	●	●	●	●	●
Designasaurus II (*See* Designasaurus)	●	●			●	●	●	●	●	●	●
Enchanted Forest			●				●	●	●	●	●
Faces (*See* Tetris)										●	●
Fantavision		●							●	●	●
Firehouse Rescue				●	●	●	●				
Five-Star Forecast (*See* Mystery Objects)	●									●	●
Fossil Hunter (*See* Mystery Objects)	●										●
Game Shop	●		●					●	●	●	●
Invisible Bugs (*See* Mystery Objects)										●	●
Jenny's Journeys			●						●	●	●
JigSaw!			●				●	●	●	●	●

(continued)

King's Rule

Little People Bowling Alley

Lunar Greenhouse
(*See* Mystery Objects)

Miner's Cave
(*See* Mystery Objects)

Murphy's Minerals
(*See* Mystery Objects)

Music Construction Set

My Grand Piano

Mystery Matter
(*See* Mystery Objects)

Mystery Objects

The New Oregon Trail

Observation and Classification
(*See* Reading—Colors and Shapes)

Patterns

Peanuts Maze Marathon

Peanuts Picture Puzzler

Perplexing Puzzles

The Puzzle Storybook

REASONING PROGRAMS

PROGRAMS	OTHER SKILLS COVERED			AGES AND GRADES							
	Reading	Writing	Arithmetic	2-4 / PreK	5 / K	6 / 1	7 / 2	8 / 3	9 / 4	10 / 5	11+ / 6+
The Royal Rules (*See* King's Rule)			●								●
School Bus Driver							●				
Stickybear Music				●	●	●	●	●	●	●	●
Stickybear Town Builder			●			●		●	●		
Sun and Seasons (*See* Mystery Objects)	●									●	●
Talking Peanuts Maze Marathon (*See* Peanuts Maze Marathon)					●	●	●	●	●		
Talking Peanuts Picture Puzzler (*See* Peanuts Picture Puzzler)			●	●	●	●	●	●			
Tetris			●				●	●	●	●	●
Think Quick!			●					●	●	●	●
Tip 'N Flip			●						●	●	●
Tonk in the Land of Buddy-Bots				●	●	●	●	●			
Weeds to Trees (*See* Mystery Objects)	●									●	●

Welltris
(*See* Tetris)

Where in Europe Is Carmen SanDiego
(*See* Where in the World Is Carmen SanDiego)

Where in the USA Is Carmen SanDiego
(*See* Where in the World Is Carmen SanDiego)

Where in Time Is Carmen SanDiego
(*See* Where in the World Is Carmen SanDiego)

Where in the World Is Carmen SanDiego

Where in the World Is Carmen SanDiego: Deluxe Edition
(*See* Where in the World Is Carmen SanDiego)

Zeroing In

1-2-3 Sequence Me

4–6 years
Grades PreK–1

Sunburst Communications, 1988, $65.00

Hardware

Apple II series, 64 KB

★ Essential: 5.25-inch disk drive

☆ Recommended: color monitor, regular keyboard or Muppet
Learning Keys

Apple Macintosh Plus, 1 MB ($99.00)

★ Essential: 3.5-inch disk drive, color monitor

Abilities Needed

Your child will probably require your help in the first few sessions
before he or she will be able to run the program independently.

This program is appropriate for the learning-disabled child.

Curriculum Areas

The program teaches reading skills by having your child place sets
of pictures or words in order so that they form a logical or common
sequence.

Reading

- *Comprehension skills*—following simple directions,
  recalling information on topics, identifying sequences of
  events
- *Decoding skills*—reading single-syllable words, dealing
  with sequence and direction, matching pictures and
  words

The Program

(Tutor). The program presents simple action sequences, such as
building a snowman, hanging a picture on a nail, and cooking an egg.
Trax, an animated little dog, is the host.

The program has three levels, which your child selects with an
easy-to-use icon menu. In each level, three boxes appear on the screen
that contain pictures, words, or both. In Level 1, your child sees three
pictures; in Level 2, he or she sees picture and words; in Level 3, he or

she sees only words. In an all-picture sequence, such as one about filling a glass of milk, your child might see a full glass, an empty glass, and a glass being filled with milk. In a picture-and-word sequence, two of the boxes contain words and one contains a picture. In an all-word sequence, all three boxes have writing in them. Your child's task is to place the boxes so that they form a correct sequence. He or she does this by putting the number *1* under the box that contains the first part of the sequence, *2* under the box that represents the middle of the sequence, and *3* under the box that represents the final part of the sequence.

If your child makes mistakes, the program is well designed to help him or her over the difficulty. For example, after your child makes two mistakes, the program tells him or her to watch while it models the correct answer. When your child enters the correct numbers, the boxes realign themselves in the correct order. Trax, the dog, applauds the final product.

Attractive graphics enhance the program, which offers practice in a skill that is emphasized in most early reading programs. The picture-and-word options help your child understand that the concept of sequence applies to both graphics and language. In the first few sessions, your child might have some difficulty adjusting to the program's design because he or she cannot move the pictures or words to their proper place in the sequence until they are numbered. Thus, your child must get used to numbering the boxes while they are out of order. For example, he or she might have to put the number *3* under the first picture because it represents the last picture in the sequence. Your child should be able to adapt to this fairly readily, but you might have to help him or her at the outset.

You can set the program for the number of problems you want your child to have in any session. The choices vary from 1 to 20.

Ace Explorer— Sequencing

8–12 years
Grades 3–6

Series
Mindplay, 1988, $49.99

Hardware

Apple II series, 48 KB

★ Essential: 5.25-inch disk drive

☆ Recommended: printer

IBM PC and compatibles, 128 KB

★ Essential: 3.5-inch or 5.25-inch disk drive, color graphics card

☆ Recommended: printer

Abilities Needed

Your child should be reading at the third-grade level in order to understand the explanations in the program.

This program is appropriate for the learning-disabled child, although a child with significant language or organizational problems might have difficulty with it.

Curriculum Areas

The program teaches reading and writing by having your child analyze different types of written material.

Reading

- *Comprehension skills*—combining sentences, recalling information on topics, identifying sequences of events, following complex directions

Writing

- *The process*—completing fictional texts, editing texts
- *The mechanics*—using elements of a word processing program

The Program

(Tutor/Tool). The program teaches reading and writing by having your child sequence a set of ideas so that there is a clear beginning, middle, and end.

In the program, your child assumes the role of explorer and deals with a science fiction–type problem, which is assigned by Mission Control. There are 60 different story missions. For instance, your child might have to explain what has happened to stores that used to be known as supermarkets. Your child culls information from a variety of sources that will allow him or her to understand the sequence of events that led to the assigned scenario. The information sources include visits to other planets, videophone interviews with aliens, and a computer bank that offers information about the planets. Your child stores the information he or she gathers in a section of the program called "Notes." In the Notes section, your child organizes and rearranges the facts so that he or she creates a logically sequenced story.

The graphics are clear, and although not particularly appealing, they effectively support the material. The objective of the game provides motivation, and the addition of a running clock adds a competitive element.

When your child makes an incorrect choice, such as selecting the wrong sequence, the program offers feedback. At times, the keyboarding requirements are demanding: Your child has to move text around in a very careful sequence in order to select the elements he or she wants to include in the final product.

When your child has successfully found the essential story parts and sequenced them correctly, Mission Control rewards him or her with a story printout and a graphic of the alien.

The program offers an editor, Story Creator, which allows your child to create and edit his or her own stories. Your child can name his or her own aliens, create clues, and invent planets. He or she can also use the available graphics to illustrate the story. The program offers a Challenge Upgrade, which allows you or your child to customize the program by varying the sound, the amount of time for play, the speed at which mission-assignment text is presented, the level of difficulty of play, and the sequence in which the assignments appear. The program also keeps a summary record of your child's performance.

ACE REPORTER and ACE DETECTIVE, two other programs in the series, use the same game plan to offer practice with different kinds of text. Your child takes on an assignment, gathers information or clues from a variety of sources, and then combines the clues to complete the assigned task.

In ACE REPORTER—MAIN IDEA AND DETAILS (1987, $49.99), your child works with the who-what-when-and-why format of a news article to practice reading for the main idea and details.

In ACE DETECTIVE—DRAWING CONCLUSIONS (1987, $49.99), your child uses the format of motive, opportunity, and means to solve crimes. He or she practices the critical reading skills of organizing information and drawing conclusions.

Alge-Blaster!

12 years and older
Grades 7 and up

Davidson, 1986, $49.95

Hardware
Apple II series, 64 KB
- ★ Essential: 3.5-inch or 5.25-inch disk drive
- ☆ Recommended: printer

Commodore 64/128, 64 KB
- ★ Essential: 5.25-inch disk drive
- ☆ Recommended: printer

IBM PC and compatibles, 128 KB
- ★ Essential: 3.5-inch or 5.25-inch disk drive, color graphics card
- ☆ Recommended: printer

ALTERNATIVE VERSION

Alge-Blaster! Plus!
Davidson, 1988, $49.95

Hardware
Apple II series, 128 KB
- ★ Essential: 3.5-inch or 5.25-inch disk drive

IBM PC and compatibles, 512 KB
- ★ Essential: 3.5-inch or 5.25-inch disk drive, color graphics card
- ☆ Recommended: printer

Apple Macintosh, 1 MB ($59.95)

Abilities Needed

Your child needs to be able to take notes during the display of problems because some information needed for solution is not available later. You will need to remind him or her to take notes.

This program is appropriate for the learning-disabled child, although a child with significant memory or organizational problems might have difficulty with it.

Curriculum Areas

The program teaches arithmetic by helping your child review and practice prealgebra and algebra fundamentals.

Arithmetic

- *Concepts*—understanding equations
- *Fundamental operations*—applying the operations to negative numbers and in equations

The Program

(Tutor). The program uses a step-by-step approach for solving algebraic problems. It covers 21 topics in 5 algebra areas, with a total of 670 problems.

In *Positive / Negative Numbers,* your child solves the following kinds of addition, subtraction, multiplication, and division problems: $8 + (-9) = -1$; $(-8)(-7) = 56$.

In *Monomials and Polynomials,* your child solves the following kinds of addition, subtraction, and multiplication problems: $5a + 6a + 7a = 18a$; $(a + 2a - 6) + (7 - a) = 2a + 1$.

In *Factoring Monomials and Trinomials,* your child solves problems such as $4a - a = a(4 - 1)$.

In *Solving Equations,* your child solves equations such as $5a - 12 = 33$ and $2x + 1 = -3$, where $a = 9$ and $x = (-2)$.

In *Solving Systems of Equations,* your child solves higher-level sets of equations, such as $a + 2b = 14$ and $a - 3b = -11$, where $a = 4$ and $b = 5$.

In each of the five areas, your child goes through three progressive activities. Your child begins with *Tutorial: Study the Steps,* which demonstrates and systematically explains each step necessary for solution. This tutorial offers two examples. For instance, for the problem *(–3) + (–7) – 4 = __* , it gives the following rules: "If all the signs are the same, add the numbers and use that sign; if the signs are mixed, add the numbers with the same signs separately."

A Practice Section: Build Your Skill guides your child through the solution of 10 problems by showing step-by-step prompts.

Finally, *Quiz Section: Solve It* challenges your child to work through 20 problems on his or her own, without prompts.

When your child makes a mistake, the message "Try again" appears on the screen. After two attempts, the computer gives the answer. However, the program offers an instructional Help option, which allows your child to access on-screen prompts at any time.

When your child successfully solves a problem, he or she is rewarded with encouraging messages such as "Congratulations" and "Good work."

Both versions of the program offer an easy-to-use editor that allows your child to add his or her own problems.

At the end of each series of problems, a scoreboard appears, which shows the problems attempted, the number of correct answers, the percentage of correct answers, and the number of incorrect answers. A review option allows your child to review and retry missed problems. Your child can save and print these records.

The program manual contains a glossary of algebraic terms.

ALGE-BLASTER! PLUS! contains more than 500 algebraic equations and problems using algebraic fractions, radical expressions, and quadratic equations. In addition, this version of the program contains a challenging graphing game.

Alphabet Circus

4–6 years
Grades PreK–1

DLM Software, 1984, $32.95

Hardware
Apple II series, 48 KB
Commodore 64/128, 64 KB
- ★ Essential: 5.25-inch disk drive
- ☆ Recommended: color monitor

IBM PC and compatibles, 128 KB

★ Essential: 3.5-inch or 5.25-inch disk drive, color graphics card

☆ Recommended: color monitor

Abilities Needed

Your child will need your help to read the on-screen instructions. After becoming familiar with the format, he or she should be able to work independently. Some of the vocabulary might be unfamiliar to your child (for example, the word *unicycle*), and you might need to offer help when these words appear. Unless your child has some mastery of spelling, you will also need to guide his or her work in the word processing game.

This program is appropriate for the learning-disabled child.

Curriculum Areas

The program builds reading and writing skills by teaching and reviewing alphabetic order, letter recognition, and simple keyboarding skills.

Reading

■ *Decoding skills*—matching and recognizing letters, linking sounds to letters, reading single-syllable words, reading multisyllable words, matching pictures and words

Writing

■ *The mechanics*—using elements of a word processing program, keyboarding

The Program

(Tutor). This program consists of six games.

In *Meet The Circus,* the Ringmaster calls up the uppercase letter that your child presses on the keyboard. The chosen letter is highlighted, and a word beginning with that letter, together with a picture, appears on the screen. For instance, your child presses *K*, and the word *Kangaroo* appears with a picture of that animal.

In *Alphabet Parade,* your child sees the alphabet appear, in sequence, one letter at a time. The Alphabet Song accompanies the presentation of the letters. At various points, the sequence stops, and your child must press the letter that should appear next. For example, he or she might see ABCD on the screen and should then press *E* to complete the task successfully.

In *Lost Letter,* your child sees a picture of a circus character or object. He or she must then press the first letter of the name of the object in the picture. For instance, the picture might be of a wagon. In that case, your child would press *W.*

In *Secret Letter,* your child and a partner take turns guessing the letter that the Ringmaster has secretly chosen. To help the players arrive at the correct choice, the program offers cues that use the alphabet sequence. For example, after pressing the letter *H,* your child might be told that the correct choice "comes before" that letter.

In *Juggler,* your child plays against the clock. A juggler throws up a letter, and your child must select the matching letter on the keyboard as fast as he or she can.

In *Marquee Maker,* your child works with elements of a word processing program. The screen, designed to look like an electronic blackboard, records simple messages that your child writes. A message cannot exceed a total of 40 letters and spaces. At any one time, your child can see only six letters or spaces on the screen.

The graphics and sound effects are appealing, and the formats of the six games are varied enough to hold your child's interest.

All the game formats, except those in *Meet the Circus* and *Marquee Maker,* require your child to meet a goal. When your child makes an error, he or she has two chances to select the correct answer; the program offers help cues. For example, in *Alphabet Parade,* the Ringmaster shakes his head after the first incorrect choice. He then shows a picture of a circus character whose name starts with the correct letter. After a second incorrect choice, the Ringmaster supplies the correct letter, and the game continues. In the word processing game, *Marquee Maker,* the program does not offer feedback or guide your child's performance.

At times, the rewards offered might be confusing to a young child, especially if he or she is not adept at number concepts. For instance, at the end of a game, a seal might balance two balls for each choice that was correct on the first try and one ball for each choice that was correct on the second try. In *Juggler*, number concepts that are even more complex are shown in the performance record.

Except in *Alphabet Parade* and *Marquee Maker,* the program keeps a record of your child's performance and shows him or her the results either after a set number of trials or at the completion of the game.

Animal Photo Fun

4–6 years
Grades PreK–1

DLM Software, 1985, $32.95

Hardware

Apple II series, 48 KB

★ Essential: 5.25-inch disk drive

☆ Recommended: color monitor

Abilities Needed

Your child will need your help to read the on-screen instructions. After becoming familiar with the format, he or she should be able to work independently. Your child might be unfamiliar with some of the vocabulary (such as the names of the desert animals *armadillo* and *scorpion*), and you might need to offer help in these cases.

This program is appropriate for the learning-disabled child.

Curriculum Areas

The program teaches reasoning and writing by helping your child to associate animals with their habitats, classify animals by habitat, and use memory skills.

Reasoning

- *Gathering information*—recalling relevant information
- *Analyzing information*—distinguishing relevant from nonrelevant cues, organizing details

Writing

- *The mechanics*—using elements of a word processing program, keyboarding

The Program

(Tutor). This six-part program teaches and reviews information about animals and their habitats.

In *Meet The Animals,* as the title suggests, your child is introduced to the subject content of the program. He or she learns six habitats and six animals that live in each one. He or she moves the Photographer's hat to a "snapshot" showing one of the six different habitats. The habitats include forest, desert, pond, jungle, ocean, and farm. Each habitat is represented by a symbol and a name. By pressing a key, your child sees one of the six different animals that live in each habitat. He or she can choose to see more animals from the same habitat or move to another habitat to find different animals.

In *Odd One Out,* your child helps the Photographer sort pictures of animals into habitat groups by identifying which one of four animals does not belong in a particular habitat.

In *Photo Safari,* a timed game, your child helps the Photographer take pictures of animals before the time runs out. He or she watches a picture of an animal appear and then must identify the animal and determine which of the six habitats is right for that animal.

In *Animal Mom Watch,* your child pairs a baby animal (for example, a fawn) with its mother (a doe). This is a memory game, with a format similar to that of Concentration, in which six covered cards are shown on the screen. Your child controls the cards he or she wants to select, and the game continues until three pairs are correctly matched.

In *Animal Rummy 1* and *2,* your child plays in a guessing game against either the computer (Rummy 1) or another person (Rummy 2). In each game, the screen displays three pictures of animals from different habitats. Pressing keys changes the animals. Your child and his or her partner take turns pressing keys until all three animals on the screen are from the same habitat.

The program's graphics and sound effects are appealing, and the formats of the six activities are varied enough to hold your child's interest.

Except for *Meet the Animals,* the activities are in game formats that require your child to meet a goal. When he or she makes a mistake, the program offers cues to help your child make the correct choice. He or she gets two chances. For example, in *Odd One Out,* the Photographer shakes his head after the first incorrect choice and shows a picture of the odd animal's habitat. If the second choice is incorrect, the program shows the right answer, and the game continues. In *Meet The Animals,* the program does not offer any feedback or control your child's performance.

At times, the rewards might be confusing to a young child, particularly if he or she is not adept at number concepts. For example, at the end of a game, the Photographer adds two horses to his filmstrip for each choice that was correct on the first try and one horse for each choice that was correct on the second try.

The program keeps a record of your child's performance, with the exception—once again—of *Meet The Animals*. He or she is shown the results either after a particular number of trials or at the completion of the game.

Ant Farm

8 years and older
Grades 3 and up

Sunburst Communications, 1987, $65.00

Hardware
Apple II series, 64 KB
★ Essential: 3.5-inch or 5.25-inch disk drive

Abilities Needed
Your child needs to be reading at the third-grade level in order to handle the on-screen instructions. Otherwise, he or she will need your help to run the program.

Curriculum Areas
The program sharpens your child's analysis of visual details and helps him or her recognize increasingly complex visual patterns. It also aids the development of memory skills.

Reasoning
- *Gathering information*—recalling relevant information, seeking information in available sources
- *Analyzing information*—distinguishing relevant from nonrelevant cues, recognizing patterns
- *Developing hypotheses*—eliminating alternatives
- *Planning strategies*—selecting relevant information to create a plan of action

Arithmetic
- *Concepts*—understanding spatial concepts

The Program

(Tutor/Tool). The program consists of mazes that represent ant farms. They are made up of connecting tunnels called workstations. Your child's job is to place each ant at its appropriate workstation. The ants work by moving in particular patterns; these patterns match segments of the maze. For instance, an ant might move in a pattern that forms a T-shape, and your child would have to place the ant in the segment of the maze that forms a T. Your child must carefully scan the parts of the maze to locate the segment where a particular ant has to work. This process becomes increasingly demanding as the mazes become more and more complex. Because of the complexity of the game, it might be best for your child to play with a partner. The program contains four parts:

In *How To Play,* the program gives your child the instructions for the game. Your child learns to use the Research Window for getting information he or she needs to solve the problem. For example, with the Research Window, your child can call up an ant's pattern of movement at any time.

In *Learn,* your child tries out the rules and principles of play. He or she practices with mazes at three levels of difficulty: easy, medium, and hard. It is critical that your child work with this part of the program; without this experience, he or she would probably find it difficult to play the game effectively.

In *Play,* your child puts all the information together and uses it to place up to nine ants in each maze selected. Among the features of this activity is the Tool Box, with which your child learns to use the computer as a tool to gain access to information or to delete information when it is no longer needed. For instance, in the Tool Box, your child can call up the Research Window. He or she can then hide the ants when the maze is so crowded that it is difficult to analyze.

In *Challenge,* your child plays with rules that become more restrictive and more complex. In this segment, there is only one correct station for each ant. When the ant is in its station, it can pick up and drop eggs. Your child places the ants so that they form an egg chain.

The program's graphics are appealing, and the game is quite challenging. The program offers variations in the complexity of the mazes and in the quantity of information your child can choose to access. For instance, in *Play,* he or she can elect whether or not to show a trace of the ant's work pattern on the screen. Without the trace, your child takes the more difficult route of relying on memory. The game demands a great deal of concentration, and your child must sequence moves carefully if he or she is to make smooth and steady progress.

Your child must be precise about the exact location for placing an ant, or the placement will not be accepted. When the placement is correct, your child is rewarded by seeing the ant happily carry out its work at its station. When the placement is not correct, your child sees cues in the form of written messages and arrows that help guide him or her to a new placement.

The program offers a wide range of options, including changing the difficulty of the mazes, turning the sound on or off, and choosing different ways in which to use the Tool Box.

Arithmetic Critters

5–7 years
Grades K–2

MECC, 1986, $39.95

Hardware
Apple II series, 64 KB
   ★ Essential: 3.5-inch or 5.25-inch disk drive

Abilities Needed
To use this program, particularly the on-screen instructions, your child should be reading at the first-grade level. If your child is reading at this level, you will have to provide only initial help.

This program is appropriate for the learning-disabled child.

Curriculum Areas
The program helps your child learn to count, measure, and use the operations of addition and subtraction. A follow-up to COUNTING CRITTERS, the program provides practice in adding single digits (the one's place numbers *1* through *9*), subtracting numbers less than 18, recognizing the numbers from 10 through 99, and measuring lengths.

Arithmetic

- *Numeration*—counting objects
- *Concepts*—recognizing terms and signs for mathematical operations
- *Fundamental operations*—operating with addition, operating with subtraction
- *Measurement*—using units of length

The Program

(Tutor). Each of four games covers a different type of arithmetic problem.

In *Animal Addition,* your child adds 2 groups of up to 9 identical animals—for instance, 7 dogs + 1 dog = __.

In *Fowl Play,* your child subtracts from 1 to 9 identical birds from groups of as many as 18 birds—for instance, 9 larks – 2 larks = __.

In *Unit Worm,* your child measures lengths, using caterpillars as the unit of measurement. For example, your child might find that the length of a worm equals two caterpillars.

In *Egg Plant,* your child fills orders for boxes of eggs to be shipped on trucks from an "egg factory." Trucks appear on the screen with egg cartons stacked on them in units of 10. For example, one truck carries 10 cartons, the next truck carries 10, and the third truck carries 8. The program asks "How many? Count them." Your child then types in the number that correctly represents the number of cartons displayed.

The strength of this program, like that of COUNTING CRITTERS, is the instructive feedback it gives when your child makes an incorrect response. When he or she makes an error, the program offers two hints and the correct answer. First the program offers a written and spoken cue to try again; then it highlights the animals and beeps the same number of times as the number to be counted; finally it shows the correct answer.

For each activity, a scoreboard appears after every set of 10 problems, showing the total number of correct answers.

Author! Author!

9 years and older
Grades 4 and up

Mindplay, 1988, $59.99

Hardware

Apple II series, 48 KB

- ★ Essential: 5.25-inch disk drive, blank disks for saving work
- ☆ Recommended: printer

IBM PC and compatibles, 128 KB

- ★ Essential: 3.5-inch or 5.25-inch disk drive, color graphics card, blank disks for saving work
- ☆ Recommended: printer

Abilities Needed

Your child should be reading at the fourth-grade level in order to understand the explanations in the program.

Curriculum Areas

The program gives your child experience with major elements of play writing, drama, and creative writing.

Writing

- *The process*—creating fictional texts, creating messages for visual material, editing texts, using organizational strategies
- *The mechanics*—using elements of a word processing program

The Program

(Tutor/Tutee). This is a sophisticated program that requires your child to think, organize, and concentrate. Your child will probably gain most from the program if he or she is knowledgeable (either through the school curriculum or from discussions at home) about different forms of writing, such as drama, poetry, and biography. Unless your child loves to write, he or she can best use it to complete creative writing assignments from school.

The program introduces your child to many of the conventions and rules of play writing in two ways. First, the program demonstrates the development of an actual play—in this case, a somewhat liberal interpretation of "Jack and the Beanstalk." The developing script for each scene appears on the lower part of the screen while accompanying graphics appear on the upper part. Second, the program provides your child with an explicit outline of the rules and conventions of play writing. The purpose of the outline is to familiarize your child with such terms as *dramatic form, leading characters,* and *conflict resolution.* These sorts of literary terms are becoming increasingly important in many school writing curricula.

After this two-step introduction, your child then goes on to write his or her own play. (At this point in the program, your child will have to switch repeatedly between the program disk and the formatted blank disks on which he or she will enter the new play.) The program asks questions to guide your child step by step through the play-writing sequence. These questions lead him or her to fill in the outline that creates the story line for the play. Next your child selects the cast of characters and the graphics that will be used for backdrops and props in the play. Finally your child creates each scene, including the stage directions and comments that he or she wants to accompany the dialogue. Numerous options allow your child to edit, save, and print the plays he or she has written.

The program offers a good range of graphics and animation. Although the pictures are not particularly appealing, they are adequate to convey basic information about the characters and their actions. The program also includes a library of props and character graphics that move and flip, a selection of backdrops, and one data disk. Remember, your child will need a blank formatted disk for each new play he or she writes and saves.

Bank Street Beginner's Filer

7–11 years
Grades 2–6

Series
Sunburst Communications, 1986, $79.00

Hardware

Apple II series, 48 KB
Commodore 64, 64 KB

★ Essential: 5.25-inch disk drive (three-disk set), printer, blank disks for storing files

☆ Recommended: two disk drives

Abilities Needed

If your child is in second grade, he or she will initially need your help to read the on-screen instructions. After becoming familiar with the format, he or she should be able to work independently.

This program is appropriate for the learning-disabled child, although a child with significant language problems might have difficulty with it.

Curriculum Areas

This program helps your child understand, create, and use simple databases. (A database is an organized set of information on a particular topic.)

Writing

- *The process*—using organizational strategies
- *The mechanics*—using study skills

Reading

- *Comprehension skills*—following directions

Reasoning

- *Gathering information*—recalling relevant information, taking notes
- *Analyzing information*—distinguishing relevant from nonrelevant cues, organizing or sequencing details

The Program

(Tool). This three-disk program teaches your child how to use a computer to collect, organize, locate, and report information.

The Program Disk familiarizes your child with the concepts of fields, records, and databases (or files). Your child learns that a database, or file, is a collection of records and that each record is divided into fields. A field defines each category of information, such as name, address, and phone number. Each record in a database contains the same fields. In this program, your child can create a maximum of 50 records, each containing a maximum of 10 fields.

The easy-to-use main menu of the Program Disk offers your child eight choices.

In *Add Record,* your child enters data into new records in a database file. He or she can also attach brief notes or comments to each record.

In *Report,* your child obtains information selected from records in the form he or she specifies. Your child can print this information in two formats: a Screen Report, which prints records the way they appear on the screen, and a Table Report, which prints the records in columns and rows.

In *Create a Field,* your child builds a database structure.

In *Change a Field,* your child renames, deletes, or rearranges fields in a database.

In *Find,* your child retrieves specific information in one to two records according to criteria he or she chooses.

In *Sort,* your child rearranges the sequence of his or her records according to alphabetic order.

In *Clear,* your child erases all or some of the records in his or her file.

In *Other,* your child loads files from a disk, saves files to a disk, or does housekeeping tasks such as retrieving, renaming, deleting, or saving.

The Beginner's Database Disk provides your child with a collection of database files for use with the program disk. Your child can practice using a database with these files. Your child uses the files just as they are; he or she does not need to add or change data. The files also serve as examples for files your child can create. For instance, *Dinosaurs* contains 17 records, each describing a different dinosaur, whereas *Books* is an example of a database that can be created for storing book reviews.

The Classroom Tools Disk offers easy-to-use tools, such as programs that catalog data disks. These tools are designed primarily for classroom use, however.

As with many programs designed for school as well as home use, the manual that accompanies the program is extensive. It offers a step-by-step tutorial for parents and teachers as well as a complete reference section on operating the program.

BANK STREET SCHOOL FILER (1986, $99.00) is an expanded version of the program for children 10 years and older (Grades 5 and up). This program is available for the Apple II series, 64 KB (with data display in 40 columns) and 128 KB (with data display in 40 or 80 columns) as well as for the Commodore 64. The increased power of this version allows your child more flexibility in creating and using databases. He or she can include as many as 50 fields in each record and can store up to 255 records in the 64-KB version, or up to 512 records in the 128-KB version. The program allows your child to sort on two fields at one time, combine files that share the same form, save part of a file, or save only the fields' names and types. He or she can also retrieve files created by BANK STREET BEGINNER'S FILER.

With this program, your child can create and use formats that are appropriate throughout his or her school years. After selecting an exact format for a report, your child can also save that format to be used again. The program allows your child to save a report on a disk and then use it in a word processing file.

Bank Street Story Book

8 years and older
Grades 3 and up

Mindscape Educational Software, 1986, $39.95

Hardware
Apple II series, 48 KB
Commodore 64/128, 64 KB
IBM PC and compatibles, 128 KB

★ Essential: 5.25-inch disk drive; joystick, mouse, or Koala Pad; blank disks for saving files

☆ Recommended: color monitor, printer

Abilities Needed
Your child should be reading at the third-grade level in order to independently read the stories on the disk. Your child will need your help to read the well-designed but extensive manual.

This program is appropriate for a learning-disabled child, although a child with significant visual-spatial problems and organizational problems might have difficulty with it.

Curriculum Areas
The program teaches writing and reading through a story processor that allows your child both to read stories in the program and to create his or her own illustrated stories.

Writing
- *The process*—creating messages for visual materials, creating fictional texts, editing texts
- *The mechanics*—using elements of a word processing program

Reading
- *Comprehension skills*—reading stories, following complex directions

The Program

(Tool). The program is a simplified word processor and drawing program that allows your child to create illustrated stories and other written materials. The range of activities includes retelling a familiar story, illustrating a report, drawing a graph, and making an animated cartoon. The drawing and the writing can be done independently, or they can be combined.

At the start, your child learns the program by reading through some of the sample stories and other texts that are on the disk. These sample texts include a Greek fable, an animated greeting card, and a fractured fairy tale.

The program includes an excellent tutorial that leads your child step by step through the processes he or she can use to create new materials. The tutorial shows him or her the key steps in sections called *Drawing, Coloring, Typing, Flipping Pages,* and *Editing.* It's important for your child to go through the tutorial carefully; it will enable him or her to use the program efficiently and productively.

After your child has learned the components, he or she will find the program easy to use. The menu is fairly extensive; your child can access any part of it by pressing the first letter of the component he or she wants—for example, *S* for Show, *R* for Read, and *H* for Help.

Illustrated writing is always appealing to children, and the potential of this program makes the appeal even greater. For example, your child can mix the colors so that he or she has a wide variety of possible colors to choose from. The program also allows your child to animate his or her creations. The word processing component can be used independently of the drawing features. However, if your child's primary goal is word processing, this program would not be the most appropriate choice.

Your child will need patience and the ability to sequence carefully if he or she is to create satisfying materials. For example, in order to put a blue box on a page, your child must go through six steps: four line steps (to create the box), one color step (to color it in), and one flip step (to turn the page).

You will need blank disks in order to save the stories that your child creates.

Bank Street Writer Plus

7 years and older
Grades 2 and up

Broderbund Software, 1986, $79.95

Hardware

Apple II series, 128 KB

★ Essential: 3.5-inch or 5.25-inch disk drive, printer

☆ Recommended: mouse

IBM PC and compatibles, 256 KB

★ Essential: 3.5-inch or 5.25-inch disk drive, printer

Abilities Needed

Your child should be reading at the third-grade level in order to read the on-screen instructions. Younger children will need your help in operating the program.

This program is appropriate for the learning-disabled child.

Curriculum Areas

The program teaches writing through the use of a complete, easy-to-use word processing system.

Writing

■ *The mechanics*—using a word processing program

The Program

(Tool). This program features pull-down menus, on-screen prompts, and commands for every function it performs. Instructions appear on the screen, so your child does not have to remember special codes, keys, or symbols.

Your child can write, revise, correct, erase, unerase, and rearrange words, sentences, and paragraphs; and copy, save, and print documents with a simple click of his or her mouse or keyboard. An on-disk tutorial that teaches word processing right on the computer screen is included.

BANK STREET WRITER PLUS offers a 40-column or 80-column format. After your child becomes more experienced in using the program, he or she can make use of single-key shortcut commands. This feature permits your child to skip over certain menus and prompts, and it allows you or your child to set up function keys to carry out your own multistep commands (macros). The program also offers a 60,000-word automatic spelling checker and an online thesaurus with synonyms and antonyms.

Bannermania

9 years and older
Grades 4 and up

Broderbund Software, 1989, $34.95

Hardware

IBM PC and compatibles, 256 KB

★ Essential: 3.5-inch or 5.25-inch disk drive, printer

Abilities Needed

Your child should be reading at the fourth-grade level to use this program independently. It is helpful for your child to have some word processing skills, such as simple keyboarding, before using the program.

This program is appropriate for the learning-disabled child.

Curriculum Areas

This inventive and attractive program teaches writing by enabling your child to create original banners and to modify ready-made banners.

Writing

- *The process* — applying supplied messages to visual material, creating messages for visual material, editing texts

The Program

(Tool). The program offers your child a way to add a professional look to school reports and other projects. The program includes over 80 banners for all occasions. Your child can add two-line messages to the banners for any idea or event in which he or she has an interest.

The program offers drop-down menus for ease of operation. Your child can *create* a new banner; *load* a ready-made banner or an original banner that has been previously saved; *edit* a banner; *change* the appearance of a banner with special effects, such as 3-D or shadows; and *print* the banner.

After your child selects or creates the banner, he or she scrolls through a series of menus offering the following options: Fonts (19), Special Effects (34 different ones, such as drop shadows, vibes, three layer, and perspective), Color (134 predesigned sets), and Shape (27 different ones, such as arch, convex, and pennant). Your child can view all the effects through a preview window at any time during the program.

He or she can also modify the size and layout of the banner so that the same message can be turned into a vertical banner, a bumper sticker, or a poster. Depending on the type of printer available, your child can print the banners in black, in one color, or in many colors.

Beamer

8–10 years
Grades 3–5

Data Command, 1984, $39.95

Hardware
Apple II series, 48 KB
  ★ Essential: 5.25-inch disk drive

Abilities Needed
Your child needs to understand the following concepts in order to use the program: Prefixes and suffixes are units of meaning. Additional parts can be affixed to words.

This program is appropriate for the learning-disabled child.

Curriculum Areas
The program teaches reading and writing by having your child analyze words. He or she breaks words into prefixes, base words, and suffixes. The program also offers practice in spelling.

Reading
  ■ *Decoding skills* — reading single-syllable and multisyllable words, analyzing words for their elements, enlarging vocabulary

Writing
  ■ *The mechanics* — spelling single-syllable and multisyllable words

The Program

(Tutor). This easy-to-use drill-and-practice program reinforces spelling as well as word-recognition skills. The theme of the program is that your child must rescue an alien who is stranded on a green asteroid. Your child rescues the alien by typing the right base word (for example, in/*complete*/ly, im/*port*/er), prefix (for example, *anti*/freeze, *con*/cave), or suffix (for example, auction/*eer*, heir/*ess*). Each time your child plays, the program randomly selects different words from a list of 400 words contained in its memory.

The program uses the concept of mastery to define success. Your child cannot finish the game until he or she answers all items correctly. When he or she makes a mistake, the computer gives the answer. That item then reappears at the end of the game list, and your child has a second opportunity to answer.

The program offers two kinds of rewards for finding the right word elements. When your child types the correct answer, a space ship "zaps" the word with a laser beam and destroys it. Then, when your child has answered all items correctly, he or she is "beamed up" to the spaceship.

You or your child can select which word element will be the focus of play in each game. As your child improves, the program presents more difficult words. He or she can attain four ranks, from Cadet (four or more missed items) to Space Fleet Admiral (all items correct). The program keeps a record of your child's work.

Blazing Paddles

5 years and older
Grades K and up

Baudville, 1988, $34.95

Hardware

Apple II series, 48 KB
Commodore 64, 64 KB

* ★ Essential: 5.25-inch disk drive; mouse, joystick, Koala Pad or Graphics Tablet; color monitor; printer; blank disks for saving work

Abilities Needed

Your child needs little or no reading ability and minimal drawing ability to use the program successfully.

This program is appropriate for the learning-disabled child.

Curriculum Areas

The program teaches reasoning and writing through the use of a powerful, easy-to-use drawing tool. Your child creates drawings and diagrams, with or without text.

Reasoning

- *Analyzing information* — organizing or sequencing details, recognizing patterns
- *Planning strategies* — making decisions

Writing

- *The process* — creating messages for visual material

The Program

(Tool). This program permits your child to draw, paint, and print high-resolution illustrations with ease. He or she learns to guide the computer and choose the directions he or she gives it in order to create the pictures planned in his or her imagination. The main menu appears around the border of the screen. Each component of the program is represented by both a title and an icon. Some of the functions your child can select are

- *Brush Set.* Allows your child to choose from among 7 different brush strokes.

- *Color Selection.* Allows your child to choose from among over 200 available colors and textured hues.

- *Drawing Routines.* Allows your child to use 14 different routines, including

  - □ Sketch — a freehand drawing mode
  - □ Dots — a routine for drawing single dots
  - □ Line — a routine for drawing individual straight lines
  - □ Lines — a routine for drawing connected straight lines
  - □ Oval 1 — a routine for drawing outlines of circles and ellipses

□ Oval 2—a routine for drawing solid-color filled circles and ellipses

□ Box 1—a routine for drawing outlines of rectangles and squares

□ Box 2—a routine for drawing solid-color filled boxes

■ *Text*. Allows your child to add short text to the picture.

■ *Window*. Allows your child to cut and paste elements of a picture.

■ *Zoom*. Allows your child to edit fine details by providing a magnified view of a small area of a picture.

■ *Spray*. Creates an "airbrush" effect by "spraying" color on the screen. This can be used for shading and for blending one color with another.

■ *Fill*. Allows your child to fill an area of a picture.

■ *Clear the Screen*. Allows your child to empty the screen by selecting the trash-can icon.

Your child works on his or her drawing in a window at the center of the screen but is still able to make other menu selections, using the icons around the screen's border. The program comes with a library of predrawn shapes (such as a tree, a car, a man, and a bicycle) that your child can add to his or her original pictures.

Blockout

9 years and older
Grades 4 and up

California Dreams / Electronic Arts, 1989, $39.95

Hardware
IBM and compatibles, 384 KB
★ Essential: 3.5-inch or 5.25-inch disk drive

Curriculum Areas
The program teaches and strengthens spatial and positional concepts through a three-dimensional game.

Reasoning
- *Analyzing information*—organizing or sequencing details, recognizing patterns
- *Planning strategies*—making decisions, formulating solutions

Arithmetic
- *Concepts*—understanding spatial concepts

The Program

(Tutee). This is a fascinating visual-spatial game in which your child tries to fill the back wall of the playing area, called "the pit," with rectangular blocks of different sizes. The pit is like a three-dimensional drawing of a room in which perspective makes the back wall look smaller than the parts of the room that are closer to you. All the walls of the pit are marked to form grids. As play begins, different rectangular blocks start to appear in the foreground. Your child can rotate these in any direction, but he or she must use the blocks to fill the back wall so that there are no empty spaces in the grid on that wall. If he or she fills in the wall completely, the layer of blocks already placed disappears, and your child still has the full space of the pit. The idea is to keep the game going as long as possible. If the pieces your child has placed do not fill in a wall completely (if there are any spaces), the incomplete layer does not disappear, and the pit starts filling up. To put it another way, the back wall gets closer and closer. When the layers build up so that they reach the near end of the pit, the game ends.

Before playing the game, your child can see a demonstration of the game and go through a practice session. We highly recommend the practice sessions for any child who isn't a master of these sorts of puzzles. A Help menu is also available to remind your child of the keys that control the various movements and to show him or her the different rotations. Your child can rotate any piece in six different directions: clockwise or counterclockwise on each of the three axes.

The menu offers several options that provide wide variation in the game. Your child can write the setup that determines the size of the pit. He or she can vary the length and width from 3 to 7 spaces, and the depth from 6 to 18 spaces. Thus, the smallest pit would be $3 \times 3 \times 6$; the largest would be $7 \times 7 \times 18$. He or she also has three choices for setting the shape of the pieces to be placed. The choices range from simple (flat pieces that are two dimensional) to more complex (extended pieces that use all three dimensions). In addition, your child can select one of three speeds at which to rotate the pieces: slow, medium, and fast. After your child makes these selections, he or she has 10 choices (0–9) for the speed of the game. The higher the number, the faster he or she must play.

As your child plays, he or she can see a scorecard on the screen that shows the number of pieces he or she has placed and the total score that he or she has earned. Your child can stop the game at any point to rest or think through a new plan of action. BLOCKOUT is a wonderful game if your child loves visual and spatial challenges.

The Boars' Store
7–9 years
Grades 2–4

Random House/American School Publishers, 1987, $39.95

Hardware
Apple II series, 64 KB
★ Essential: 5.25-inch disk drive
☆ Recommended: color monitor

Abilities Needed
Your child should be reading at the second-grade level in order to read the on-screen instructions. He or she should have a basic understanding of the value of different coins and bills and should have mastered basic addition and subtraction skills before using the program.

This program is appropriate for the learning-disabled child.

Curriculum Areas
The program teaches arithmetic and reasoning by having your child play a simulation game in which he or she counts coin values and makes change.

Arithmetic
■ *Fundamental operations*—operating with addition, operating with subtraction
■ *Measurement*—using units of money

Reasoning
- *Gathering information*—taking notes
- *Analyzing information*—distinguishing relevant from nonrelevant cues

The Program

(Tutor). In this program, your child goes shopping in the Boars' store and makes purchases from an inventory of over 100 items. He or she then goes to the cash register to total the purchases. In paying, he or she can either give the exact amount or pay a larger sum and determine the amount of change due. There are four main menu choices.

In *Counting Coins—With Help,* your child chooses items to buy and then indicates how many coins he or she needs to purchase the items. As your child pays for each item, the cash register selects the item and shows the correct amount—for example, cupcake = $0.12, pen = $0.02.

In *Counting Coins—On Your Own,* your child plays the same game as above, except that the cash register shows a total only after complete payment has been made. Your child must keep track—either in his or her head or with paper and pencil—of the total value of the coins needed.

In *Making Change—Subtracting,* your child chooses items to buy and is given a larger amount of money than the total purchase price. Your child subtracts to determine the correct change and indicates how many coins are needed to give the correct change. For example, your child makes four purchases for a total of $5.36; the program then says, "You have $10.00. The total cost is $5.36. How much change should you receive? Use paper and pencil."

In *Making Change—Counting Up,* your child chooses items to buy and is given a larger amount of money than the purchase price. Then he or she must count up from the total cost to the amount of money given. For example, if the total purchase was $0.57, the program says, "You have $0.75. The total cost is $0.57. How much change should you receive? Let's count up to $0.75."

The program features appealing, high-resolution graphics; color; sound; and animation. Your child can easily move around within each section of the program. However, he or she cannot escape an activity until it has been completed.

Your child must meet a goal in each segment of the program. When your child makes a mistake, the program gives him or her two chances to correct it. After the first try, a message and help cue appear: "Sorry, try again. Solve the problem with paper and pencil." After the second incorrect try, the computer shows the correct answer. The program also offers consistent and well-designed help screens when your child makes a mistake. For example, if he or she enters incorrect change, the help screen shows the correct change and compares it to your child's incorrect choice.

The program rewards your child verbally by showing the message "That's correct." It also requires your child to fine-tune his or her answers in order to show the best use of the coins. If your child enters the correct change but could use fewer coins, this message appears: "That's correct. Try fewer coins."

The program offers three increasingly demanding levels of play. Level 1 allows the purchase of only two items with a total cost of under $1.00. Level 2 allows the purchase of only three items with a total cost of under $5.00. Level 3 allows the purchase of four items with a total cost of under $10.00. Ten different activities—such as Birthday Party, Under Sea, Circus, and Halloween—ask your child to purchase related items. For example, if your child selects Birthday Party, he or she is shown both related items (such as a cupcake, ice cream, and a present) and unrelated items (a ticket, a diving tank, and a witch's hat). Your child can choose any item, but he or she must try to select items that go with the theme.

The Boars Tell Time

5–7 years
Grades K–2

Random House/American School Publishers, 1987, $39.95

Hardware
Apple II series, 64 KB
   ★ Essential: 5.25-inch disk drive

Abilities Needed

The program requires relatively little reading, so even if your child is not yet skilled in reading, you can easily show him or her how to work with the program independently.

This program is appropriate for the learning-disabled child.

Curriculum Areas

The program teaches and offers practice in telling both analog and digital time.

Arithmetic

■ *Measurement*—using units of time

The Program

(Tutor). In all three segments of the program, you or your child can choose to work with time in units of hours, half hours, quarter hours, or five minutes.

In *Telling Time,* your child sees an analog clock that is set to a particular time. He or she must set a digital clock to the equivalent time.

In *Setting the Clock,* your child sees a digital clock that is set to a particular time. He or she must then set an analog clock to the equivalent time.

In *Time Trials,* which is in a quiz-type format, randomly generated times appear on an analog clock. Your child must enter the correct time on a digital clock. When he or she is correct, the Boar rewards your child with an animation sequence. By pressing the Escape key, your child can see his or her score up to that point.

The program has appealing graphics, and it is generally easy to operate. You have the option of turning the sound on or off. Although it is similar to MECC's CLOCK WORKS, it requires far less reading. There is no time pressure in any of the games, so your child can take all the time he or she needs to make a decision.

In *Setting the Clock,* the minute hand moves even if your child has elected to work with units of hours. Your child might be focused only on the hours and not notice the minutes. If he or she forgets to account for the minutes, he or she might then make a number of incorrect choices, so you will need to watch and offer guidance. *Telling Time* and *Setting the Clock* both offer feedback. In each, the program tells your child each time he or she is wrong but does not supply hints about the correct answer. After three incorrect choices, the program tells your child the correct answer.

Chariots, Cougars and Kings

8–10 years
Grades 3–5

Hartley Courseware, 1985, $39.95

Hardware
Apple II series, 48 KB
  ★ Essential: 3.5-inch or 5.25-inch disk drive
  ☆ Recommended: color monitor
IBM PC and compatibles, 256 KB ($59.95)
  ★ Essential: 3.5-inch disk drive, color graphics card
  ☆ Recommended: color monitor

Abilities Needed
This program is appropriate for the learning-disabled child, although a child with significant language problems might have difficulty with it.

Curriculum Areas
The program builds comprehension skills by having your child read familiar stories and then answer questions about them.

Reading
  ■ *Decoding skills*—reading words in text, defining words
  ■ *Comprehension skills*—combining words into sentences, combining sentences, recalling information on topics, recalling details from stories, reading stories, identifying sequences of events, identifying main ideas, reading fictional texts

Reasoning
  ■ *Developing hypotheses*—making inferences and deductions, determining cause and effect

The Program

(Tutor). The program contains 20 short stories paired with good color graphics. Some of the themes include "How Did the Unicorn Get His Horn?" "What Is A Black Hole?" and "The King Who Wanted Everything Gold." After reading the stories, your child must answer different kinds of comprehension questions. If he or she answers fewer than 40 percent of the questions correctly, the story is terminated.

Your child can reread the story at any time during the presentation. Throughout the presentation, the program offers hints when your child makes a mistake—for example, it shows the section of the story that contains the correct answer so that your child can reread it.

So that you can easily pinpoint your child's difficulties, the program shows the number of correct items in each specific comprehension category when your child's record is displayed.

An extensive options menu allows you or your child to vary the program. You can alter the number of tries allowed before the correct answer is given (two is standard), change the hints that will be offered when your child gives an incorrect answer, ask the program to explain the correct answer, and make it possible for your child to rewrite the text of any story. You can also change the percentage of questions that must be answered correctly before a story is terminated, and you can determine whether the order of questions is random or parallel to the order in which the answers occur in the story.

The program also offers your child the option of creating his or her own stories and questions.

Children's Writing and Publishing Center

9 years and older
Grades 4 and up

The Learning Company, 1988, $59.95

Hardware

Apple II series, 128 KB

   ★ Essential: 3.5-inch or 5.25-inch disk drive, printer

   ☆ Recommended: color monitor

IBM PC and compatibles, 384 KB ($69.95)

★ Essential: 3.5-inch or 5.25-inch disk drive, color graphics card, printer

☆ Recommended: color monitor

Abilities Needed

To use this program, particularly the extensive on-screen instructions, your child should be reading at the third-grade level. It will also be useful if your child has some familiarity with the keyboard.

This program is appropriate for the learning-disabled child.

Curriculum Areas

The program offers practice in written communications skills through the use of a simple-to-use desktop publishing system.

Writing

■ *The process*—creating fictional texts, creating nonfictional texts, editing texts, using organizational strategies

■ *The mechanics*—spelling single-syllable words, spelling multisyllable words, constructing phrases and sentences, using punctuation and capitalization, using a word processor, proofreading

The Program

(Tool). This program offers a user-friendly word processor that is integrated with a graphics library of over 150 pictures and 22 predesigned headings. The focus is on essential steps to writing well: gathering and organizing thoughts, writing them out, and then editing them.

The word processor in the program is versatile and features colorful, easy-to-read menus that offer many options. Your child can adjust the column format to either single column (for reports, stories, or letters up to four pages long) or double column (for a newsletter of up to one page). He or she can cut and paste text, choose from eight different fonts to vary the style of text, and choose whether to insert pictures from the graphics library into the text. The program automatically wraps text around the pictures placed in the document.

The program can store and save documents as well as print them in black and white or color (if a color printer is available). It offers

WYSIWYG (what you see is what you get) displays, easy-to-follow screens, and online help for beginning writers.

The program can also interface with several compatible picture disks, potentially increasing the number of illustrations available to your child. These picture libraries include any graphics disks that are compatible with the early edition of PRINT SHOP as well as ART GALLERY I AND II (Unison World), MINIPIX 1 and 2 (Beagle Brothers), GRAPHICS SCRAPBOOK 1, 2 and 3 (Epyx), and the 23-disk GRAPHICS LIBRARY (Big Red).

Circus Math

7–8 years
Grades 2–3

Series
MECC, 1985, $59.00

Hardware
Apple II series, 48 KB
   ★ Essential: 3.5-inch or 5.25-inch disk drive
   ☆ Recommended: printer

Abilities Needed
Before using this program, your child should have prior information about the place values of numbers. You will have to show him or her how to enter the answers correctly.

This program is appropriate for the learning-disabled child.

Curriculum Areas
The program teaches arithmetic by offering practice in whole-number addition. Problems involve up to four digits and three addends.

Arithmetic
   ■ *Fundamental operations*—operating with addition

The Program
(Tutor). Using a circus theme, the program offers five activities. The five games are sequenced progressively, from easy to hard, but none offer problems that involve regrouping (carrying). Each level includes problems from the previous level in addition to more difficult problems.

In *Clown Maker,* your child solves whole-number addition problems that have up to two 2-digit addends and answers of less than 100—for example, 31 + 21 = ___. The game consists of 20 problems.

In *Clown Car,* your child solves problems that have up to three 2-digit addends—for example, 43 + 43 + 21 = ___. The game consists of 20 problems.

In *High Wire,* your child solves problems that have one single-digit addend and one addend of either three or four digits—for example, 3223 + 4 = ___. The game consists of 20 problems.

In *Cannon Shoot,* your child solves problems that have two 3-digit addends and problems that have a 2-digit addend plus a 3- or 4-digit addend—for example, 322 + 111 = ___ and 24 + 1528 = ___. The game consists of 25 problems.

In *Elephant Walk,* a timed review drill of 20 items, your child solves problems from the four preceding levels.

As in other MECC programs, this program offers structured help in reaching the right answer. When your child makes a mistake, the cue words "Try Again" appear on the screen. If he or she makes a second error, "Try Again" reappears, and the column containing the error is boxed and highlighted.

The program offers positive rewards for correct answers: Your child gets the opportunity to make a clown face, rescue a clown from a high wire, and shoot a cannonball.

You can set the program to keep a record of your child's work so that you can easily assess progress. If a printer is available, you can print and save these records. Several other options allow flexibility. You can adjust the total time for completion of review problems in *Elephant Walk* and the time allotted for each problem step, you can select either vertical or horizontal presentation for the problems, and you can select the printer feature for record keeping.

CIRCUS MATH is the second program in the seven-part *Mastering Math* series. Each program ($59.00 each) presents progressively harder material.

EARLY ADDITION (1984), for children 6–7 years old (Grades 1–2), teaches one- and two-digit addition in a drill-and-practice format. Your child works on whole-number addition problems with sums of 10 or less and on adding zero and a single-digit number. As rewards for correct answers, your child gets to help firefighters put out a blaze, make airplanes fly, and race his or her jumping frog against the computer's.

ADDITION LOGICIAN (1984), for children 8 years old (Grade 3), teaches addition problems that involve regrouping (carrying). By successfully completing the problems, your child wins points that enable him or her to play logic games against the computer.

SPACE SUBTRACTION (1985), for children 6–8 years old (Grades 1–3), teaches whole-number subtraction facts with no regrouping (borrowing). As rewards for correct answers, your child can design his or her own space creatures, land a lunar module, and play outer-space games. This program requires 64 KB of memory.

SUBTRACTION PUZZLES (1984), for children 8 years old (Grade 3), teaches whole-number subtraction problems that involve regrouping. When your child gives correct answers, he or she gets to solve peg-jumping and tracing puzzles, cross the ocean in a balloon, capture genies in a bottle, and try finding out the names of mysterious creatures. This program requires 64 KB of memory.

MULTIPLICATION PUZZLES (1985), for children 8–9 years old (Grades 3–4), teaches multiplication facts as well as problems with missing factors, both with and without regrouping. As rewards for correct answers, your child gets to rescue a castaway on a desert island, locate and capture a rabbit raiding a carrot patch, and try turning out the lights in a house with a "mind" of its own. This program requires 64 KB of memory.

QUOTIENT QUEST (1985), for children 9 years old (Grade 4), teaches division problems that involve up to four digits, with and without remainders. For completing problems successfully, your child gets to rearrange totem poles, trap a jewel thief, and search for chimpanzees. This program requires 64 KB of memory.

Clock Works

5–8 years
Grades K–1

Series
MECC, 1986, $59.00

Hardware

Apple II series, 64 KB

★ Essential: 3.5-inch or 5.25-inch disk drive

Abilities Needed

To use this program independently, your child should be reading at the second-grade level because time is occasionally expressed in written-out form—for instance, quarter to three. Even if he or she is reading at the second-grade level, your child might need your help to read the on-screen instructions.

This program is appropriate for the learning-disabled child.

Curriculum Areas

The program teaches arithmetic skills by introducing and reviewing the measurement of time. Your child learns ways to express time, the relationship between analog- and digital-clock settings, and time intervals (five minutes, ten minutes, and so on).

Arithmetic

- *Numeration*—counting sequentially
- *Concepts*—understanding relational concepts
- *Measurement*—using units of time

The Program

(Tutor). The program consists of four parts that teach and review measurement of time.

In *What's the Time,* the screen shows an analog clock that is set to a particular time. Your child practices telling time by selecting, from four possible choices, the one that correctly represents the time setting on the clock. The choices can appear in number form (3:30), in written form (three-thirty), or in both forms.

In *Set the Clock,* your child again works with an analog clock. In this segment, he or she is assigned a time and must then set the hands of the clock so that the clock face matches the assigned time.

In *Digital Drill,* your child works with a digital clock and learns the relationship between analog and digital clocks. He or she sees times that are either shown on an analog clock or written out in words. He or she then sets the digital clock so that it matches the assigned time.

In *Clock Factory,* your child designs his or her own alarm clock by selecting such features as the type of numerals (Arabic vs. Roman), the number of time intervals shown on the face, the number of numerals shown on the face (for example, four vs. twelve), the shape of the clock (for example, a coffee pot or a house), and the time the alarm will ring. After making the selections, your child sees the completed clock on the screen. The clock starts to tick and continues until the alarm goes off.

The graphics and sounds are appealing, and the formats are designed to give your child varied practice with most of the key aspects of telling time.

Except for *Clock Factory,* the game formats require your child to meet a goal. When your child makes a mistake, he or she can try twice to set the clock hands correctly or to pick the right time. The program does not offer any clues or help. After the second try, the computer sets the hands of the clock or shows the correct time choice. In *What's the Time,* if your child repeats errors, he or she eventually sees the right answer because it is the only choice left. The repeated corrections can be useful if your child makes a few consecutive errors on the same problem. If, however, he or she shows a consistent pattern of repeated errors over many trials, the program is probably too difficult for him or her at this time.

An appealing reward in *Clock Factory* is that the computer plays a tune related to the shape your child chooses for the clock face. For example, if the face is like a teapot, the computer plays "I'm a Little Teapot."

You can customize the program for your child's level in several ways: You can vary the time intervals with which your child works (for instance, 15 minutes or 30 minutes), the forms used to express time (for example, 3:00 vs. three o'clock), and the clock-face designs your child can choose in the final activity.

MEASURE WORKS (1989, $59.00, Apple II series, 128 KB) is the second program in this series. The program is for children 8–10 years old

(Grades 3–5). In the program, your child learns to use measurements in both the American and the metric systems that involve volume, weight, and size (heights, perimeters, and areas).

Code Quest

9 years and older
Grades 4 and up

Sunburst Communications, 1985, $65.00

Hardware
Apple II series, 48 KB
  ★ Essential: 5.25-inch disk drive
  ☆ Recommended: color monitor
Commodore 64, 64 KB
IBM PC and compatibles, 128 KB
  ★ Essential: 5.25-inch disk drive, color monitor

Abilities Needed
Your child should be reading at the third-grade level in order to use the program independently.

Curriculum Areas
The program teaches reasoning by having your child use systems of codes to uncover clues to the hidden identities of different objects.

Reasoning
  ■ *Gathering information*—recalling relevant information, seeking information in available sources, taking notes
  ■ *Analyzing information*—distinguishing relevant from nonrelevant cues
  ■ *Developing hypotheses*—making inferences and deductions, eliminating alternatives
  ■ *Planning strategies*—making decisions, formulating solutions, managing resources

Reading
  ■ *Comprehension skills*—playing word games

The Program

(Tutor). The program offers a choice of seven different, progressively more difficult, code options. Your child must break the codes in order to understand the clues.

In *Transposition Cipher,* the code consists of words that are written backwards and spaced differently from the actual words in the clue. For instance, the words *this one* might appear as *e nos i ht.*

In *Number Substitution Cipher,* the code substitutes numbers for letters. For example, *36-21-22 35* might stand for the words "not a."

In *Substitution Cipher,* the code substitutes one letter of the alphabet for another letter. For example, *bpoa* might stand for "more."

In *Military Intelligence Type Cipher,* the code substitutes words for letters. For instance, the word *cake* might stand for the letter *T.*

In *Twisted Path Cipher,* the code appears in a box grid, and your child ciphers it by following a mazelike pattern through the grid.

In *Picture Cipher,* each letter in the clue is the first letter in the name of a pictured object.

In *Super Sleuth,* no new codes appear. Instead, the computer randomly offers any of the other six codes.

With each code, your child searches for six clues that will help him or her identify a mystery object. For example, the mystery object might be *fire.* The first clue might be "smoke and flame," whereas the next one might be "warms your house." Your child can select a different code to search for each hint. Because there are six hints for each mystery object, he or she might use all the codes on any one problem.

In searching for each clue, your child can use a help key, which gives hints that smooth the search. But the goal is to guess the mystery object with as few clues as possible and with minimal use of the help key. Your child has only one chance to guess the mystery object. When your child feels there is enough information, he or she enters an answer, and the computer indicates whether it is right or wrong. If it is wrong, the game ends, and your child can start a new mystery search. A flaw in the design of the program is that if your child mistypes a letter when he or she enters an answer, the program treats the answer as an incorrect guess, and the game ends.

Although not exciting, the graphics are clear, and they do support the program. Because the focus is on the problem at hand and on using the codes, your child is not likely to consider them a detriment.

One option allows your child to save a game that is in progress. Another special option allows your child to enter his or her own mystery objects and clues. This option, together with the range of codes, makes the game highly variable. The program maintains its appeal over many sessions of play.

The program requires time, patience, and the ability to work in a sequenced, orderly fashion. However, codes are endlessly fascinating to children, and the program is a tantalizing one if your child has this interest.

ColorMe: The Computer Coloring Kit

3–10 years
Grades PreK–5

Mindscape Educational Software, 1985, $44.95

Hardware
Apple II series, 128 KB
IBM PC and compatibles, 256 KB
  ★ Essential: 5.25-inch disk drive (two-disk set), Koala Pad, mouse or joystick
  ☆ Recommended: color monitor, printer

Abilities Needed
Because the program uses simple icons for directions, a beginning reader can use it independently. If your child is a prereader, you will initially need to explain the program.

This program is appropriate for the learning-disabled child.

Curriculum Areas
This program teaches reasoning and writing by having your child experiment with line, color, and composition in drawing, coloring, and composing pictures.

Reasoning

- *Analyzing information* — organizing details, recognizing patterns
- *Planning strategies* — making decisions

Writing

- *The process* — creating messages for visual material
- *The mechanics* — using elements of a word processing program

The Program

(Tool). This coloring and drawing program is designed so that your child can either create original art or "cut and paste" dozens of predrawn pictures.

The program consists of two disks. The Program Disk allows your child to create original freehand art with a mouse-controlled (or joystick-controlled) crayon. The Picture Disk contains ready-made drawings, which your child can either cut and paste into his or her own pictures or simply color and print. All pictures can be displayed in both outline and filled-in form.

The program offers an easy-to-use text option that allows your child to add short captions and messages to his or her artwork.

You or your child can vary the following: the size of the crayon (four sizes), the color of the crayon (if you have a color monitor), the size of the letters in text (four sizes), and the drawing style (two functions, one appropriate for large areas and the other appropriate for small areas).

Your child can erase his or her work by setting the crayon color to match the background color (white) and then drawing over what he or she wants to erase. This procedure "whites out" the individual lines. To erase the entire screen in one step, your child activates the Erase Page option with the mouse or the joystick.

You can extend the program with other available products. COLORME PICTURE DISKS, such as *Rainbow Brite, Shirt Tales, The Hugga Bunch,* and *TinkTonks* increase the number of predrawn pictures your child can use. The COLORME SUPPLY BOX, which allows your child to create stickers, includes supplies for making stickers, buttons, coloring books, and greeting cards.

Colors and Shapes

2–4 years
Grade PreK

Series
Hartley Courseware, 1984, $35.95

Hardware

Apple II series, 128 KB
  ★ Essential: 3.5-inch or 5.25-inch disk drive, color monitor
IBM PC and compatibles, 256 KB
  ★ Essential: 3.5-inch or 5.25-inch disk drive, color graphics card, color monitor

Abilities Needed

If your child is very young, he or she will need your help in getting used to the program. After your child understands the format, he or she should be able to operate the program independently.

This program is appropriate for the learning-disabled child.

Curriculum Areas

The program provides practice in matching colors and shapes.

Reading

  ■ *Comprehension skills*—following simple directions

Arithmetic

  ■ *Numeration*—matching objects to objects

The Program

(Tutor). The program contains four activities.

In *Color Craze,* your child sees a sample of a particular color and then a row of different-colored squares. He or she selects the square that matches the sample.

In *Bats and Bears,* the format is similar to that of *Color Craze,* but in this game, your child matches shapes.

In *Ugly Bug,* your child deals simultaneously with color and shape. The screen shows the face of an "ugly bug" whose eyes, nose, and mouth are made up of different-colored shapes. Then sets of features appear, and your child must select the set that matches the facial features of the ugly bug.

In *Pick a Part,* your child sees an object, such as a car, that is made up of different-colored shapes. Then he or she sees four choices, three of which are needed to make a duplicate of the object. As your child selects the needed pieces, they move up on the screen and combine to form a figure exactly like the model.

The program's graphics, sound, and color are appealing, and picture menus make the program easy to use. In addition, it can help your young child become familiar and comfortable with computer games.

If your child takes a long time to respond, the program completes the task in progress. When your child answers correctly, the shapes move into place so that your child knows that he or she is correct. When the choice is incorrect, the program highlights the right choice.

You can vary the difficulty level of the games (three settings), the speed of the games (nine settings), the number of plays per game, and the number of games to be played. You can also turn the sound on or off.

Hartley's *Early Discoveries* series contains two additional programs for slightly older children.

In CONSERVATION AND COUNTING (1985, $35.95), for children 3–5 years old (Grades PreK–K), your child does four math-related activities that build an understanding of quantity. The games focus on one-to-one correspondence, conservation of numbers, number-numeral relationships, and matching sets—all with numbers less than 10. Each game has three levels of play. Using picture menus, your child selects his or her activity and level.

In OBSERVATION AND CLASSIFICATION (1985, $35.95), for children 3–5 years old (Grades PreK–K), your child observes and classifies familiar objects. In three games, your child selects the object that is different from others, the object that is the same size as the one shown, or the one that belongs to the same class as a group shown. Your child selects his or her own difficulty level. This program also introduces simple on-screen record keeping.

Comparison Kitchen

3–6 years
Grades PreK–1

DLM Software, 1985, $32.95

Hardware

Apple II series, 48 KB

★ Essential: 5.25-inch disk drive

☆ Recommended: color monitor

IBM PC and compatibles, 128 KB

★ Essential: 3.5-inch or 5.25-inch disk drive, color graphics card

☆ Recommended: color monitor

Abilities Needed

To use this program independently and understand its menus, your child should be reading at the first-grade level. If your child is a pre-reader, you will initially need to explain how to play the games. After becoming familiar with the format, a prereader should be able to work independently. Before using this program, your child should understand the concepts *same* and *different*.

This program is appropriate for the learning-disabled child.

Curriculum Areas

This program teaches arithmetic through games that help your child learn about sizes and amounts and that offer practice in discrimination of objects by color, shape, and size.

Arithmetic

- *Concepts* —understanding spatial concepts, understanding relational concepts
- *Applications* —using estimation

The Program

(Tutor). The program offers six activities.

In *Cookie Hunt,* your child must use classification skills to find and match cookies. He or she looks at a group of four cookies and decides which one matches a sample cookie presented by the Chef. The matches get progressively harder as they move from differences based on size, shape, or both to differences based on specific attributes (kind of icing, number of raisins).

In *Bake Shop,* your child helps the Baker make a cookie that matches a sample cookie in shape and then helps decorate the cookie so that it matches in color as well.

In *Which Is Less,* your child watches the Baker cut slices from three cakes. Your child must choose which of the three then contains the least amount of cake.

In *Same or Different,* a timed activity, your child has to work as fast as possible to determine whether pairs of baked goods are the same or different. The problems get progressively harder because the differences distinguishing each set of baked goods become more subtle.

In *Bake Off 1* and *Bake Off 2,* your child plays guessing games against either the computer (*Bake Off 1*) or a partner (*Bake Off 2*). In each game, your child sees nine different sizes of cake, ranging from one slice to a whole cake. Your child must guess which one of the nine choices matches a hidden piece that the Baker is holding. The program offers hints, using the concepts *smaller* and *larger,* to help your child arrive at the correct choice. It also provides visual cues, such as crossing off the incorrect choices, to aid your child's selections.

The graphics and sound are appealing, and the formats of the six segments are varied enough to hold your child's interest.

The Chef and the Baker appear in all the games to offer visual feedback, which is especially helpful for a prereading child. All the games are in a format that requires your child to meet a goal. When your child makes a mistake, visual, written, and sound cues indicate the error. For example, the Baker shakes his head no, the words "That's not it. Try again" appear, and the computer beeps. Your child gets a second chance to answer correctly. If he or she makes a second mistake, the computer offers the right response. In both *Bake Off* games, all the cakes that have been eliminated by the cues "smaller than that" or "larger than that" are crossed off in blue.

When your child chooses correctly, the rewards include some of the following: the Baker nods his head yes, the computer plays a tune like "The Muffin Man," or the words "You're right. They match" appear. Your child also scores points for correct answers. At times, the rewards might be confusing to a young child, particularly if he or she is not adept at number concepts. For example, at the end of *Bake Shop*—after five cookies have been made—a scoreboard appears. It shows that your child has earned two cookies for each choice that was correct on a first try and one cookie for each choice that was correct on a second try.

The program keeps a record of your child's performance and shows him or her the results after every group of five problems.

Coordinate Math

9 years and older
Grades 4 and up

MECC, 1987, $59.00

Hardware
Apple II series, 128 KB
★ Essential: 3.5-inch or 5.25-inch disk drive

Abilities Needed
Your child must be reading at the third-grade level in order to independently follow the lengthy instructions.

Curriculum Areas
The program teaches arithmetic and reasoning through the use of map coordinates that involve locations on land and at sea.

Arithmetic
- *Concepts*—understanding spatial concepts
- *Applications*—using visual representations, using estimation, applying measurement to simulated real-life situations
- *Measurement*—using units of length

Reasoning
- *Analyzing information*—organizing or sequencing details
- *Developing hypotheses*—making inferences and deductions, eliminating alternatives
- *Planning strategies*—making decisions, selecting relevant information to create a plan of action, formulating solutions

The Program

(Tutor). The program contains three segments.

In *Nomad,* your child has to drive a car to Grandma Nomad's house. She loves to move and is always in a new city and in a new location. Your child sees a map on the screen that employs either map coordinates (which use the four directions of north, south, east, or west) or graph coordinates (which use numbers on the x- and y-axes). He or she starts at the airport. The program tells him or her grandma's new location, and your child must get from the airport to the house by steadily giving the computer directions for the turns to be taken at each intersection.

In *Snark,* your child faces a character, Snark, who loves to hide in a 10-by-10 grid on the computer screen. Your child has to type in the coordinates on the x- and y-axes as well as the size of a radius that will define a circle. The computer then tells your child whether Snark is inside or outside the circle he or she has constructed. Your child has 12 tries in which to find Snark. He or she can play the game at one of three difficulty levels: With Erase, all the points that have been eliminated disappear from the screen, making the search easier; with Review What You've Done, your child can go over the results of earlier moves he or she has made; and with You're on Your Own, your child searches for Snark without any graphics help.

In *Radar,* your child is captain of a rescue boat that is trying to reach and save a runaway ship at sea. The runaway ship is destroyed if it either reaches the center of the screen or moves off the radar screen. Your child can play the game in two ways. When he or she plays using angle headings, the headings are always measured in the 360 degrees of a circle; when he or she plays using coordinate headings, your child has to direct his or her ship by entering pairs of coordinates that represent the north/south plane and the east/west plane. If your child's plan is successful, he or she receives congratulations from the computer; if it is not, there is a major crash as the runaway ship meets disaster.

The program provides good correction and guidance when your child encounters difficulty, and varying levels of play allow you or your child to adjust the demands to his or her growing level of skill. The options available in each game help to maintain your child's interest in the material. You can turn the sound on or off.

The program provides a motivating set of games that allow your child to practice map skills. However, he or she must exercise care and patience in order to get the most benefit from the material.

Counting Critters

3–6 years
Grades PreK–1

MECC, 1985, $39.95

Hardware
Apple II series, 64 KB
   ★ Essential: 3.5-inch or 5.25-inch disk drive

Abilities Needed
Before using this program, your child should be able to recognize the digits *1–20* and be able to count groups or sets of animals.

This program is appropriate for the learning-disabled child.

Curriculum Areas
This program teaches beginning arithmetic skills to your child by offering activities in number recognition and counting.

Arithmetic
   ■ *Numeration* — matching numbers to objects, counting objects, counting sequentially

The Program
(Tutor). The program offers your child practice in recognizing written numbers from 1 to 20, matching numbers with groups of objects from 1 to 20, and identifying and counting groups of objects from 1 to 10. Five games provide practice in these skills, each in a different way.

In *Matching Magic*, your child matches numbers between 1 and 20. For example, the number 5 is shown on the screen, along with four digits, such as 3, 5, 2, and 7. Your child finds the match. The program then shows a set of the same number of objects — for example, 5 doves.

In *Counting Safari*, your child counts 1 to 12 safari animals as seen by a chimpanzee from his tree in the jungle.

In *Pet Store,* your child counts the number of 1 to 12 identical puppies that correctly matches a number shown on the screen, and then places the dogs in Suzy Shopkeeper's window.

In *Counting Pond,* your child matches the number of identical fish (from a set that shows two different kinds of fish) to a number shown on the screen. These fish feed a frog in the pond.

In *Circus Puzzles,* your child identifies a number that completes a sequence. The program then reveals a dot-to-dot puzzle based on that number sequence.

Although the graphics in this program are not as captivating as those in more recent programs, it handles incorrect responses quite well. The program offers progressive hints to help your child find the right solution. Until he or she gives the right answer, your child gets a series of 3 hints: First the program highlights the wrong answer and removes it from the remaining choices. Animated characters shake their heads no; sometimes the program counts the number of animals in the set out loud. Finally the screen shows the correct answer.

Create with GARFIELD!

9 years and older
Grades 4 and up

DLM Software, 1986, $29.95

Hardware
Apple II series, 64 KB
Commodore 64/128, 64 KB
   ★ Essential: 5.25-inch disk drive, printer, blank disks for
      saving work

Abilities Needed
Your child should be reading at the fourth-grade level to follow the program instructions and to use the program independently.

    This program is appropriate for the learning-disabled child.

ALTERNATIVE VERSION

Create with GARFIELD! Deluxe Edition
DLM Software, 1988, $39.95

Hardware

Apple II series, 64 KB

Commodore 64/128, 64 KB

   ★ Essential: 5.25-inch disk drive (two-disk set), color monitor, printer, blank disks for saving work

IBM PC and compatibles, 256 KB

   ★ Essential: 5.25-inch disk drive (two-disk set), color graphics card, color monitor, printer, blank disks for saving work

---

Curriculum Areas

The program teaches writing by stimulating creative thinking and offering practice in writing. It helps your child develop a sense of design, balance, sequence, and spatial relationships.

Writing

- *The process*—creating simple written messages, applying supplied messages to visual materials, creating messages for visual material
- *The mechanics*—keyboarding, using a word processing program

The Program

(Tool). The original program includes about 75 pieces of built-in art and captions, featuring Garfield and his friends, for making cartoons, labels, and posters or personalized items such as books, letterhead, and announcements.

To create a cartoon, your child first selects a background. Then he or she chooses characters and props; sets up comic situations, such as Garfield teasing Odie or falling head over heels for Arlene; and adds either preprogrammed or original captions. By creating a separate initialized data disk, your child can save the cartoons as well as print out his or her creation.

You can vary the following features: seven backgrounds (including a room, Garfield's bed, Jon's easy chair, and so on), six characters (Garfield, Pooky, Jon, Odie, Arlene, and Nermal), twelve prop pictures (for example, a TV and a refrigerator), preprogrammed quotes from Garfield (for example, "Nap attack," "I need a little push now and then," "Why me?"), and "cartoon" words ("Wham," "Crash," "Bonk").

The program offers an easy-to-use word processor so that your child can write his or her own captions or even original short stories to go with the pictures.

CREATE WITH GARFIELD! DELUXE EDITION offers over 200 pieces of art and special features, including changeable borders, a variety of typefaces for writing captions, and an electronic feature that displays the cartoons continuously, frame after frame. It comes with an Activities booklet that illustrates the many uses of the program, including ID tags for school supplies, invitations and place cards, personalized notes and address labels, reward labels for work well done, and signs and announcements.

Crossword Magic

8 years and older
Grades 3 and up

Series
Mindscape Educational Software, 1985, $59.95

Hardware
Apple II series, 64 KB
   ★ Essential: 5.25-inch disk drive, printer
IBM PC and compatibles, 128 KB
   ★ Essential: 3.5-inch or 5.25-inch disk drive, printer
Apple Macintosh, 512KB ($49.95)
   ★ Essential: 3.5-inch disk drive, printer

Abilities Needed
This program is appropriate for the learning-disabled child.

Curriculum Areas

The program teaches reading skills by allowing your child to create customized crossword puzzles on different subjects for class projects, special occasions, or specific interests.

Reading

- *Decoding skills*—analyzing words for their meanings, enlarging vocabulary, defining words
- *Comprehension skills*—playing word games

Writing

- *The process*—creating simple written messages

The Program

(Tutee). This utility program lets your child create crossword puzzles on any topic—for example, a geographical puzzle on Africa or a mathematical puzzle using equations as clues. Puzzle size can vary; the largest puzzle your child can create occupies a 20-by-20 grid. As your child enters each word, it is displayed on the screen and is connected in the puzzle format with previously entered words. Then your child writes a clue for each word to be used in the puzzle. Clues can be up to 98 characters long. Your child can edit and review the clues before saving the puzzle.

Your child can save all puzzles for future play and can print them for use when he or she is away from the computer. After the words have been typed into the puzzle grid on the screen, they are difficult to read—partly because of colored text. If you are using a color monitor, turn off the color to improve the resolution. The puzzle printouts are produced in easier-to-read uppercase letters. Your child can include a reduced-size answer grid in the printout, and he or she can also specify that it be on a separate page.

CROSSWORD MAGIC PUZZLE DISKS are available for use with version 4.0 of CROSSWORD MAGIC that runs on the Apple II and uses 64 KB of memory ($39.95; or $79.95 for a package that also includes CROSSWORD MAGIC). This package provides ready-made puzzles in six different curriculum areas. The six programs are *Mathematics* (problems and terms), *Science* (vocabulary), *Social Studies* (history, geography facts, and vocabulary), *Language Arts* (parts of speech),

Reading (literature-based questions), and *Spelling* (common stumpers). As in CROSSWORD MAGIC, you can print or modify these puzzles to suit individual needs.

Decimal Concepts

8–11 years
Grades 3–6

Series
MECC, 1988, $59.00

Hardware
Apple II series, 128 KB
   ★ Essential: 3.5-inch or 5.25-inch disk drive

Abilities Needed
This program is appropriate for the learning-disabled child, although a child with significant visual-spatial problems might have difficulty with it.

Curriculum Areas
The program concentrates on decimals and teaches place value, rounding decimal numbers, ordering and comparing decimal numbers, and placing decimal numbers along a number line.

Arithmetic
   ■ *Concepts*—understanding spatial concepts, understanding relational concepts, understanding equations
   ■ *Applications*—using visual representations, using estimation

The Program
(Tutor). The program offers three games:

In *Maze Runner,* your child moves a runner as quickly as possible from the beginning of a maze to the end. The maze, however, is invisible. The program displays pieces of the maze only as the runner bumps into one of its walls. Your child gives directions to the runner that allow him to get around the obstacles and out of the maze. At the end of the maze, the program gives your child information about his or her performance. At this point, the work with decimals begins. For example, he or she might see that the runner ran the maze in 38.12 seconds and then see a series of questions about that number. One set of questions asks your child to convert the decimal to words (in this instance, thirty-eight and twelve hundredths) by selecting which one of four choices is the same as the number.

In *Decimal Duel,* your child plays against either a partner or the computer. Each player has a 10-by-10 grid (a square with 100 boxes), and each is assigned a number that must be reached but not exceeded. For example, the program might assign your child the number *0.23* and assign the partner *0.36*. Each player is then presented with a series of choices. For instance, your child might be given the set *0.15*, *0.08*, and *0.02*. He or she chooses a number, and the boxes in the grid fill up to that number. The choices continue until one player reaches, but does not exceed, the assigned number.

In *Decimal Bounce,* your child sees two number lines. The line at the top of the screen shows numbers in decimal form (for instance, 0.1, 0.2, 0.3), and the line at the bottom of the screen shows numbers in fractional form expressed in tenths (for instance, $\frac{1}{10}$, $\frac{2}{10}$, $\frac{3}{10}$). A ball containing a particular number (for instance, 0.83) drops down from the top of the screen. Your child directs the ball so that it lands at the appropriate point on the bottom line (in this case, between the fractions $\frac{8}{10}$ and $\frac{9}{10}$). Your child also does the reverse conversion, in which he or she must place fractions correctly on the decimal line at the top.

This attractively packaged program offers your child appealing games and gives immediate feedback about his or her understanding of decimals.

During play, your child receives written feedback for a correct answer. If he or she makes a mistake, the program offers different levels of cuing. In *Maze Runner,* your child is told to "Try again," and he or she can do so until the correct choice is made. In *Decimal Duel,* the program gives your child information such as whether he or she has entered numbers that go beyond the target number. In *Decimal Bounce,* the program tells your child why the placement he or she has made is incorrect.

You can vary several options in the program: content level, the number of problems, and speed of play. You can also turn sound on or off. An information section explains how the games are played. Your child sees a summary of his or her performance when play is complete.

This program is part of MECC's *Conquering Math* series, which contains 10 programs ($59.00 each). In the Concepts programs, your child learns the basic concepts of the math processes—for example, decimal concepts. In the Conquering programs, your child applies the basic math operations to the concepts—for instance, adding and subtracting with decimals.

In FRACTION CONCEPTS (1987), for children 8–10 years old (Grades 3–5), your child works in the "fraction factory" to learn about the functions of numerators and denominators, the expression of equivalent fractions in different terms, the addition of fractions to make a whole, and the terminology specific to fractions.

In FRACTION PRACTICE UNLIMITED (1987), for children 9–11 years old (Grades 4–6), your child practices advanced fraction drills, such as reducing fractions to their lowest terms, classifying fractions by type or size, comparing fractions by size, and renaming fractional numbers.

In CONQUERING WHOLE NUMBERS (1987), for children 8–11 years old (Grades 3–6), your child practices the four basic operations on whole numbers. The problems involve numbers with multiple digits and regrouping.

In CONQUERING FRACTIONS (+, –) (1988), for children 9–13 years old (Grades 4–8), and CONQUERING FRACTIONS (×, ÷) (1988), for children 10–13 years old (Grades 5–8), your child focuses on using the four basic operations of addition, subtraction, multiplication, and division with fractions.

In CONQUERING PERCENTS (1989), for children 10–13 years old (Grades 5–8), your child explores percentage concepts and the process of solving percentage problems.

In CONQUERING RATIOS AND PROPORTIONS (1989), for children 9–13 years old (Grades 4–8), your child explores ratio concepts and uses proportions to solve word problems. The program is set in Medieval Europe, so your child gets a taste of twelfth-century culture.

In CONQUERING DECIMALS (+,–) (1988), for children 9–13 years old (Grades 4–8), and CONQUERING DECIMALS (×, ÷) (1988), for children 10–13 years old (Grades 5–8), your child focuses on using the four basic operations of addition, subtraction, multiplication, and division with decimals.

Designasaurus

5 years and older
Grades K and up

DesignWare / Britannica Software, 1987, $39.95

Hardware
Apple II series, 128 KB
Commodore 64, 64 KB ($29.95)
   ★ Essential: 5.25-inch disk drive, printer
Apple IIGS, 768 KB (1988, $49.95)
   ★ Essential: 3.5-inch disk drive (two-disk set), mouse, printer
   ☆ Recommended: two 3.5-inch disk drives
IBM PC and compatibles, 512 KB
   ★ Essential: 3.5-inch or 5.25-inch disk drive, color graphics card, printer, mouse

---

ALTERNATIVE VERSION

Designasaurus II
DesignWare / Britannica Software, 1990, $39.95

Hardware
IBM PC and compatibles, 512 KB
   ★ Essential: 3.5-inch or 5.25-inch disk drive, printer, mouse

---

Abilities Needed
Your child should be reading at the third-grade level to operate this program independently. For early readers or prereaders, you will initially have to help read the instructions. After becoming familiar with the format, your child should be able to work independently.

This program is appropriate for the learning-disabled child.

Curriculum Areas

The program teaches reasoning and reading through background information and a simulation game about dinosaurs.

Reasoning

- *Analyzing information* — distinguishing relevant from nonrelevant cues, comparing facts and categories, organizing or sequencing details
- *Planning strategies* — making decisions, selecting relevant information to create a plan of action

Writing

- *The process* — creating messages for visual material

Reading

- *Decoding skills* — reading words in text
- *Comprehension skills* — reading nonfictional texts

The Program

(Tool/Tutor). The program offers three enjoyable activities for learning about dinosaurs and creating new and interesting creatures.

In *Build-A-Dinosaur,* your child creates his or her own prehistoric giant. Your child is met by a paleontologist at the Museum of Natural History, who helps him or her select bones for the head, neck, body, and tail from the museum's collection of fossilized dinosaur bones. Your child pieces the bones together and then gives his or her creation a name. He or she can print out the dinosaur in three different sizes along with such paleontological information as age, classification, and likelihood of survival.

In *Print-A-Dinosaur,* your child can print out 12 different dinosaurs in 3 sizes (8½ inches by 11 inches for reports, 11 inches by 17 inches for posters, and 17 inches by 22 inches for jumbo displays). Each dinosaur printout comes with a description of, and information about, that dinosaur.

In *Walk-A-Dinosaur,* your child controls a Brontosaurus, a Stegosaurus, or a Tyrannosaurus rex as it travels through five different ecosystems — perhaps the Alberta Plains, the Jurassic forests, or the Precambian swamps of 200 million years ago. Your child guides his or her dinosaur through these journeys, making choices along the way that will ensure the dinosaur's survival. The dinosaur must eat the correct foods, avoid certain predators, and watch for natural disasters. Each decision your child makes affects the delicate ecological balance. Your child must pay attention to variables such as vegetation, carnivores, and herbivores. If your child successfully guides his or her dinosaur through all five ecosystems, he or she is awarded a Certificate of Completion and is enrolled in the Dinosaur Hall of Fame. He or she can print out the diploma.

The topic of dinosaurs is fascinating, and your child can have lots of fun while learning about biological classifications, food-chain theories, ecological balance, and prehistoric events.

DESIGNASAURUS II (available only for the IBM PC and compatibles) offers four activities with enhanced graphics.

In *Create,* your child can create his or her own real or imaginary dinosaur.

In *Survive,* your child sees how his or her newly created dinosaur survives in this new time and place.

In *Time Travel,* your child's creation is transported to another time and place. Four prehistoric eras and eight ecological systems (for example, rainforest and desert) are represented.

In *Print,* your child can print out his or her creations.

Digitosaurus

8–10 years
Grades 3–5

Sunburst Communications, 1988, $65.00

Hardware

IBM PC and compatibles, 256 KB
   ★ Essential: 5.25-inch disk drive, color graphics card
IBM P/S 2, 256 KB
   ★ Essential: 5.25-inch disk drive

Abilities Needed

Your child should be reading at the third-grade level to use this program independently. After becoming familiar with the format, he or she should be able to work alone by reading only a few words. For the more difficult levels of the program, your child should have a good grasp of math operations and should be using this program to achieve automaticity.

This program is appropriate for the learning-disabled child.

Curriculum Areas

The program teaches arithmetic by having your child review the basic calculation operations with whole numbers. It teaches your child to compare several problems at once in order to determine which problem yields the largest number as solution.

Arithmetic

- *Concepts*—understanding relational concepts
- *Fundamental operations*—operating with addition, subtraction, multiplication, and division
- *Applications*—using estimation

The Program

(Tutor). Your child helps Digitosaurus, a dinosaur, grow older and wiser by solving math problems. He or she adds years to the dinosaur's age by first identifying which of three problems on the screen yields the highest number and then by solving that problem correctly.

The program presents all the problems in the same way, but it offers three levels of problem difficulty.

In the *Easy Level,* your child might see addition problems using one-digit numbers, such as $2 + 3 = $ __.

In the *Medium Level*, your child might see addition problems using two-digit numbers or a combination of one- and two-digit numbers, such as $17 + 9 = $ __.

In the *Hard Level*, your child might see addition problems using 2 two-digit numbers, such as $23 + 45 = $ __.

By solving problems correctly, your child helps the dinosaur accumulate years (points): 50 years if your child selects and answers the problem correctly on the first try; 40 years if the problem selected is the largest and correct on the second try; 35 years if the problem selected is the second largest and answered correctly on the first try; 25 years if the problem selected is the second largest and answered on the second try; 20 years if the problem selected is the smallest and answered on the first try; 10 years if the problem selected is the smallest and answered on the second try; and 0 years if the problem selected is not correct after two tries.

If your child makes an error in solving a problem, he or she is told so and given a second try. If a second mistake occurs, the computer offers the right answer.

After each set of 10 problems, your child receives a score and enters the Digitosaurus Hall of Fame.

The program allows you or your child to choose the type of math operation to be reviewed, set the level of difficulty of the problems (easy, medium, or hard), and turn the sound on or off. Your child can also select whether he or she enters the numbers in the answers from left to right or right to left.

The Dinosaur Discovery Kit

3–8 years
Grades PreK–3

First Byte / Davidson, 1989, $39.95

Hardware

Apple Macintosh, 512 KB

★ Essential: 3.5-inch disk drive, printer

☆ Recommended: mouse

IBM PC and compatibles, 512 KB

★ Essential: 3.5-inch disk drive or 5.25-inch disk drive (two-disk set), color monitor, color graphics card, printer

☆ Recommended: mouse

The program is compatible with several speech accessories, ranging in price from $50.00 through $150.00, made by Covox (503-342-1271), Hearsay, Inc. (718-232-7266), and Street Electronics Corporation (805-684-4593). Although not essential for operating the program, these accessories provide higher-quality, more natural voice sounds than the program offers.

Abilities Needed

If your child is a prereader, he or she will initially need your help to follow the instructions. After becoming familiar with the format, he or she should be able to work most of the program independently.

This program is appropriate for the learning-disabled child.

Curriculum Areas

This program teaches writing and reading by having your child construct and color pictures of dinosaurs and create stories to accompany the pictures. Additionally, the program provides practice in visual discrimination skills through a Concentration-type matching game.

Writing

- *The process*—creating messages for visual material, creating fictional texts
- *The mechanics*—spelling single-syllable and multisyllable words, constructing phrases and sentences

Reading

- *Decoding skills*—linking sounds to letters and words, reading single-syllable words, matching pictures and words, blending clusters of letters into sounds, reading words in text
- *Comprehension skills*—following simple directions, combining words into sentences, combining sentences, reading and listening to stories

The Program

(Tool/Tutor). This speech-enhanced program with its easy-to-use picture icons smooths the way for a prereader or beginning reader. Zug, the talking Megasaurus, acts as your child's guide to learning about dinosaurs while your child builds early reading and writing skills. The program offers three activities.

In *Coloring Book,* your child colors dinosaur scenes by selecting a crayon in response to a prompt word that is both written on the screen and spoken. For example, the key word *trees* appears on the screen, and the program says the word aloud. Your child then selects the green crayon from 12 available colors. Trees appear in his or her picture, and the program both says and shows the words *green trees.* When the picture is finished, the program writes out and tells a dinosaur fact related to the picture. Your child can print out the picture and text.

In *Story Maker,* your child creates a story and picture by selecting icons to represent characters, actions, and objects. First he or she selects a story from among three choices: Dinosaur Land, Zug's Party, and Stuck. Then he or she selects picture objects, such as trees, mountains, and different kinds of dinosaurs to complete a scene. These story symbols can be used to create a picture or to complete a sentence. As your child constructs the picture, a sentence like the following might appear: "A Tyrannosaurus rex with big teeth arrives. To get him to smile, Zug had to give him the biggest __." Your child supplies the last word by choosing from the story symbols. He or she might, for example, select a balloon or a present. That symbol is then added to the picture. When the picture is complete, your child can go on to the following choices:

- Read Story. The program reads the story and builds the picture as your child created it. Your child can repeat the story as many times as desired.

- See Story. The screen displays only the text of the story.

- Hear Story. Your child hears the text spoken, sentence by sentence, and sees the completed picture.

- Print. Your child prints out the picture, the story, or both.

In *Dinosaur Match,* a Concentration-like game, your child matches dinosaurs of all kinds and sizes. When he or she has matched all the dinosaurs, he or she can print out an award certificate for the winner. Your child selects exactly the kind of game he or she wants to play by making the following choices: He or she can choose to match real dinosaurs, dinosaur shadows, or pictures of Zug in different costumes; he or she can set the level of play at Easy or Hard; and he or she can choose to play alone, with a friend, or against Zug. If your child selects Zug as an opponent, he or she can determine Zug's level of ability (silly, smart, or very smart).

This is an especially appealing program because it features the ever-fascinating topic of dinosaurs and because it offers excellent multicolor graphics, sound, and help cues. The speech feature reads all the program text, including menu choices, story sentences, and individual words. The program offers other options as well: You can turn the sound on or off, you can change the volume, and you can enter your child's name at the beginning so that the program speaks it throughout as a reward for good work.

The program has the potential to grow with your child through the early childhood years. The youngest children can easily use the picture icons, and older children who can read will enjoy the stories and dinosaur facts.

Dinosaurs

2½–5 years
Grades PreK–K

Advanced Ideas, 1984, $39.95

Hardware
Apple II series, 64 KB
Commodore 64, 64 KB ($34.95)
   ★ Essential: 5.25-inch disk drive
IBM PC and PS/2 and compatibles, 256 KB
   ★ Essential: 5.25-inch disk drive, color graphics card

Abilities Needed
Before using this program, your child should be familiar with the names of the six dinosaurs covered in the program and also, perhaps, information about which ate plants and which ate meat.

This program is appropriate for the learning-disabled child.

Curriculum Areas
The program introduces your young child to basic computer use while offering practice in the prereading skills of matching, sorting, classification, counting, and pattern and letter recognition.

Reading
- *Decoding skills*—matching and recognizing letters, matching pictures and words

Arithmetic
- *Numeration*—matching objects to objects
- *Concepts*—understanding spatial concepts

Reasoning

■ *Analyzing information*—comparing facts and categories, organizing details, recognizing patterns

The Program

(Tutor). Five games, featuring six dinosaurs, are progressively sequenced from easy to hard.

In *Matching,* your child matches the target dinosaur to its twin.

In *Sorting,* your child sorts the dinosaurs into two groups, those that ate meat and those that ate plants.

In *Classifying,* your child groups the dinosaurs on the basis of the environments they lived in—land, sea, or air.

In *Counting and Matching,* your child matches a picture of a target dinosaur or dinosaurs with its correct twin from among six choices.

In *Pattern and Letter Recognition,* your child matches the picture of each dinosaur with its name.

The dinosaurs move across the screen from left to right, offering your child an introduction to the reading directionality he or she will encounter in reading and writing.

The program does not manage errors well in that it does not offer hints or cues when your child makes a mistake. Until he or she offers the correct choice, the game will not continue. For the youngest children, the absence of instructions is potentially frustrating unless you are present to provide direction.

In all other ways, the program is easy to use and offers a stimulating topic, positive reinforcement for correct answers (the dinosaurs stomp, swim, or fly across the screen), and an entertaining introduction to basic computer operations, such as using the keyboard.

Easy as ABC

3–6 years
Grades PreK–1

Spinnaker Educational Software,
Division of Queue, Inc., 1984, $39.95

Hardware

Apple II series, 64 KB
Commodore 64, 64 KB

★ Essential: 5.25-inch disk drive

☆ Recommended: color monitor

Apple Macintosh, 128 KB

★ Essential: 3.5-inch disk drive

☆ Recommended: color monitor

IBM PC and compatibles, 64 KB

★ Essential: 5.25-inch disk drive, color graphics card

☆ Recommended: color monitor

Abilities Needed

Your child can operate this program independently because no reading is required.

This program is appropriate for the learning-disabled child.

Curriculum Areas

This program is designed to teach the alphabet to young children.

Reading

- *Decoding skills*—matching and recognizing letters, dealing with sequence and direction

The Program

(Tutor). This easy-to-use program of five games provides your child practice with the ABC's. Using the picture menus, your child can select games without your help.

In *Match Letters,* your child picks up letters shown at the bottom of the screen to match letters in a target word. Each letter is dropped onto the dash directly below its matching letter. For instance, the target word is *ZEBRA*; the choices are R Z E B A.

In *Dot to Dot,* your child makes colorful pictures by finding letters in alphabetic order. Each time your child selects a letter in the right order, a line connects the dots.

In *Leapfrog,* your child makes a frog leap into the air by finding missing letters. Three frogs are shown; two of them hold letters. Your child determines which of six choices is the letter the middle frog needs to complete a three-letter sequence. Your child might see, for instance, the sequence $L \_ N$, with the choices being D K M H O C.

In *Lunar Letters,* your child plots the course to a distant planet by picking up six different letters in alphabetic order and dropping them into the Universe. The letters are shown, out of order, at the bottom of the screen.

In *Honey Hunt,* your child fills a beehive with honey by flying a bee into one of four flowers. The correct flower has matching uppercase and lowercase letters—for example Ll.

The program indicates when your child has made a mistake. For example, in *Matching Letters,* the computer beeps; in *Leapfrog,* the frog eats the incorrect letter; in *Dot to Dot,* a letter lights up and blinks. Your child then has a second chance to make a selection.

The program rewards your child for correct choices with both visual and aural feedback. Musical tunes accompany most activities. In *Leapfrog,* the frog leaps up into the air when the right letter is selected for the sequence. In *Honey Hunt,* the bee drinks honey from the hive.

Easy Graph

8 years and older
Grades 3 and up

Grolier Electronics / Houghton Mifflin, 1984, $49.95

Hardware
Apple II series, 64 KB
Commodore 64, 64 KB
IBM PC and compatibles, 64 KB
★ Essential: 5.25-inch disk drive, printer

ALTERNATIVE VERSION

Easy Graph II
Grolier Electronics / Houghton Mifflin, 1988, $60.00

Hardware
Apple II series, 64 KB
★ Essential: 5.25-inch disk drive, printer

Abilities Needed
Your child should be reading at the third-grade level in order to use the program independently.

This program is appropriate for the learning-disabled child.

Curriculum Areas

The program teaches fundamental graphing concepts. Your child learns to read and understand graphs and use them for displaying information.

Arithmetic

- *Applications*—creating and using visual representations

The Program

(Tutor/Tool). This easy-to-use program takes your child through each step of graphing. He or she learns to represent information using graphs and charts and learns how to make three different kinds: pictographs, bar graphs, and pie charts. The program has four parts.

In *Introduction,* your child learns what graphing is all about and how information looks when it is put into each of the three different types of graphs.

In *Learn to Use Easy Graph,* your child learns to read graphs and make them. The program defines each type of graph: A pictograph uses pictures or symbols to represent numbers; a bar graph uses wide, solid lines to show the numbers; and a pie chart pictorially compares parts of a whole. The program discusses the different purposes of the three kinds of graphs through examples. For instance, a birthday party with four guests might demonstrate the use of a pictograph. The birthday cake is cut into 12 pieces so that everyone can have 2 pieces, with some cake left over for later. The computer says, "Let's make a pictograph to show who ate the birthday cake. Janice ate 2 slices, Carlos ate 1 slice, Maria ate 2 slices, and Doug ate 3 slices. There are 4 slices left."

In *Practice Using Easy Graph,* your child practices making each kind of graph. Using a step-by-step approach to preparing a graph, the program helps your child define the goal. "Using a pictograph, I want to compare the __ of several __." Your child then fills in the blanks with appropriate topics—for instance, "I want to compare the populations of several states."

In *Create Your Own Graphs,* your child uses the simple graphing tool to create and print graphs of his or her own information.

Easy Graph lets your child compare up to eight subjects at a time. He or she can choose to display the data in a pictograph, with 20 symbols to select from, or in a bar graph or pie chart.

The updated EASY GRAPH II version uses a five-step, fill-in-the-blanks tutorial to teach your child how to present information visually. This program offers four types of graphs: pictographs, bar charts, line graphs, and pie charts. Your child enters his or her information, and the program scales and plots the data.

This well-designed program complements the teaching of graphing skills in school. After your child understands the principles of graphing, he or she can use the program to illustrate a broad range of topics for homework assignments and other schoolwork.

Enchanted Forest

9 years and up
Grades 4 and up

Sunburst Communications, 1985, $65.00

Hardware
Apple II series, 64 KB
Tandy 1000, 256 KB
★ Essential: 5.25-inch disk drive, color monitor
IBM PC and compatibles, 128 KB
★ Essential: 5.25-inch disk drive, color graphics card, color monitor

Abilities Needed
Your child should have third-grade reading ability in order to handle the on-screen instructions and text. Even a child with this level of reading ability might need your help in reading the extensive manual. Your child should also be able to draw maps because this skill is necessary for keeping track of the information he or she will be getting throughout the program.

Curriculum Areas
The program teaches reasoning through a game in which your child learns principles of logic, including negation (for instance, "NOT the small ones"), conjunction ("the white ones AND the small ones"), and disjunction ("the large one AND/OR the circle").

Reasoning
■ *Gathering information*—recalling relevant information, seeking information in an available source, taking notes

- *Analyzing information*—distinguishing relevant from nonrelevant cues, comparing facts and categories
- *Developing hypotheses*—making inferences and deductions, formulating rules and generalizations, eliminating alternatives
- *Planning strategies*—making decisions, selecting relevant information to create a plan of action, formulating solutions

The Program

(Tutor). The program uses the enticing theme of a wicked witch who must be defeated. The witch's spell has changed the forest animals into geometric shapes and has hidden them in enchanted ponds. Your child, along with 12 "friends" built into the program, must free the animals and reach the witch's castle. The program has three main sections.

In the *Witch's School,* your child learns the rules of the game and practices them. Using the categories of shape, size, and color, your child learns the concepts of negation, conjunction, and disjunction. He or she becomes familiar with solving problems such as identifying "all the shapes that are not small" and "shapes that are all purple and all large." The three categories cover two sizes (large and small), four colors (purple, black, green, and white), and four shapes (square, triangle, circle, and rectangle).

In *Forest and Storm,* your child searches for the animals hidden in the enchanted ponds. He or she moves in any of four directions: north, east, south and west. Your child's job is to locate one of the ponds and then, using on-screen cues about the geometric figures, determine what geometric figure is in the pond. When your child can describe all the animals in the pond, the next step is to reach the witch's computer, where he or she will enter the information about the ponds and try to free the animals.

During the search, your child might encounter a storm, which results in the loss of three friends. The friends are then changed into geometric figures and join the animals that your child has to set free. The program is set up so that there is a 15 percent chance of a storm after your child makes three moves in the forest. Your child continues to face storms over the course of the journey. Should he or she lose all the computer friends, the game is over, and the witch is victorious.

In *Witch's Computer,* your child's goal is to enter the logical connectives that define the set of figures in a particular pond. If your child knows the secret, he or she can free the animals. If your child's logic is incorrect, he or she loses all the unfreed ponds. Once a pond is freed, however, your child can't lose it by making mistakes. The cycle is repeated until your child frees all the ponds. In this segment of the program, your child can also get a status report that includes such information as the number of animal ponds, the animals that have been freed, and the number of friends lost.

The game is exciting and complex, and it lends itself to endless variations. It takes time to play, requires concentration, and must be taken seriously if it is to be both useful and fun. It can be played much more effectively if your child takes notes on the information as he or she is receiving it.

The graphics and animation support the content. They are not outstanding, but they need not be in a program such as this, in which the focus is on sophisticated thinking.

In *Forest and Storm,* the program tells your child whether his or her decision about the geometric figure is correct or not. Your child can keep working on the game until he or she is correct. In *Witch's Computer,* when he or she enters an incorrect logical connective, your child loses all the unfreed ponds.

Your child can play the game alone or with a partner. An extensive manual offers a range of additional productive ideas for exploring the domain of logic.

Estimation: Quick Solve I

9 years and older
Grades 4 and up

Series
MECC, 1990, $59.00

Hardware
Apple II series, 128 KB
   ★ Essential: 3.5-inch or 5.25-inch disk drive

Abilities Needed

Your child should be reading at the third-grade level in order to follow the written material independently. The program assumes your child understands the concept of estimation and can use decimals, fractions, whole numbers, and percentages.

This program is appropriate for the learning-disabled child, although a child with significant visual-spatial and organizational problems might have difficulty with it.

Curriculum Areas

This program teaches arithmetic by offering repeated practice in the important skill of estimation.

Arithmetic

- *Concepts*—understanding relational concepts
- *Fundamental operations*—applying the operations to whole numbers, decimals, fractions, and percentages
- *Applications*—using estimation

The Program

(Tutor). Using a game format to solve a series of estimation problems, your child competes either against a friend or against one of six players that "live" inside the computer. The players have different personalities, and each one offers your child different tips on how to work with estimation problems.

At the start of the game, a game board appears on the screen. It has three columns, each one labeled with the type of problem that will appear in that column—for instance, decimals or percentages. Each column has four rows: The top row contains the number 10; the second row, the number 20; the third row, the number 30; and the bottom row, the number 40. These numbers stand for the points your child earns by solving a problem in that particular row. The problems in the lower rows, which earn more points, must be solved faster, and the estimates must be closer to the answers than those in the top rows. The program has three parts.

In *Rules,* your child is introduced to the host of the game, Esther Mation, who explains the rules. Games are set for two rounds, with 12 problems each round.

In *Quick Solve,* your child plays the game. When the game begins, the computer decides whether your child or the partner will start. A problem then appears on the screen. It is from one of the boxes in the game board, and it is worth the number of points in that box. For example, the problem might be a picture with a set of black squares and white squares. The computer presents a written message that asks your child to "Estimate the percentage of squares that are black." Your child presses a letter on the keyboard when he or she is ready to answer. If your child doesn't answer quickly enough, he or she loses a turn, and the other player can answer. To earn points, estimates must be within an acceptable range.

In *Player Profiles,* your child sees profiles of the computer's inhabitants, against whom he or she can play.

The play aspects of this game are well designed, and they add to, rather than detract from, the skill being practiced.

When an answer is not correct, the player is told that the estimate is "not close enough," and the other player then has the chance to solve the problem.

If the estimate is close enough, the computer tells this to the player in a written message and awards the player the points he or she has earned. It also displays a line that shows an acceptable estimate range for the problem. For example, if the exact answer is 16 percent, the line might show a range of 10 percent to 20 percent. At times, a bonus question appears, and the player at the moment has the chance to earn extra points. The game is set to be played for 2 rounds, with 12 problems in each round. The player with the most points wins.

Several options provide variation. You or your child can select the categories to be played, the problem types, the time settings, and the number of rounds per game.

ESTIMATION: QUICK SOLVE II, the second program in this series, (1990, $59.00) is for children 10 years and older (Grades 5 and up). In this program, your child earns points for estimating problems involving time, measurement, money, and graphs.

Fantavision

9 years and older
Grades 4 and up

Wild Duck, 1991, $59.95

Hardware
Commodore Amiga, 256 KB
IBM PC and compatibles, 256 KB

★ Essential: 3.5-inch or 5.25-inch disk drive, mouse, and color monitor

Note: The program is to become available for the Apple II series (128 KB) and the Apple II GS (256 KB) in October 1991, from Roger Wagner Publishing.

Abilities Needed
Although the program demands little reading because all the pull-down menus include picture icons, the concepts behind the program and its use are sophisticated. A younger child will need your help to read the manual and learn how to use the program.

Curriculum Areas
This program teaches reasoning and writing skills by having your child use animation techniques to create movies and dazzling special effects on the computer screen.

Reasoning
■ *Analyzing information*—organizing or sequencing details, recognizing patterns
■ *Planning strategies*—making decisions, selecting relevant information to create a plan of action

Writing
■ *The process*—creating messages for visual material
■ *The mechanics*—using elements of a word processing program

The Program
(Tool). This program allows your child to draw anything on one frame and then instantly animate it or transform it into something else in the following frames. For an action sequence, your child draws the first and

last frames. For example, in frame one, your child draws a plane in the air. In frame two, he or she draws a plane on a runway. Then the computer generates up to 64 intervening frames to complete the action so that the plane appears to come in for a realistic three-point landing. The possibilities for creating such projects as movies, cartoons, and film strips are endless.

The program offers about 20 different functions, all presented in picture icons. Using a mouse or a joystick, your child simply clicks on the functions that he or she wants to activate. Among the functions that your child can activate with icons are Draw, Insert, Delete, Draw Circles, and Draw Rectangles. Your child also uses icons to access the Text Writer, the Color Palette (14 colors and patterns), and Dimensions (solid shapes, lines, or dots).

Your child can view his or her creations frame by frame by selecting the Filmstrip icon. He or she can also select, frame by frame, objects that he or she wants to manipulate with the Goodies or Edit menu. The Goodies menu includes such processes as Zoom, Flip, Squash, Turn, and Lean. Your child selects the Edit menu to add text to the artwork on the screen. The Edit menu includes processes such as Undo, Cut, Paste, Copy, Clone, and Zap.

Your child can use four animation modes for variety: Normal, Background, Lightning, and Trace (to create special effects).

The program comes with an extensive manual that clearly explains all the options and how to work with them.

Firehouse Rescue

3–7 years
Grades PreK–2

Fisher-Price / Gametek / IJE, 1988, $14.95

Hardware

Apple II series, 128 KB

★ Essential: 5.25-inch disk drive

☆ Recommended: color monitor, joystick

IBM PC and compatibles, 256 KB

★ Essential: 3.5-inch or 5.25-inch disk drive

☆ Recommended: color monitor, joystick

Abilities Needed

If your child is a preschooler or prereader, he or she will initially need your help to read the directions. After becoming familiar with the format, your child should be able to work independently.

This program is appropriate for the learning-disabled child, although a child with significant visual-spatial problems might have difficulty with it.

Curriculum Areas

The program teaches reasoning through a game that offers practice in decision-making skills and recall of details. Your child also strengthens hand-eye coordination.

Reasoning

- *Gathering information* —recalling relevant information
- *Analyzing information* —distinguishing relevant from nonrelevant cues
- *Developing hypotheses* —eliminating alternatives
- *Planning strategies* —making decisions, selecting relevant information to create a plan of action

The Program

(Tutor). Your child takes on the job of a firefighter-in-training. He or she drives the firetruck through different mazes rescuing either Little People or pets from various locations. After your child drives the firetruck out of the firehouse and into a maze, he or she uses the four direction arrow keys (Right, Left, Up, and Down) to choose the direction in which he or she wants the firetruck to move. The house your child must reach signals him or her by flashing the word *house*. The program offers four progressive levels of play.

In *Level 1,* your child drives through four single-screen mazes. Each of the mazes has one house, and there is no time limit.

In *Level 2,* your child drives through three multiscreen mazes. All the mazes have two houses, and there is no time limit. When your child rescues the people or pets in the first house, he or she must go on to the second house to complete the maze.

In *Level 3,* your child drives through the same mazes as in Level 2 but with the added challenge of a 50-second time limit. A time bar at the bottom of the screen shows the time remaining. If time runs out before the rescue is complete, your child can try the maze again.

In *Level 4,* your child drives through the Level-3 mazes with a 50-second time limit, but he or she must also find a hidden key at each flashing house. Your child must pick up the key before entering the house.

A rather loud noise accompanies the firetruck as it moves along the paths. This sound could be distracting to some children, and you have the option of turning off the sound at any time.

First Letter Fun

3–6 years
Grades PreK–1

MECC, 1985, $39.95

Hardware
Apple II series, 64 KB
   ★ Essential: 3.5-inch or 5.25-inch disk drive

Abilities Needed
To use this program, your child must be able to recognize all the letters of the alphabet, and he or she should know some initial-letter sounds. In the beginning, a preschooler might need your help to understand the games.

   This program is appropriate for the learning-disabled child.

Curriculum Areas
The program teaches reading-readiness skills. Using games with clear designs and simple graphics, the program provides practice in matching initial letters to sounds. It includes all the letters of the alphabet except Q and X.

Reading
   ■ *Decoding skills*—linking sounds to letters and words, reading single-syllable words

The Program
(Tutor). The program offers four games, each one centered on a particular theme. Each story shows an animated sequence of events.

In *Farm,* the program highlights one of 10 farm-related pictures (for example, a horse, a gate, an apple). Your child must identify the correct beginning sound of the name of that object from among four letters. He or she can identify the letter either by choosing from a selection box or by typing the correct letter on the keyboard.

The other three games have different topics, but they use the same format as *Farm.*

In *Circus,* your child sees pictures of circus animals.

In *Magic,* he or she sees pictures related to magic.

And in *Park,* your child sees pictures of objects or activities related to recreation.

The program gives your child three tries at choosing the right letter, but it offers no hints or clues. After the third incorrect answer, the program shows the correct letter and also shows the complete word under the picture of the object.

The program offers clear, positive rewards for good work. At the end of each sequence, it shows all the pictures and corresponding sounds that your child matched correctly during the game.

The program offers only one option: You can change the letters from all uppercase to all lowercase so that your child learns to recognize letters in both forms.

First Letters and Words   *3–6 years*
Grades PreK–1

Smartworks / Davidson, 1988, $39.95

Hardware
IBM PC and compatibles, 512 KB
   ★ Essential: 5.25-inch disk drive, color graphics card, mouse
   ☆ Recommended: printer

Abilities Needed
Because the program simulates speech and reads all the material aloud (in addition to showing it on the screen), your child can easily operate the program without your help. However, he or she should know how to use a mouse.

The program is appropriate for the learning-disabled child.

Curriculum Areas

The program teaches beginning reading skills by giving your child practice in matching uppercase and lowercase letters, relating letters to words, and playing simple word games.

Reading

- *Decoding skills*—matching and recognizing letters, linking sounds to letters and words, reading single-syllable words, matching pictures and words, enlarging vocabulary
- *Comprehension skills*—playing word games

The Program

(Tutor). Ted-E-Bear is your child's guide through the four activities in this program. Ted-E-Bear talks throughout the program, offering your child instructions, explanations, and special reward messages.

In *Card Circus,* your child helps circus performers with their acts by matching uppercase and lowercase letters. For example, the letter *A* appears on the screen, accompanied by four choices on cards: *b, J, W,* and *a.* When your child correctly matches the uppercase *A* and the lowercase *a,* Ted-E-Bear pronounces the letter.

In *Magic Letter Machine,* your child presses a letter on the keyboard, and the letter appears on the screen as if it were being drawn by a pencil on paper. Ted-E-Bear says the name of the letter and sends it to his magic machine. Then the letter appears on the screen together with a picture of an object whose name begins with that letter and a short sentence, such as "R is for rocket."

In *Dinosaur Surprise,* your child learns colors and the names of body parts. An outline drawing of a dinosaur appears on the screen. The program displays the name of a body part (for example, "head") and Ted-E-Bear says the name aloud. By clicking the mouse on the color palette, your child selects a color to fill the specified body part, and Ted-E-Bear says the name of the color. When your child has completed the whole dinosaur, the dinosaur's name is spoken and displayed at the top of the screen. If a printer is available, you can print and save these pictures.

In *Who Am I?* your child plays a guessing game with the computer. Ted-E-Bear provides short descriptions of a mystery animal or object, and your child uses them to identify it and type in its name. For example, Ted-E-Bear might say, "I am small and gray. I love to eat cheese. I hate cats! Who am I?" When your child has correctly named the animal, Bear spells the word and says, "I am a mouse."

Because of the highly structured content, it is almost impossible for your child to make errors. The program rewards him or her with speech, music, special messages, colorful graphics, and animation in every activity. You can customize the program by creating spoken messages specifically for your child. Then messages such as "Keep up the good work, Michael" or "Good job, Michael" will appear intermittently throughout the game. You can also change the volume of Ted-E-Bear's voice or turn it off.

Fish Scales

4–8 years
Grades PreK–3

DLM Software, 1985, $32.95

Hardware
Apple II series, 48 KB
   ★ Essential: 5.25-inch disk drive
   ☆ Recommended: color monitor

Abilities Needed
Your child should be reading at about second-grade level in order to understand the menus and use this program independently. If your child is a prereader or is reading below second-grade level, he or she will need your help to follow on-screen directions, cues, and rewards.

   This program is appropriate for the learning-disabled child.

Curriculum Areas
The program teaches arithmetic by having your child measure height, length, and distance and use estimation to compare measurements.

Arithmetic
   ■ *Numeration*—matching numbers to objects
   ■ *Concepts*—understanding relational concepts
   ■ *Applications*—using estimation
   ■ *Measurement*—using units of length

Reading

- *Comprehension skills*—following simple directions

The Program

(Tutor). Your child is welcomed by a friendly fisherman, who appears in all six games and offers visual feedback to prereaders.

In *Fish Jump,* your child uses a measuring stick with a scale of 1 through 9 to make a fish leap out of the water to different heights. Your child presses a number on the keyboard, the measuring stick shows that number of units, and the fish jumps to that height.

In *Today's Catch,* your child uses the same measuring stick to compare the lengths of several colorful fish. The fisherman pulls a fish from his basket and holds it up to the measuring stick. Your child measures the fish and presses the number from 1 through 9 that represents the correct length.

In *Look and Hook,* your child catches a passing fish by setting the fishhook to the correct depth. The fisherman shows a number, which is the depth of the next fish, and your child moves the hook to that depth.

In *Which Fish?* your child measures several fish of different lengths. The fisherman presents a number from 1 through 9 and five fish. Your child finds the fish whose length matches the number.

In *Fishing Dock,* your child measures distances in order to find the fish closest to the dock. The fisherman shows two fish. Your child measures the distance from the dock to each fish by counting the white squares along a line drawn from the fish to the dock.

In *Fishing Derby,* your child plays a guessing game of skill and chance, either alone or with another player. Players compete to catch the most fish. Your child casts for fish by pressing a number on the keyboard from 1 through 9. If a fish is hiding where he or she casts, that fish is caught.

When your child makes a mistake, the fisherman shakes his head no, and the program displays written hints on the screen. For example, in *Today's Catch,* the words "Too short" or "Too long" appear; in *Fishing Dock,* numbers appear along the distance lines for your child to count. Your child then gets a second chance to answer correctly. If he or she makes a second error, the fisherman offers the right answer.

Your child gets various rewards for correct answers. The program plays tunes such as "My Bonnie Lies over the Ocean," the fisherman nods his head yes, and the measuring stick displays a blinking red line at correct numbers. After your child catches or measures a series of five fish, he or she is rewarded with points (two fish for a correct answer on the first try; one fish for a correct response on the second try). The program displays the scores in a scoreboard.

You can turn off both the sound effects and the screen directions. The latter option is useful for prereaders, who might be confused by all the written text.

Friendly Filer

9 years and older
Grades 4 and up

Grolier Electronics / Houghton Mifflin, 1984, $80.00

Hardware
Apple II series, 128 KB
IBM PC and compatibles, 128 KB
★ Essential: 5.25-inch disk drive, extra blank disks for creating your own databases
☆ Recommended: printer

Abilities Needed
Your child should be reading at the fourth-grade level in order to independently follow the tutorial that guides his or her use of the program.

This program is appropriate for the learning-disabled child, although a child with significant language problems might have difficulty with it.

Curriculum Areas
The program offers your child the opportunity to understand, create, and use databases (organized sets of information on particular topics).

Writing
■ *The process*—using organizational strategies
■ *The mechanics*—using study skills

Reading
■ *Comprehension skills*—following complex directions

Reasoning

- *Gathering information* —recalling relevant information, taking notes
- *Analyzing information* —distinguishing relevant from nonrelevant cues, organizing or sequencing details

The Program

(Tool/Tutor). This program teaches and offers practice in the invaluable skills of organizing and retrieving information. The menu has four major segments.

In *Introduction,* InfoImp tells your child how the program is organized. This section is a carefully organized tutorial in which your child goes through each step of the filing system. For example, he or she sees names of different fruits and their prices scattered all over the screen. InfoImp then shows your child how this information can be organized in neat and useful ways, such as by alphabetic order or price.

In *Learn to Use Friendly Filer,* your child learns how to sort a file and how to select records. He or she becomes familiar with the basic vocabulary of storing and retrieving information, learning terms such as *file, record,* and *field.* Your child learns that a file is made up of many records and that each record is made up of fields. For example, a file on jungle animals might have 40 or 50 records, each one representing information on a different animal. The record on each animal contains the same fields. In this instance, they might be animal name, weight, diet, and habitat.

In *Practice with Friendly Filer,* your child continues the tutorial by practicing the concepts he or she has learned up to this point. This segment allows your child to sort files and select records. This segment also offers a Challenge component in which the program presents questions that test your child's ability to use the Friendly Filer. Your child can choose questions at a Beginner, Intermediate, or Expert level.

In *Using Friendly Filer,* your child actually creates databases. The segment offers the following options:

- Create a file. He or she can name the file and decide what fields it will have and how many records he or she will enter.
- Edit a file. He or she can add, change, or delete records.
- Search a File. He or she can select, sort, or print records.

The program is well designed and offers your child steady and careful guidance through the complex terrain of data management. Although the material is presented in a clear, businesslike form, the program offers little in the way of graphics or animation. This presentation is appropriate, however, because a database is a serious tool. Unless your child has already learned database-management skills in school, he or she will probably need several training sessions before feeling comfortable with the program.

This is the sort of program that can grow with your child because the skills it develops become increasingly sophisticated with practice. At the outset, your child is likely to welcome your guidance when the time comes to create and use his or her own files. He or she is also likely to enjoy working on the program with friends because the partnership can yield good discussions and lead to the creation of richer filing systems.

The information your child sees on the screen at any one time is naturally only a small part of a file. He or she might need some time to get accustomed to scrolling through information. The program assumes that your child's written-language skills are relatively sophisticated and pose no significant problems. For example, if your child misspells the words he or she enters, the program will accept the misspellings.

The program can be used for pleasurable activities, such as keeping the records of a party your child might be planning. In the main, however, the program is a valuable tool that your child can use to organize information on any major subject in the curriculum.

The FRIENDLY FILER SOCIAL STUDIES ACTIVITIES DISK and the SCIENCE AND NATURE ACTIVITIES DISK are also available for use with the program ($19.95 each). These database files contain information that complements school curricular activities. The Social Studies Disk offers information on explorers, Native Americans, Canadian provinces, famous people, and more. The Science and Nature Disk can be used to create databases on nutrition, rocks and minerals, the animal kingdom, world energy resources, edible plants, and inventions.

Fun from A to Z

3–6 years
Grades PreK–1

MECC, 1985, $39.95

Hardware
Apple II Series, 64 KB
★ Essential: 3.5-inch or 5.25-inch disk drive

Abilities Needed
Your prereading preschooler can operate this program independently. He or she will not need to read because menu choices and scores are given in picture form. Keyboard manipulation is simple.

This program is appropriate for the learning-disabled child.

Curriculum Areas
This program offers your child practice in distinguishing letters of the alphabet, in matching uppercase and lowercase letters, and in learning the sequence of the alphabet.

Reading
■ *Decoding skills*—matching and recognizing letters, dealing with sequence and direction

Writing
■ *The mechanics*—keyboarding

The Program
(Tutor). The program consists of three activities.

In *Birds,* your child learns to discriminate letters and match uppercase and lowercase letters. For example, your child sees a lowercase *v* and selects, from among four choices, the capital *V*. By selecting the correct letter, your child helps a lost songbird find its way home. The bird takes the correct letter and flies home to the birdhouse.

In *Dots,* your child learns the sequence of letters by connecting dots, in alphabetic order, to form pictures.

In *Runners,* your child helps rabbits win races by selecting the letter that completes a randomly chosen segment of the alphabet—for example, *c, d, ?, f.*

The program is well designed, and the graphics and sounds are appealing.

The program allows unlimited time for your child to answer, and he or she has two or three chances to select the right letter. In *Birds* and *Dots,* the correct letter is shown on the screen after your child has made two unsuccessful tries. In *Runners,* the program offers hints if your child selects the wrong letter. First a question mark appears in the place of the missing letter. After a second mistake, the computer fills in the correct letter and highlights it. Your child must then match the letter shown on the screen.

Sound and animation (for example, the bird flies to its house, a musical bird chirps a tune) offer your child positive rewards and motivation to continue.

You can adjust the program to suit your child's abilities by varying the letters to be matched, the kinds of letters presented (uppercase, lowercase, or mixed-case), the number of dots to be labeled in a puzzle, the number of dot puzzles presented, and the puzzle size.

The program shows a record of what your child has covered in any session. As in all MECC programs, which are designed for school as well as for home use, the manual is extensive.

Game Shop

8 years and older
Grades 3 and up

Microsoft Software, 1990, $49.95

Hardware
IBM PC and compatibles, 512 KB
- ★ Essential: two 5.25-inch disk drives (four-disk set) or one 3.5-inch disk drive (two-disk set), color graphics card
- ☆ Recommended: color monitor, mouse, blank disks for saving work or a hard-disk drive

Abilities Needed
Although your child of 8 to 10 years of age can enjoy playing the games, he or she should probably be over 10 years old to use the programming options that can modify the games.

This program is appropriate for the learning-disabled child, although a child with significant timing and visual problems might have difficulty with it.

Curriculum Areas

The program offers a set of attractive games involving visual and sequencing skills. It includes a programming language—Microsoft QuickBasic—that allows your child to learn to modify and customize the games. Your child can learn and practice computer programming in a stimulating environment, seeing immediate payoff for the ideas and skills being learned.

Reasoning

- *Gathering information*—recalling relevant information, seeking information in reference sources
- *Analyzing information*—organizing or sequencing details, recognizing patterns
- *Planning strategies*—making decisions, selecting relevant information to create a plan of action

Arithmetic

- *Concepts*—understanding spatial concepts
- *Applications*—creating and using visual representations

The Program

(Tutor/Tool/Tutee). The program contains six appealing, well-designed games.

In *QBlocks,* a customized version of Tetris (see the Tetris review), blocks float down and start filling up a well. Your child is challenged to keep the well from filling up with the blocks for as long as possible by rotating and positioning them as they fall so that they form compact rows. As your child scores more points, the game gets faster so that the challenge level keeps increasing.

In *QBricks,* a type of paddleball, your child, either alone or with a partner, faces a wall of bricks and deflects balls so as to clear the wall. The ball speed increases with every level, and the paddles shorten above a certain level.

In *QSpace,* Starbases orbiting the planet Saurus are under attack from enemy fire. Your child protects the Starbases by firing his for her own interceptor missiles to destroy incoming ones. The enemy attacks the planet in waves, each coming more rapidly than the one before it and containing more missiles.

In *QMaze,* your child works with a set of mazes. Racing against a friend or against the clock, he or she must find a path that allows a successful exit. Monsters can be added to the maze to increase the level of difficulty: If the monster catches your child, he or she loses the game.

In *QShips,* a duel on the high seas, your child has the mission of destroying the opponent's ships by varying the angle and speed of a cannon. He or she must take into account wind, the ship's speed, and surface conditions. With each turn, your child either fires a cannon or moves his or her ship to avoid the opponent's cannon fire.

In *QSynth,* a music program, your child records and plays back songs by pressing keys on a keyboard he or she sees on the monitor. Your child can save up to 50 songs on a disk and play them back. He or she can also use the song editor to edit the music.

The games are well designed and, without any additional programming, offer considerable variety in challenge level.

Each game allows your child to customize a wide number of features using Microsoft QuickBasic. In *QBricks,* for instance, your child can modify the block patterns, the length of the paddle, the number and shape of the special bricks in the pattern, the end of the level bonus multiplier, the color of the ball or the paddle, and the ball speed. Your child can vary a comparable range of features in all six games. The program suggests the best changes for each game.

In order to truly understand how to carry out the programming, your child should read the well-organized and quite extensive *Learn BASIC Now* book that comes with the program. The book is designed to be used step by step along with the program, and it offers your child an excellent introduction to a computer programming language. If your child is not eager to or skilled enough to systematically follow a manual, you might have to help him or her use the book.

This is the type of program your child can use, and use in different ways, for many years. A child under 10 will likely be content to play the games themselves and concentrate on improving visual skills and speed of response. He or she is also likely to enjoy having a wide range of games to play with a partner. Older children are likely to be attracted to the control and problem solving that the programming language offers. This program is an unusual and productive mixture of fun and learning.

Get to the Point

9–12 years
Grades 4–7

Sunburst Communications, 1985, $65.00

Hardware
Apple II series, 48 KB
  ★ Essential: 5.25-inch disk drive
IBM PC and compatibles, 128 KB
  ★ Essential: 5.25-inch disk drive, color graphics card
IBM PS/2, 256 KB
Tandy 1000, 256 KB
  ★ Essential: 5.25-inch disk drive

Abilities Needed
This program is appropriate for the learning-disabled child, although a child with significant visual-spatial problems might have difficulty with it.

Curriculum Areas
The program teaches arithmetic by giving your child practice in using estimation and in all the fundamental operations on decimals having from one to six places.

Arithmetic
  ■ *Concepts*—understanding relational concepts
  ■ *Fundamental operations*—applying the operations with decimals
  ■ *Applications*—using estimation

The Program
(Tutor). The program is a "decimal feast" that offers three main courses.

In *Point of Order,* the "appetizer," your child plays a game in which he or she estimates decimals. At the start of the game, your child chooses to play with decimals of from two to six places. For example, if he or she chooses to work with decimals of two places, he or she might then see the numbers *.03* and *.55.* Your child's task is to enter a decimal between these two numbers, with the goal of keeping the game going for as many turns as possible. If your child selects the number *.54,* for example, the next numbers that appear on the screen will be *.54* and *.55.* At this point, no other numbers can be entered, and so the game ends. On the other hand, if he or she enters a number such as *.28,* the next numbers will be *.28* and *.55,* allowing the game to continue. To be successful, your child must really think about the interval range and the best estimate to enter in order to keep the game going. At any point, your child can press the question mark key to see a list of past guesses that he or she has made.

In *Point in Question,* the "main course," your child applies one of the four basic operations of addition, subtraction, multiplication, or division to decimals. He or she works at one of four levels of difficulty: one-place decimals to four-place decimals.

In *Counterpoint,* the "dessert," your child plays a game similar to that in *Point of Order.* This time, however, your child plays with a partner. Each partner has the chance to select the decimal number he or she wants the other to guess. In this case, one child turns around while the other enters a decimal number between 0 and 1; the first child then turns back to the computer and has to guess the number that was entered.

The program offers well-designed problems in an important aspect of arithmetic. The games are appealing and serve to maintain motivation. All the problems appear in "missing operand" form. That is, one number in the problem and the answer are given; the missing number is the other operand. For example, your child might see $.08 + \_\_ = .11.$ To solve this addition problem, your child actually has to use subtraction. If he or she has difficulty understanding the relationships among the basic operations, the format might pose a problem.

The program offers good feedback throughout. In *Point of Order,* for example, the program won't accept an entry that doesn't fit within the interval. In *Point in Question,* if your child is correct, the program displays the message "You found it in one trial." If your child is incorrect, the message says "Wrong," and the program tells your child how his or her entry affects the problem. In the example above, for instance, if your child entered *.04,* the computer would display $.08 + .04 = .12.$

Goofy's Railway Express

2–4 years
Grade PreK

Series
Walt Disney Computer Software, 1990, $14.95

Hardware
Commodore 64/128, 64 KB
  ★ Essential: 5.25-inch disk drive, color monitor
IBM PC and compatibles or IBM PS/2, 256 KB
  ★ Essential: 3.5-inch or 5.25-inch disk drive, color graphics card, color monitor

Abilities Needed
In the first few sessions, your child will need your help in learning to run the program. You will also need to be available to enter the copy protection code at the beginning of each play session.

This program is appropriate for the learning-disabled child.

Curriculum Areas
The program teaches your child about colors and shapes, and it shows him or her how these characteristics appear in common objects.

Arithmetic
  ■ *Concepts*—understanding spatial concepts

Reasoning
  ■ *Analyzing information*—recognizing patterns

The Program
(Tutor). The program uses the ever-attractive Disney characters and animation to help your preschooler learn about colors and shapes. The program presents the material by way of a train ride in which Goofy and Mickey pass through various landscapes. The program has no menu, and your child moves through it in a preset way. The program consists of two major segments.

In *Selecting Objects,* your child chooses geometric shapes and sees how the shapes can appear in nature. As the train moves along, some of its smoke puffs contain geometric shapes such as triangles, circles, and semicircles. When a shape appears, your child can choose whether to press the Spacebar. If he or she does press the Spacebar, the shape then moves to a different place and changes into an object that fits the scene. For example, a circle might move to a tree and become a hole that is an owl's home, or a semicircle might fall to the ground and become a mushroom. In each scene, your child can press the Spacebar to see eight different objects. By waiting to press the Spacebar until later in the scene, your child can see new shapes that have not been presented before.

In *Boarding Passengers,* four other Disney characters are waiting at various depots to join Goofy and Mickey on the train. Above each character is a geometric shape. Your child must press the Spacebar when he or she sees a matching shape. The train then stops, and the character with that shape boards the train.

At the start, you can select one of three speeds to set the pace of the program. Although you can't select from a menu, you or your child can easily leave the program running while you take a break and resume work when you are ready. You can easily turn the music and sound effects on or off.

Programs for this age range typically require your child to simply match shapes and colors. In contrast, this program shows your child—in an entertaining manner—how these characteristics can be detected in real-world objects. Because your child can't make a mistake, he or she is likely to find the program appealing and not the least bit frustrating.

Initially, you'll probably need to show your child how to use the Spacebar and how to delay pressing it in order to see different objects on the tours through the various scenes. The program has an unusual copy protection system which, because it is too difficult for a young child to use, requires you to be available to start the program each time your child plays it.

This is not an ambitious program, but it is a highly appealing, reasonably priced one that your very young child can turn to over and over for the fun of transforming shapes and colors into meaningful objects. The material also lends itself to discussions about the changes you are watching. The manual contains additional suggestions about using the program to interact with your child.

▼

MICKEY'S RUNAWAY ZOO (1990, $14.95) is a second program in this series. Designed for children 3–5 years old (Grades PreK–K), it focuses on teaching the numbers *1* through *9*. It uses the theme of recapturing animals that have escaped from a zoo. Your child practices counting the animals as he or she rounds them up. The numbers in the scenes are clustered so that they involve either *1* through *5* or *6* through *9*. Once again, it is almost impossible for your child to make an error, so the program causes no strain for a young child.

DONALD'S ALPHABET CHASE (1990, $14.95) is a third program in this series. Designed for children about 3–5 years old (Grades PreK–K), it focuses on teaching the uppercase letters of the alphabet. Pets in the shape of letters (for example, a frog curled up to form the letter *A*) have slipped out of a toybox and Donald has to catch them. He can only do so if your child presses the letter on the keyboard that matches the letter-shaped animal he or she sees on the screen. Each time your child helps Donald capture an animal, the letter moves up to its place in the alphabet sequence that appears at the top of the screen. Because there are only a few letters in each scene, your child does not have to deal with the whole alphabet at once.

The Grammar Examiner

10 years and older
Grades 5 and up

DesignWare / Britannica Software, 1986, $39.95

Hardware
Apple II series, 64 KB
Commodore 64, 64 KB ($29.95)
  ★ Essential: 5.25-inch disk drive
  ☆ Recommended: color monitor, joystick
IBM PC and compatibles, 64 KB
  ★ Essential: 5.25-inch disk drive, color graphics card, color monitor
  ☆ Recommended: joystick

Abilities Needed

Some of the paragraphs in the program require a seventh-grade reading level. For these segments, a younger child will need your help.

Curriculum Areas

The program offers your child practice in essential grammar skills.

Writing

- *The process*—editing texts
- *The mechanics*—using elements of a word processing program, analyzing sentences for grammar, using punctuation and capitalization

The Program

(Tutor). This board-game program simulates a climb up the career ladder of newspaper journalism. In this game, your child takes the role of a cub reporter on a major newspaper. Four built-in game boards are available: *The New York Times, The Tribune, The Daily News,* and *The Comical.* The computer randomly selects the number of moves your child makes and advances his or her marker. The type of square your child lands on determines both the path to the top of the newspaper hierarchy and the kind of task your child will be required to answer. Some squares result in promotions or demotions—for example, "You write a story on the stock market and get rich. You gain $161 in pay." Other squares require your child to answer a multiple-choice grammar question or to edit a paragraph to correct errors. The program offers over 150 multiple-choice questions and paragraphs.

One negative feature is that the program offers no explanations of grammatical rules. If your child makes mistakes, he or she receives no information about why his or her answer was incorrect.

Rewards for successful answers are pay raises and promotions from cub reporter to editor-in-chief.

The program offers an Editor option, which allows your child to create new game boards and to add stories and grammar questions. This feature also allows you to make the program more profitable for a younger child by entering easier grammar tasks in simpler language and at lower reading levels.

Your child can play the game alone, against the computer, or against up to four challengers. If your child opts to play against the computer, you can vary the number of questions it gets right or the number of mistakes it corrects when it edits a paragraph.

Grammar Gremlins

8–11 years
Grades 3–6

Davidson, 1986, $49.95

Hardware
Apple II series, 64 KB
- ★ Essential: 3.5-inch or 5.25-inch disk drive
- ☆ Recommended: printer

IBM PC and compatibles, 128 KB
- ★ Essential: 3.5-inch or 5.25-inch disk drive, color graphics card
- ☆ Recommended: Printer

Abilities Needed
Your child should be reading at the third-grade level in order to follow the material he or she will see on the screen.

This program is appropriate for the learning-disabled child, although a child with significant language or visual-spatial problems might have difficulty with it.

Curriculum Areas
The program tests for and teaches skill in capitalization, punctuation, plurals, contractions, parts of speech, and sentences.

Writing
- ■ *The mechanics*—analyzing sentences for grammar, using punctuation and capitalization

Reading
- ■ *Decoding skills*—analyzing words for their elements

The Program
(Tutor). The program has four major segments, two of which are tests and two of which teach the material. It covers 60 rules in more than 600 practice sentences.

In *Pretest,* your child is tested on all the skills that will be taught in the program. The test is in a multiple-choice format, in which your child must choose the correct answer from among four choices. If the item tests plurals, for example, your child might see the sentence "Betty bought two blue __." He or she would choose from *books*, *bookes*, *book's*, and *bookses* to complete the sentence. At the end of the test, the program analyzes your child's performance so that you can see which skills he or she has mastered and which require additional practice. You might find, for example, that he or she has achieved 90 percent or higher on everything but parts of speech and capitalization. You can use these results to guide the tasks your child works on as he or she uses the program.

In *Build Your Skill,* your child selects a skill to work on (capitalization, punctuation, plurals, and so on). The program then shows your child the major rules for that skill. For example, in plurals, it tells him or her when the plural is formed by adding *s* (as in *dogs*) and when it is formed by adding *es* (as in *dishes*). After reviewing the rules, your child answers a series of 20 multiple-choice items in which he or she applies the rules.

In *Grammar Gremlins Game,* your child works with the same skills, but in a game format. He or she sees a haunted house with closed windows. Behind the windows are the answers that your child needs to complete sentences correctly. The faster your child works, the more points he or she can earn. As in *Build Your Skill,* only a single skill is tested at any one time. For example, all the problems could be on parts of speech. You or your child can make this selection at the start of the game. At times, a gremlin appears, allowing your child to earn extra points. Your child can play the game at two levels: the simpler Novice level or the more difficult Advanced level.

In *Review Test* (similar to *Pretest*), your child is tested on how well he or she has learned the skills presented in *Build Your Skill* and *Grammar Gremlins*.

The material is well designed, and the games supply motivation for learning a set of skills that children would often like to avoid learning. Apparently, the developers of the program also tried to increase motivation by having all the major words in a sentence start with the same letter—for instance, "Christy got three colored cards for Columbus Day." This doesn't seem to be necessary, but it doesn't detract from the teaching.

The teaching segment *Build Your Skill* is, appropriately, the only one that responds to your child's answers. If his or her choice is correct, the answer moves up from the choices at the bottom of the screen and enters the sentence. If the choice is incorrect, the computer tells your child to make another selection. If the second choice is incorrect, the computer highlights the correct answer.

At the end of a session in *Build Your Skill,* your child sees a scoreboard that lists the number of problems attempted, the number answered correctly, and the percentage answered correctly.

The options allow you or your child to print the results, to turn the sound on or off, and to select one of four levels of difficulty. An easy-to-use editor also allows your child to add his or her own practice sentences and grammar rules.

Four additional GRAMMAR GREMLINS DATA DISKS (1986, $19.95 each)—one for each grade from grades 3 to 6—are available from Davidson for use with the program.

Grammar Toy Shop

8–9 years
Grades 3–4

MECC, 1990, $59.00

Hardware
Apple II series, 128 KB
★ Essential: 3.5-inch or 5.25-inch disk drive
☆ Recommended: color monitor, printer

Abilities Needed
Your child should be reading at the third-grade level to use the program independently.

This program is appropriate for the learning-disabled child, although a child who has significant language problems might have difficulty with it.

Curriculum Areas
The program teaches writing and reading by focusing on grammatical concepts such as subject-verb agreement, verb tense and agreement, and the basic parts of speech.

Writing

- *The mechanics*—constructing phrases and sentences, analyzing sentences for grammar

Reading

- *Comprehension skills*—combining words into sentences, combining sentences, playing word games

The Program

(Tutor). The program has three major segments.

In *Silly Toys,* your child plays a game in which he or she builds sentences to create a story about silly things that a toy does. At the start, your child selects 1 of 10 toys such as a penguin, a bear, or a cat. The beginning words of a sentence appear on the screen. For instance, your child might see the words *My cat.* He or she then sees "sentence endings" and has to choose one that makes a complete sentence. (Some of the endings will form an incomplete sentence if they are chosen.) When the story is complete, the computer tells your child "Good work, you have made one silly toy."

In *Toy Wishes,* your child analyzes sentences for their parts of speech. The segment covers nouns, action verbs, adjectives, and pronouns. Your child sees a sentence such as "A hippo that rides tigers is the best toy in the world." The word *hippo* might be highlighted, and he or she places it in one of two boxes: nouns or action verbs. Next the word *ride* might be highlighted, and your child places that word in the appropriate box.

In *Word Flip Express,* your child combines the skills used in *Silly Toys* and *Toy Wishes* to play a game that can be either timed or untimed. The game involves filling the cars of a train so that the words are in correct order. For example, a train might have two sets of words.

| That | wear | is | quiet |
| Pigs | pig | red | hats |

Your child has to reorder the words so that they form complete sentences—in this instance, "Pigs wear red hats" and "That pig is quiet." The number of words that must be shifted varies from problem to problem.

The material is clearly presented on easy-to-read screens. The focus on toys, although not detrimental to the program, in no way supports the concepts being taught. The use of a color monitor adds visual appeal to the program.

The program provides good feedback to your child. In *Silly Toys,* if he or she is incorrect, the computer says "No" and shows the correct choice. In *Toy Wishes,* the computer responds to a first incorrect choice by saying "No, try again." After your child makes a second incorrect choice, the computer offers the correct answer.

In *Word Flip Express,* your child earns a score and raises it with each correct answer. The program offers the verbal reinforcement of "Great score."

The options available allow you to set the number of problems and the level of mastery and to determine whether to view the results on the screen, print them out, or both. You can also turn the sound on or off. In addition, the menu offers a choice called Toy Shop Tops in which you can see your child's results on the *Word Flip Express* game.

Your child might enjoy playing this program as a kind of word game, but most likely he or she will use it to reinforce grammar concepts being taught in school.

Hide 'N Sequence: Elementary Level

8–10 years
Grades 3–5

Sunburst Communications, 1985, $75.00

Hardware
Apple II series, 64 KB
Commodore 64, 64 KB
   ★ Essential: 5.25-inch disk drive (two-disk set)
   ☆ Recommended: printer

OTHER LEVELS

Hide 'N Sequence: Middle School Level
10–13 years, Grades 5–8
Sunburst Communications, 1985, $75.00

Hide 'N Sequence: High School Level
13–17 years, Grades 8–12
Sunburst Communications, 1985, $75.00

Abilities Needed
If your child is in the lower grades, you will initially need to explain this program because the instructions are complicated. After your child becomes familiar with the format, he or she should be able to work independently.

This program is appropriate for the learning-disabled child, although a child with significant language problems might have difficulty with it.

Curriculum Areas
The program teaches reading and writing by helping your child organize ideas, predict sequences, and analyze cause and effect.

Reading
- *Comprehension skills*—following complex directions, identifying sequences of events, reading fictional texts, reading nonfictional texts

Writing
- *The process*—creating fictional texts, creating nonfictional texts
- *The mechanics*—using elements of a word processing program, using a word processing program

The Program
(Tutor). This program offers an unusual language game that develops your child's understanding of sequence in different types of written material.

Your child unscrambles a story sentence by sentence. Three cartoonlike storytellers (Harry, Ollie, and Anna) present your child with a choice of three sentences. Your child must select the sentence most likely to come next in a variety of writing styles. The program covers four styles: narration (stories, fables, and fairy tales), exposition (explanation, how-to articles, and recipes), description (describing people, places, and things), and persuasion (arguments, advertisements, and speeches). For example, your child chooses the story entitled "Explain Zoobie Cookies." The first sentence reads, "A few weeks ago, I decided to take a vacation in my rocket ship." The three storytellers then present sentences that might come next. Harry says, "I landed on the Planet Zoobie"; Ollie states, "And that's all there is to it!"; and Anna offers, "When you finish the cookie dough, roll it into little balls."

The program provides the first sentence in each story. Your child then selects, sentence by sentence, what should come next. He or she tries to match the way an author originally wrote the story. After the sequence is completed, your child checks by comparing his or her sequence with the original.

If the sentences are out of sequence, the program highlights misplaced sentences and tells your child "Try another storyteller." Your child can make as many changes as he or she wants and rearrange the sentences at will. He or she checks and changes the sentences until the sequence is correct.

When your child creates the correct sequence on the first try, the program offers the following reward message: "You found the hidden sequence. Congratulations. You matched the original on the first try." If your child needs five checks and changes before the sequence is correct, the program offers "Right on check #5."

The program offers a built-in word processor that allows your child to write up to 12 of his or her own stories for use in the game.

How the West Was One + Three x Four

9 years and older
Grades 4 and up

WINGS for learning, a Sunburst Company; 1988; $65.00

Hardware

Apple II series, 64 KB

★ Essential: 3.5-inch or 5.25-inch disk drive

IBM PC and compatibles, 128 KB

★ Essential: 5.25-inch disk drive, color graphics card

IBM PS/2, 256 KB

Tandy 1000, 256 KB

★ Essential: 3.5-inch disk drive

Abilities Needed

Your child should be reading at the fourth-grade level in order to follow the on-screen instructions, which are both lengthy and complex.

Curriculum Areas

The program teaches arithmetic and reasoning by having your child solve complex, multistep math problems. The problems are similar to those in early algebra, but the vocabulary of algebra is not used. To solve the problems, your child not only has to use a variety of operations but has to use them in a way that allows him or her to find the best possible solution.

Arithmetic

- *Concepts*—recognizing terms and signs for mathematical operations, understanding equations
- *Fundamental operations*—operating with addition, subtraction, multiplication, and division
- *Applications*—analyzing word problems with multiple operations, applying measurement to simulated real-life situations

Reasoning

- *Gathering information*—recalling relevant information, seeking information in available sources

- *Developing hypotheses*—eliminating alternatives
- *Planning strategies*—making decisions, selecting relevant information to create a plan of action, formulating solutions, managing resources

The Program

(Tutor/Tool). The program is in a game format that is similar to many board games. The main menu offers several choices, including ones that allow your child to change players and view the scores of top players.

In *Learn How,* the program offers an extensive explanation of how to play, which your child can use if he or she desires.

In *Play Game,* your child plays the following game. Two vehicles, a stagecoach and a locomotive, are traveling along a "trail." The trail is an on-screen path along which six towns are located. Each vehicle attempts to reach the end of the path before the other one does. Your child is the driver of the stagecoach. The computer or another child directs the locomotive. The program is designed so that your child can also work in partnership with another child against the computer.

At each player's turn, three on-screen spinners come up with a combination of numbers. For example, they might produce the numbers *1, 2,* and *6.* The player must apply two of the four basic arithmetic operations to these numbers in order to construct an equation, which allows the stagecoach to move. Doing this can be challenging. In addition to knowing how to set up equations, your child must also figure out the best possible equation. Constructing an equation that yields the highest number is not necessarily the best strategy. For example, if your child set up the equation $6 \times 2 + 1$, he or she could move 13 spaces. But there might be a shortcut at space 8 that would allow your child to advance much farther on the board. In such a case, he or she would do far better to set up the equation $1 \times 2 + 6$ because that would yield *8.*

As in all good games, the rules complicate the play. For example, if your child lands on a spot where another player has landed, the other player is bumped back two towns. In addition, if your child solves any equation incorrectly, he or she loses that turn and cannot move forward.

The teaching aspect of the program is strong and extremely well designed. After your child completes a move, the computer tells him or her whether more efficient moves were possible, and it demonstrates how to make a more efficient move. If your child made the best possible move, the computer tells your child that.

During the course of a game, your child can seek up to two hints. One hint, the "possible" hint, allows your child to ask the computer whether it is possible to use a particular equation to get to a particular point. The other hint, the "form" hint, lets your child ask the computer to show the move it would make at the moment.

At the end of the game, your child gets a summary of the play that tells him or her about both good and bad points of play. He or she might see, for example, "You never missed a problem," but "Don't forget to use the shortcuts." Your child can print out the summary if a printer is available.

Your child can set the complexity of play by telling the computer whether he or she wants the computer to play "well but not great" or to play "as well as possible." The program saves the results of top players.

This is a demanding but exciting game. If your child is skilled in math and enjoys working with mathematical problem solving, he or she is likely to be captivated by this program.

I Can Write!

7 years
Grade 2

Series
Sunburst Communications, 1988, $59.00

Hardware
Apple II series, 128 KB
- ★ Essential: 3.5-inch or 5.25-inch disk drive, 20-column Magic Slate or Magic Slate II, printer

Abilities Needed
Unless your child has become quite familiar with word processing in school, he or she will need your help for an extended period of time before he or she is able to use the program independently. Your child also needs to read at the second-grade level in order to read the text in the program on his or her own.

This program is appropriate for the learning-disabled child.

Curriculum Areas

The program teaches writing skills by offering words, phrases, and sentences that your child adds to and edits in order to create appealing written materials.

Writing

- *The process*—completing fictional texts, completing nonfictional texts, creating messages for visual materials, editing texts
- *The mechanics*—constructing phrases and sentences, using a word processing program

Reading

- *Decoding skills*—reading words in text
- *Comprehension skills*—following simple directions, reading stories

The Program

(Tool). The program is designed to help your child make the transition to using a word processing program independently. It is essentially a data disk of 25 simple files to be used in conjunction with Sunburst's Magic Slate or Magic Slate II 20-column word processing program. The files have such titles as *Colors, Links, Soup, Monster Soup,* and *My Monster.*

As the program systematically guides your child through the files, he or she gradually picks up more and more ideas about the writing process. He or she also learns key word processing operations, such as loading files, editing, saving files, and printing files.

Most of the files are relatively open ended, and your child can use them repeatedly, creating different texts each time. In a file like *Monster Story,* for example, your child can create any number of creatures. Many of the other files use the theme of monsters, which have a never-ending appeal for children. The goal of the program, however, is to familiarize your child with different types of written materials. The files call for such texts as recipes, word puzzles, rhymes, and descriptions. In combination, the files provide your child with models for a wide variety of texts.

Keep in mind that some of the files, particularly the ones at the start of the program, are designed for the classroom. These include files such as *Title Page, My Photo,* and *My Address. Title Page,* for example, asks your child to type in Name, Teacher, Grade, School, and Year. It's unlikely that he or she would want to use this file more than a few times. Skipping such files, however, should not affect the benefits your child derives from using the other files repeatedly.

The program requires you to help your child more than other programs do. But you needn't teach everything the extensive manual covers. For example, the file called *Is / Round* has your child read texts and change *is* to *was* and *round* to *square*. The aim is twofold: The first objective is to teach the Replace function on the word processor, and the second is to help your child recognize the way in which changes in a single word can change the meaning of a sentence. You can choose to bypass some of these goals without diminishing the program's value as a rich source of models that your child can use to guide his or her writing.

BE A WRITER! (1988, $59.00) is one in a series of programs that share the same format as I CAN WRITE! but it is designed for children 8 years old (Grade 3). It, too, requires the use of the 20-column Magic Slate or Magic Slate II word processing program. Overall, it makes many more explicit demands on grammar skills than I CAN WRITE! For example, your child must know grammatical terms such as *verb tense* and *pronoun* and must use these terms to guide his or her editing. If grammar is a major component of your child's school curriculum, you might find this program to be a useful and pleasant way to offer him or her the necessary practice.

Jenny's Journeys

9–11 years
Grades 4–6

MECC, 1986, $39.95

Hardware

Apple II series, 64 KB

   ★ Essential: 3.5-inch or 5.25-inch disk drive

   ☆ Recommended: mouse

IBM PC and compatibles, 256 KB

   ★ Essential: 3.5-inch or 5.25-inch disk drive

   ☆ Recommended: mouse

Abilities Needed

Your child should be reading at the fourth-grade level in order to use this program independently. He or she should be able to deal with tasks that have multiple components.

Curriculum Areas

The program teaches reasoning by offering your child practice in map-reading skills, including using a map index, finding locations, and planning efficient routes.

Reasoning

- *Gathering information*—recalling relevant information, seeking information in available sources, taking notes
- *Planning strategies*—making decisions, managing resources

Arithmetic

- *Concepts*—understanding spatial concepts
- *Applications*—creating and using visual representations

The Program

(Tutor/Tutee). Your child plays three games while driving through Aunt Jenny's town, Lake City. Each game is more difficult than the previous one.

In *Short Errands,* the easiest game, your child must find a location in Lake City without crossing Central Avenue, the main thoroughfare. For example, your child might see the following instructions on the screen: "You are now at the corner of East 4th Avenue and Elm Street. Your task is to get to the Clothing Shop at 292 East Pine Street." At this level of play, your child can ask for help.

In *Journey Across Town,* your child must find a location that lies across Central Avenue. Sometimes he or she must negotiate a construction detour to reach the location.

In *Shopping Trip,* the hardest game, your child must find, and park at, six different locations in as few moves as possible, and then return to start. Your child might see the following instructions on the screen: "You are at the corner of Fifth Avenue and Oak Street. Park at the Airport, Fish Shop, Hat Shop, Museum, Newspaper Building, and Police Station before returning."

In order to complete the journey successfully, your child must deal with multiple aspects of the trip. For example, he or she has to remember information during the trip, keep track of the gas level in the car, and plan a route so that the car won't run out of gas. An empty tank ends the game immediately.

Except in *Short Errands,* the program does not offer help when your child makes mistakes. He or she has to select another direction in which to travel, without any guidance. If your child doesn't repeatedly look at the map of Lake City, he or she can easily get lost. The program does not tell your child, at the beginning of a trip, to write down the address of the starting point of the journey. Unfortunately, he or she cannot retrieve it after the journey begins, which can leave him or her without a reference point. You might want to warn your child about this omission.

JIGSAW! The Ultimate Electronic Puzzle

7 years and older
Grades 2 and up

Series
DesignWare / Britannica Software, 1990, $39.95

Hardware
Apple II series, 512 KB
Apple IIGS, 768 KB (additional Image Library Disk 2 available for $19.95)
Apple Macintosh, 512 KB
IBM PC and compatibles, 512 KB
   ★ Essential: 3.5-inch disk drive (two-disk set)
   ☆ Recommended: color monitor, mouse, printer

Abilities Needed
Your child should be reading at the second-grade level in order to read the on-screen instructions. After becoming familiar with the format, he or she should be able to work independently.

This program is appropriate for the learning-disabled child, although a child with significant visual-spatial or organizational problems might have difficulty with it.

Curriculum Areas

The program teaches reasoning through a new set of techniques and strategies for solving jigsaw puzzles. Because the model and your child's work are never on the screen at the same time, the program places greater demands on memory than do programs for solving traditional puzzles. In working with traditional puzzles, your child selects one piece at a time and adds it to the puzzle in a slow, steady order. In this program, all the pieces are always visible on the screen, resulting in a more complex visual field and more information. Simplifying this visual array is a challenge.

Reasoning

- *Gathering information*—recalling relevant information, seeking information in available sources
- *Analyzing information*—organizing or sequencing details, recognizing patterns
- *Planning strategies*—making decisions

Arithmetic

- *Concepts*—understanding spatial concepts

The Program

(Tool). The program gives your child the opportunity to construct jigsaw puzzles on the computer. It features easy-to-use pull-down menus and consists of four main segments.

In *File,* your child performs operations that allow him or her to access and work on the puzzles. This segment also permits him or her to open, close, and cancel puzzles. If a printer is available, your child can print and save the puzzles.

In *Puzzle,* your child selects a picture, from among 24 pictures, that will serve as the model for a puzzle. The pictures represent easily recognizable subjects that range from animals (a dog) to nature scenes (a bridge across a river) to famous landmarks (the Golden Gate Bridge, Mount Rushmore) to art masterpieces to the alphabet.

In *Level,* your child determines how difficult the puzzle will be. He or she can choose to do a puzzle with 8 pieces (easiest), 15 pieces, 40 pieces (standard), or 60 pieces (the ultimate challenge).

In *Goodies,* your child selects a range of options, such as whether or not to include sound or whether to save the puzzle. This segment also offers your child a choice of approach: He or she can elect to take the Easy Way (in which he or she can restore the original picture to help guide the work) or the Hard Way (in which the picture initially appears in scrambled form so that your child doesn't know what it looks like until he or she fully completes the puzzle).

The picture breaks into the specified number of pieces, and all the pieces remain on the screen in a jumbled pattern. Unlike the irregularly shaped pieces of traditional puzzles, each piece in these puzzles is a rectangle. Your child indicates where he or she wants to move the pieces. The program rearranges the pieces with each decision he or she makes until the original picture is restored.

As your child works, the bottom of the screen displays percentages indicating how much of the puzzle he or she has completed correctly. When the puzzle is finished, the computer congratulates your child on his or her success. Incorrect moves are possible, and a piece moves to whatever position your child sends it to. When your child places a piece incorrectly, the percentages on the bottom of the screen do not change. For the most part, however, it is up to your child to realize, by scanning the picture, that the placement is incorrect.

The graphics in this program are outstanding, and they appeal to all ages. The pictures have a richness and a range of detail rarely seen on the computer screen. The program also lends itself to partnership work. Your child will probably enjoy discussing arrangements and planning a strategy with another person.

THE BERENSTAIN BEARS: JIGSAW! JUNIOR (1990, $24.95) is a scaled-down version of JIGSAW! appropriate for children 4–10 years old (Grades PreK–5). It is available only for the IBM PC and compatibles and requires 512 KB of memory. The program offers 10 puzzles featuring wonderfully animated pictures of the Berenstain Bears. Although your child can divide the puzzles—as in the original game—into 8 pieces (easiest), 15 pieces, 40 pieces (standard), or 60 pieces (the ultimate challenge), the pictures are simpler. Your child can save and print the puzzles after they are completed.

Jumping Math Flash

6–9 years
Grades 1–4

Mindscape Educational Software, 1988, $39.95

Hardware
Apple II series, 48 KB
- ★ Essential: 5.25-inch disk drive
- ☆ Recommended: color monitor, printer

Abilities Needed
Your child should be reading at the second-grade level to operate this program independently. Otherwise, he or she will initially need your help to read the on-screen instructions. After becoming familiar with the format, your child should be able to work alone.

This program is appropriate for the learning-disabled child, although a child with significant visual-spatial and timing problems might have difficulty with it.

Curriculum Areas
The program teaches arithmetic with an arcadelike drill-and-practice game that reinforces the four basic math operations. In addition to practicing fundamental math facts, your child reviews the rules of math operations.

Arithmetic
- *Fundamental operations* — operating with addition, subtraction, multiplication, and division

The Program
(Tutor). Your child completes math games by maneuvering a little fish, Jumping Math Flash, along an underwater course. He or she sees a problem and a sea full of numbers; one of the numbers is the solution to the problem. Your child not only has to maneuver Jumping Math Flash through the grid of numbers but also must guide the fish past enemy

sea creatures. Flash must find the answer before the enemy attacks and eats him! Each game has 20 problems. Your child earns points each time Jumping Math Flash reaches the correct answer without being tagged.

Each game has progressive levels of play. There are 21 levels of addition and subtraction problems and 22 levels of multiplication and division problems. For each level of play, the program offers a description of the problems—the operation to be used, the range of numbers included, and the format (arrangement) of the problems. For example, the problems might be addition problems using numbers from 0 through 10 in a regular format. Your child must answer 18 of 20 problems correctly in order to advance to the next level.

The program offers a useful teaching feature in which it states the level, gives a definition, and supplies an example of the kind of problem your child will be working on. For example, he or she might see: "Level A (regular addition), 'Adding zero to a number doesn't change its value,' $7 + 0 = 7$."

The program does not mark errors until the round ends. After each round of play, your child sees a summary sheet that displays all the problems. A mark appears next to each problem he or she answered incorrectly.

You or your child can choose different problem formats, such as regular ($3 + 1 = \_$), missing addends ($4 + \_ = 7$), or regular with help. The help formats offer your child important math information. Your child can also select three different speeds of play (slow, medium, and fast). The higher the game speed, the more points your child accrues.

When play is complete, the program rewards your child for being a high scorer by adding his or her name to the Top Ten list.

Kidswriter
Golden Edition

7–10 years
Grades 2–5

Spinnaker Educational Software, Division of Queue, Inc.; 1989; $49.95

Hardware
Apple IIGS, 787 KB
  ★ Essential: 5.25-inch disk drive, color monitor, printer
  ☆ Recommended: mouse
IBM PC and compatibles and IBM PS/2, 512 KB
  ★ Essential: 5.25-inch disk drive, color monitor, color graphics card, printer
  ☆ Recommended: mouse

ALTERNATIVE VERSION

Kidswriter
Spinnaker Educational Software, Division of Queue, Inc.; 1984; $39.95

Hardware
Apple II series, 48 KB
Commodore 64/128, 64 KB
  ★ Essential: 5.25-inch disk drive, color monitor
  ☆ Recommended: mouse
IBM PC and compatibles, 64 KB
  ★ Essential: 5.25-inch disk drive, color monitor, color graphics card
  ☆ Recommended: mouse

Abilities Needed
Your child should be reading at the second-grade level to follow the menu directions independently.

This program is appropriate for the learning-disabled child.

Curriculum Areas
The program teaches writing by providing practice in selecting topics, organizing ideas, expressing ideas clearly, constructing sentences and paragraphs, and rewriting.

Writing

- *The process*—creating messages for visual material, editing texts
- *The mechanics*—constructing phrases and sentences, using elements of a word processing program

The Program

(Tool). This program enables your child to create and print illustrated storybooks. He or she selects and colors a picture chosen from over 200 pictures with a wide range of subjects. He or she can place the picture anywhere on the screen, against a selected background, and can use up to 15 different pictures on the background at the same time. Your child does some simple word processing to write a caption or a short story to go with the scene. He or she can link the picture-story "pages" together to create a storybook of many pages.

To create a picture, your child selects the function he or she wants to use from a menu such as the following:

- (S)cene change
- (F)orward to the next object
- (B)ack to see the last object
- (P)ick up this object
- (E)rase picture
- (D)one—write a story now

As he or she writes stories with the built-in word processor, your child learns the fundamentals of word processing and editing, such as moving the cursor, inserting, deleting, and wordwrapping.

A limitation in the design of the program is that your child is restricted to the preset number of pictures contained in the program. This, in turn, restricts the choice of story topics. However, the program does provide flexibility in that it permits your child to vary the background scenes (for example, a farm, a theater, a planet in outer space), the pictures (10 picture sets representing categories of images, such as animals), the color (16-color palette), and the size of the picture (4 sizes available).

In contrast to the original KIDSWRITER program, which lacked a printer function, KIDSWRITER GOLDEN EDITION allows your child to print his or her work. This is a significant improvement. Your child is also able to save his or her stories and pictures.

KIDTALK

5–11 years
Grades K–6

First Byte/Davidson, 1988, $49.95

Hardware
Apple IIGS, 512 KB
  ★ Essential: 3.5-inch disk drive, color monitor
  ☆ Recommended: mouse, printer
Apple Macintosh, 512 KB
  ★ Essential: 3.5-inch disk drive
  ☆ Recommended: mouse, printer
IBM PC and compatibles, 512 KB ($39.95)
  ★ Essential: 5.25-inch disk drive, color monitor
  ☆ Recommended: printer

Abilities Needed
In order to use this program independently, your child should be reading at the second-grade level. A younger child will need your help to enter his or her story texts.

This program is appropriate for the learning-disabled child.

Curriculum Areas
This program teaches writing through use of a speech-enhanced word processing tool. Your child learns the relationships between letters, sounds, words, and sentences.

Writing
  ■ *The process*—creating simple written messages, creating fictional texts, editing texts
  ■ *The mechanics*—constructing sentences and phrases, using punctuation and capitalization, keyboarding, using a word processing program, proofreading

Reading
  ■ *Decoding skills*—linking sounds to letters and words, reading words in text

- *Comprehension Skills*—combining words into sentences, combining sentences

The Program

(Tool). This program offers, without requiring additional hardware, a "talking" word processor that allows your child to hear whatever text he or she enters on the keyboard. The program's voice and intonation are robotlike, but your child is not likely to be bothered by the artificial quality. The excitement of being able to write and hear his or her stories, reports, plays, poems, and messages overshadows the issue of voice quality.

Your child can revise text using the standard editing operations of cut, copy, and paste. And he or she can access menus in two forms, text menus and picture menus. If your child is reading at about second-grade level, he or she can use the pull-down text menus. If your child is younger, he or she can use the graphics-oriented "picture box" menus.

The program features six main menu selections.

In *Notebook,* your child opens a page of the notebook to create, organize, print, and store his or her work.

In *Speak,* your child selects the way in which he or she wants the computer to read the written text. It can speak a single letter at a time, say each word, or read each sentence of a document.

In *Fix-It,* your child edits documents, using the cut, copy, paste, and pick-all functions.

In *Control Panel,* your child changes how the computer speaks the text and how it displays the text.

In *Dictionary Tricks,* your child uses inventive spellings to manipulate word pronunciation. In the "Sounds-Like" dictionary, your child changes the spelling of any word so that it sounds better. For example, *library* sounds better when spoken as "lie brary." In the "Secret Code" dictionary, your child enters a word and also a code word that the program will substitute for the original word when it speaks the text. For example, when the program encounters the word *beautiful*, it substitutes the code word *ugly*.

In *Help,* your child learns to use KIDTALK independently, aided by easy-to-use talking help screens and guided tours.

The program offers three options for the way in which it reads your child's writing aloud. It reads text as a block after keyboard entry, as individually highlighted words, or letter by letter, word by word, or sentence by sentence. Speech can be varied for tone (high or low), pitch (low, medium, or high), speed (fast, medium, or slow), gender (male or female), and volume (loud or soft). Voice changes can be made within a single document to create plays and conversations. You can display and print documents in three letter sizes (large, medium, and small).

King's Rule

9 years and older
Grades 4 and up

Series
WINGS for learning, a Sunburst Company; 1985; $65.00

Hardware
Apple II series, 64 KB
   ★ Essential: 3.5-inch or 5.25-inch disk drive
   ☆ Recommended: color monitor
Commodore 64, 64 KB
IBM PC and compatibles, 128 KB
IBM PS/2, 256 KB
   ★ Essential: 5.25-inch disk drive
   ☆ Recommended: color monitor

Abilities Needed
Your child should be reading at the fourth-grade level in order to use this program independently.

Curriculum Areas
The program teaches reasoning through a series of games in which your child has to uncover the rules that govern increasingly complex sequences of numbers. Your child learns to generate and test hypotheses.

Reasoning
- *Analyzing information* — distinguishing relevant from nonrelevant cues, organizing details
- *Developing hypotheses* — making inferences, formulating rules and generalizations, eliminating alternatives
- *Planning strategies* — making decisions, formulating solutions

Arithmetic
- *Concepts*—understanding relational concepts, understanding equations
- *Fundamental operations*—operating with addition, subtraction, multiplication, and division

The Program

(Tutor). This program consists of six games. In each game, your child sees three numbers that illustrate a secret rule. He or she generates hypotheses about the rule and tests them either by entering three more numbers or by selecting from supplied examples those sets that follow the rule.

In *Castle Gate,* a game involving addition and subtraction, your child sees a set of three numbers between 1 and 10—for example, *3, 5, 7* (a set in which each number is larger by 2 than the preceding number). He or she then sees other sets—for instance, *2, 4, 6; 2, 4, 8;* and *6, 4, 2*— and has to figure out which one of them follows the same rule.

In *Guards' Room,* the same format is used, but the game involves multiplication and division. The number series now moves up or down in multiples such as *1, 5, 25* (in which each number in turn is multiplied by 5) or *18, 6, 2* (in which each number in turn is divided by 3).

In *Game Parlor,* your child now plays with all the rules that apply to the first two games. In addition, 10 new rules are introduced. One of the new rules, for instance, might be that all the numbers end in 9, so that a sequence could be *9, 19, 29.*

In *Magician's Study,* your child moves into equations: The third number in the series is now the result of an operation on the first two numbers; in addition, it might sometimes also be the result of an operation on the first two numbers plus the use of a constant. Your child deals with problems in which the basic formula underlying the numbers might be $[A \times B + 1]$ or $[7 \times (A + B)]$.

In *Royal Suite,* your child tests out alternative hypotheses. The sequences start to become tricky because two or more rules might apply. Your child, for instance, might see the sequence *10, 20, 30,* in which it appears that the numbers are increasing in multiples of 10. In fact, the rule might be that the numbers are increasing in multiples of 5. He or she could test this hypothesis by typing in *5, 15, 25.*

In *The King,* your child has to figure out a rule that can apply to one, two, or all three of the numbers. Your child might see the sequence *1, 2, 3,* for instance, and determine that the rule is that the middle number is an even number.

The program tells your child when he or she has made a mistake. At that point, your child has three options: He or she can repeat the problem, select a different problem at the same level of difficulty, or select a different problem at a lower level of difficulty. The program offers good help cues: Your child can select the Help option, which gives additional instances of the rule to be defined; Recap, which reviews the hypotheses generated so far; or Quiz.

All six segments are in a game format. In each, your child acquires tokens as a reward for figuring out a sufficient number of problems. A certain number of tokens earn him or her admission to the next, more difficult, room of the Castle. On-screen messages give feedback.

The program offers several options that allow variation in the program. Your child can select the difficulty level of the problems and can also work in either of two modes. In one mode, your child enters a sequence of numbers that he or she thinks fits the rule; in the other mode, a quiz offers sets of numbers, and your child selects the set that fits the rule. He or she can also turn the sound on or off.

This is a challenging game that will hold the interest of children—and adults—who enjoy playing around with math problems. It requires patience and a love of numbers, and it lends itself to play by two or more players. You should encourage note taking, a key skill in higher-level schooling, as a help in planning effective strategies.

THE ROYAL RULES (1987, $75.00), is the second program in the series. A sequel to KING'S RULE, the program presents more challenging mathematical rules for older children (11 years and older, grades 6 and up). If your child solves five problems in each of three quizzes, the program rewards him or her with the right to create new rules. These rules are added to a library of rules that can be used to challenge others using the program.

Little People Bowling Alley

3–7 years
Grades PreK–2

Fisher-Price / GameTek / IJE, 1988, $14.95

Hardware

Apple II series, 128 KB

★ Essential: 5.25-inch disk drive

☆ Recommended: color monitor

IBM PC and compatibles, 256 KB

★ Essential: 3.5-inch or 5.25-inch disk drive

☆ Recommended: color monitor

Abilities Needed

If your child is a preschooler or a prereader, he or she will initially need your help to read the instructions. After becoming familiar with the format, your child should be able to work independently.

This program is appropriate for the learning-disabled child.

Curriculum Areas

The program teaches reasoning and arithmetic through a game in which your child builds skills in spatial relationships and basic addition. He or she also strengthens hand-eye coordination.

Reasoning

■ *Planning strategies*—making decisions, selecting relevant information to create a plan of action

Arithmetic

■ *Fundamental operations*—operating with addition

■ *Concepts*—understanding spatial concepts

The Program

(Tutor). The program is an arcade-style bowling game. Your child can play either alone or with a partner. The goal of the game is to knock down all six pins in the alley with one or two rolls of the bowling ball. The bowling alley has markings to help your child learn where to position his or her bowler in order to make each roll a successful one. The more pins knocked down in each frame, the more points are scored. The person scoring the most points at the end of 10 frames wins that game. The program offers two progressive levels of play. In Level 1, your child can throw only a straight ball down the alley. In Level 2, he or she deals with the more advanced curve ball. The timing of the backswing and the release influences the path of the ball down the alley.

Your child has the option of either keeping score or having the computer keep score. Self-scoring allows your child to practice simple addition. With this option, the two numbers to be added (the total points from the previous frame plus the points earned in the present frame) flash on the screen. Your child types in the correct answer. If he or she makes a mistake in adding the scores, the computer gives the correct answer. When your child adds the two sets of numbers correctly, the computer offers the written message "Correct!"

Players earn points for the number of pins knocked down: A gutter ball earns no points, a spare can earn a total of 6 points when balls 1 and 2 together knock down 6 pins, and a strike can earn a total of 12 points if balls 1 and 2 together knock down all 12 pins. At the end of each game, your child sees a message such as "Well done, Stefanie." The name of the winning bowler and his or her score are entered into the Hall of Fame list that your child sees at the end of each game.

The Magic Cash Register

7–11 years
Grades 2–6

MetaComet Software, 1984, $34.95

Hardware
Apple II series, 64 KB
  ★ Essential: 5.25-inch disk drive, printer
  ☆ Recommended: color monitor

Abilities Needed
This program is appropriate for the learning-disabled child.

Curriculum Areas

The program uses a cash-register model to teach your child to handle money and make change. The real-life setting of running a cash register provides your child with practice in the arithmetic operations of addition, subtraction (with carrying and borrowing), and multiplication.

Arithmetic

- *Concepts*—recognizing terms and signs for mathematical operations
- *Fundamental operations*—operating with addition, subtraction, and multiplication
- *Measurement*—using units of money

The Program

(Tutor/Tool). In this interactive program your child acts as the cashier of his or her store. Your child decides what kind of store to open, what items to offer for sale, how to price them, when to hold a sale, and so on.

The Wizard begins by stocking the cash register with money (both coins and bills). Your child has to first "cash-in" and open the store (for instance, a supermarket) by counting and typing in the amount of each type of money in the register. Then, for each customer, he or she enters the names of items sold, the quantities sold, and the prices (for instance, one banana at $.25 and four oranges at $.25 each). Finally, your child calculates the total cost (.25 + $1.00 = $1.25), accepts payment, makes change, and prints a receipt. At the end of the games, your child needs to "cash-out"—that is, count all the money in the register and calculate the total income for the day.

The program can analyze your child's mistakes in step-by-step demonstrations. The Wizard provides immediate feedback when an error is made by showing your child how to set up the problem, indicating which digits are incorrect, offering a step-by-step guide through the problem, and finally displaying the correct answer.

The program offers two modes of operation: Instant Answers allows the computer to carry out the calculations, and Use Your Brain requires your child to do the math.

Your child can save records of the skills he or she has practiced.

Magic Spells

6–12 years
Grades 1–7

The Learning Company, 1985, $39.95

Hardware

Apple II, 64 KB

- ★ Essential: 5.25-inch disk drive, blank disks for saving word lists
- ☆ Recommended: printer

Apple IIGS, 512 KB

- ★ Essential: 3.5-inch or 5.25-inch disk drive, blank disks for saving word lists
- ☆ Recommended: printer

IBM PC and compatibles and IBM PS/2, 256 KB

- ★ Essential: 3.5-inch or 5.25-inch disk drive, color graphics card, blank disks for saving word lists
- ☆ Recommended: printer

Abilities Needed

This program is appropriate for the learning-disabled child.

Curriculum Areas

This program offers your child practice in spelling.

Writing

- *The mechanics*—spelling single-syllable words, spelling multisyllable words, using elements of a word processing program

The Program

(Tutor). Your child sharpens his or her spelling skills by unscrambling words and reproducing flashed spelling words while visiting a magical kingdom populated by knights, ladies, musicians, and unicorns. The program features large, easy-to-read text and use of both uppercase and lowercase letters.

The *Royal List* contains over 500 words divided into six levels for grades 1–6. Levels 1 and 2 have five word lists of 10 words each. Levels 3–6 have five word lists of 20 words each. A special level for frequently misspelled words has five word lists of 10 to 20 words each. The lists are based on a patterned approach to spelling. For instance, Level 1, List 1, contains words in the *-am* (*ham*), *-an* (*ran*), *-at* (*cat*), and *-ad* (*bad*) families. Level 2, List 3, contains words in the *-end* (*bend*), *-ink* (*drink*), and *-ank* (*blank*) families.

The *Castle of Spells* has two games. In each game, your child initially views the list of words selected.

- In *Scramble Spells,* your child unscrambles letters by typing them in the right order to make a word—for instance, *awrorn* (*narrow*) or *ethy* (*they*).

- In *Flash Spells,* your child views a word on the screen for one to nine seconds. Then the word disappears, and your child recalls and reproduces it by typing it.

When your child misspells a word, a question mark appears in each space where he or she placed an incorrect letter. Your child has a second chance to spell the word before the computer shows the correct answer. Your child can access help at any time by pressing the * key. Each time he or she presses this key, the computer shows where one of the letters in the scrambled word belongs. At the completion of each word list, your child sees all the words he or she misspelled and can opt to play again with only those words.

Your child earns special colored banners and a look at animated castle characters each time he or she spells a word correctly on the first try. He or she earns special rewards, such as seeing a unicorn dance to a tune, by spelling all the words in the list correctly. Graphics are clear and attractive.

The program has an easy-to-use editor, Spells Writer, which allows you to create, view, edit, delete, and print lists of your child's personal spelling words. These must be saved on a separate disk. You can vary the levels of words (1–6 and special), specify the number of seconds for which a word is displayed (1–9), and turn the sound on or off.

Math and Me

3–6 years
Grades PreK–1

Davidson, 1987, $29.95

Hardware
Apple II series, 128 KB
- ★ Essential: 3.5-inch or 5.25-inch disk drive
- ☆ Recommended: color monitor, mouse, printer

IBM PC and compatibles, 256 KB
- ★ Essential: 3.5-inch or 5.25-inch disk drive, color graphics card
- ☆ Recommended: color monitor, mouse, printer

ALTERNATIVE VERSION

Talking Math and Me
Davidson, 1988, $49.95

Hardware
Apple IIGS, 512 KB
- ★ Essential: 3.5-inch disk drive

Abilities Needed
Your child should be able to count groups of objects and should be familiar with the digits *0* through *9*.

This program is appropriate for the learning-disabled child.

Curriculum Areas
The program introduces your child to beginning arithmetic concepts such as counting and to the basic arithmetic operation of addition with single-digit numbers. It also introduces concepts of equality and inequality, such as *same, different, more than, less than, larger than,* and *smaller than.*

Arithmetic
- *Numeration*—matching numbers to objects, counting sequentially
- *Concepts*—understanding spatial concepts, understanding relational concepts
- *Fundamental operations*—operating with addition

The Program

(Tutor). The program offers four activities. The first three are important for math readiness, and the fourth involves a basic math operation. Each area has three different games, with each game building systematically from easy to more difficult.

In *Shapes,* your child recognizes and matches four shapes (circle, triangle, rectangle, and square).

In *Numbers,* your child counts, matches objects with numbers, and applies the concepts of *more* and *less* to numbers.

In *Patterns,* your child recognizes sequences of objects or numbers. For instance, he or she must fill in the missing number in the sequence *6, __, 4, 3.*

In *Addition,* your child counts and adds single-digit numbers from 0 to 9.

The program makes use of animated color graphics and sound to offer a balanced selection of early math concepts in a variety of formats, affording a chance for practice without boredom.

An appealing animated monkey comes on the screen to indicate correct responses. When your child makes a mistake, he or she gets a second chance. If the error is repeated, the program offers the correct answer. A young child will initially need your help to understand some of the cues: For instance, when he or she makes a mistake, the words "Try again" appear at the top of the screen.

There is no way to keep a record of what your child has done in any session.

The program can print a colorful certificate when your child completes an activity. An accompanying coloring book relates to the program material.

In the TALKING MATH AND ME version (available only for the Apple IIGS, 512 KB), the computer speaks many of the written cues, which eliminates the need for you to explain matters to your pre-reading child.

Six MATH AND ME workbooks, two at each grade level from PreK to 1, are also available ($3.95 each).

Math Blaster Mystery

10 years and older
Grades 5 and up

Davidson, 1989, $49.95

Hardware
Apple II series, 128 KB
- ★ Essential: 3.5-inch or 5.25-inch disk drive
- ☆ Recommended: color monitor, printer

Apple Macintosh, 1 MB
- ★ Essential: 3.5-inch disk drive
- ☆ Recommended: color monitor, printer

IBM PC and compatibles and IBM PS/2, 256 KB
- ★ Essential: 3.5-inch or 5.25-inch disk drive, color graphics card
- ☆ Recommended: color monitor, printer

Curriculum Areas
This program teaches your child a four-step strategy for solving math word problems. It helps develop critical-thinking skills by having your child apply inductive and deductive reasoning.

Arithmetic
- ■ *Concepts*—recognizing terms and signs for mathematical operations, understanding equations
- ■ *Fundamental operations*—operating with addition, subtraction, multiplication, and division; applying these operations to decimals, fractions, percentages, negative numbers, and equations
- ■ *Applications*—analyzing word problems
- ■ *Measurement*—using units of time, weight, length, and money

Reasoning
- ■ *Analyzing information*—distinguishing relevant from nonrelevant cues
- ■ *Developing hypotheses*—making inferences and deductions, eliminating alternatives
- ■ *Planning strategies*—formulating solutions

The Program

(Tutor). Using a mystery theme, the program offers four activities that help develop logical thinking.

In *Follow the Steps,* your child is introduced to a method for solving math word problems. The program presents word problems and demonstrates how to break them into four workable steps. In each step, your child gets to select the correct answer from four choices.

- In Step 1 your child should ask the question "What does the problem ask you to find?"

- In Step 2 your child should ask the question "What information is needed to solve it?"

- In Step 3 your child needs to "find the correct expression" to solve the problem.

- In Step 4 your child needs to "find the correct solution" to the problem.

There are four levels of difficulty (25 problems for each level). Level One problems include the four math operations with whole numbers, and addition and subtraction with fractions. Level Two problems include the four math operations with fractions and decimals. Level Three problems include fractions, decimals, percentages, ratios, and proportions. Level Four problems include percentages, decimals, fractions, probabilities, interest and principal, and equations.

In *Weigh the Evidence,* your child develops a strategy for breaking problems into smaller parts. He or she moves bricks of different weights from one scale to another until they equal a targeted weight (for example, $3 + 12 + 49 = 64$).

In *Decipher the Code,* your child makes inferences, tests hypotheses, and draws conclusions to solve a problem. He or she uses knowledge of math facts to find numbers in mystery equations. For example, your child sees the following on the screen: $?3 + ?5 = 6?$ He or she has to fill in the correct digits: $43 + 25 = 68$.

In *Search for Clues,* your child discovers a mystery number by searching for clues in a room full of objects and characters. Your child uses clues to determine the mystery number. For example, your child sees: "n is odd, n<1, and n is a multiple of 5. What number is n?"

The program offers excellent "hint" screens when your child makes a mistake. He or she can select instructions, definitions, formulas, or an on-screen pop-up calculator to help reach the correct answer.

Your child can be promoted from Computer Cadet to Chief Problem Solver by earning points for correct answers. The program displays encouraging messages for correct solutions.

At the end of each activity a scoreboard appears with your child's rating and scores. The program lets you keep cumulative records, either on screen or printed out, to assess your child's progress, and it can also print an Award Certificate with your child's name, activity completed, level, and detective status.

Several additional features make this sophisticated package even more attractive: Graphics offer appealing figures and high resolution, and the easy-to-use editor allows you or your child to enter original word problems. Note that if you are using a color monitor, the text is displayed in colored print, which might be distracting.

Math Blaster Plus

6–11 years
Grades 1–6

Davidson, 1987, $49.95

Hardware

Apple II series, 128 KB

Apple IIGS, 512 KB

★ Essential: 3.5-inch or 5.25-inch disk drive

☆ Recommended: printer, mouse, color monitor, blank disks for saving records

IBM PC and compatibles, 256 KB

★ Essential: 3.5-inch or 5.25-inch disk drive, color graphics card

☆ Recommended: printer, mouse, blank disks for saving records

Abilities Needed

To use this program, your child should recognize digits from 0 through 9 and be reading at the first-grade level. The youngest children will definitely need sustained help from an adult to understand the game requirements and play.

ALTERNATIVE VERSION

New Math Blaster Plus!
Davidson, 1990, $49.95

Hardware
Apple Macintosh, 1 MB ($59.95)
  ★ Essential: 3.5-inch disk drive
  ☆ Recommended: printer, mouse
IBM PC and compatibles, 512 KB
  ★ Essential: 3.5-inch or 5.25-inch disk drive, color graphics card
  ☆ Recommended: printer, mouse

This program is appropriate for the learning-disabled child, although a child with significant memory problems might have difficulty with it.

Curriculum Areas
The program offers practice in the fundamental math operations of addition, subtraction, multiplication, and division and in applying the operations to fractions, decimals, percentages, and equations.

Arithmetic
  - *Concepts*—recognizing terms and signs for mathematical operations, understanding equations
  - *Fundamental operations*—operating with addition, subtraction, multiplication, and division; applying these operations to decimals, fractions, percentages, and equations

The Program
(Tutor). There are four activities, covering the four basic math operations, plus a review activity. The games, using outer-space themes, build sequentially and offer 750 different problems. The six levels of progressive difficulty are based on elementary grade levels 1–6. The problems can be presented in a vertical format, a horizontal format, or a mixture of the two formats.

In *Countdown,* your child sees and hears a math fact (for instance, $5 + 4 = 9$). When ready, he or she makes the answer portion of the problem disappear. Your child then types in the right answer. Each fact family offers 25 problems.

In *Ignition,* your child sees a math problem with the answer missing (for instance, 6 + 3 = __). He or she types in the correct answer.

In *Lift-Off,* your child sees a problem that has a missing part (for instance, 6 + __ = 7). He or she has two opportunities to provide the correct answer. Encouraging visual and spoken messages provide a reward after every five correct answers.

In *Orbit,* your child sees three randomly selected problems from the file. One term is boxed in each problem. The child must find the boxes that contain mistakes. Correct answers are rewarded with appealing graphics. After every eighth problem your child solves correctly, a scoreboard appears.

In *Blasternaut,* a fast-action arcade-style review game, your child gets an opportunity to build speed and accuracy in math operations. A problem appears at the top of the screen, and a different answer choice is shown in each of four space stations. Choosing the correct answer quickly allows Blasternaut to land successfully on a space station. Your child scores points based on speed and level of difficulty of play. The program offers encouraging messages as reinforcement, along with an animated Blasternaut, after every five correctly answered problems.

The program offers a nice balance of problems in all basic math operations, and for children who have mastered the underlying math concepts it offers a good review of operations.

When your child gives an incorrect answer in *Countdown*, the program offers no instructive feedback; he or she must continue to select other answers until the right solution is reached. This approach might lead to frustration. Generally, in the other activities, your child has two chances to reach the correct solution for each problem. The program responds to mistakes with flashing lights and spoken cues such as "Try again."

The sound, color, and animated graphics provide effective incentives. Some of the games will be too complicated for younger children. For example, in *Blasternaut*, your child has to look at the top and bottom of the screen simultaneously to be successful.

At the end of all activities except *Countdown*, a scoreboard appears, providing your child with an opportunity to redo any problems that were incorrectly answered.

You can format a blank disk to keep a record of your child's work in any session. If a printer is available, you can print out these records.

You can also print scoreboards and colorful Certificates of Excellence. An easy-to-use editor lets you add more problems to all five activities.

Twelve supplementary MATH BLASTER workbooks for grades 1–4 are available at $4.95 each.

The NEW MATH BLASTER PLUS! version (1990, available only for the IBM PC and compatibles, 512 KB, and the Apple Macintosh, 1 MB) offers enhanced outer-space graphics, sound, and animation. It includes an additional activity, *Number Recycler*, in which your child unscrambles mixed-up equations.

Math Maze

6–11 years
Grades 1–6

DesignWare / Britannica Software, 1983, $39.95

Hardware
Apple II series, 64 KB
Commodore 64, 64 KB ($29.95)
  ★ Essential: 5.25-inch disk drive, color monitor
  ☆ Recommended: joystick
IBM PC and compatibles, 64 KB
  ★ Essential: 5.25-inch disk drive, color graphics card, color monitor
  ☆ Recommended: joystick

Abilities Needed
Your child should be reading at the third-grade level to read the on-screen instructions. A younger child will need your help to learn the game. Once familiar with the format, he or she should be able to work independently .

This program is appropriate for the learning-disabled child, although a child with significant visual-spatial, organizational, or timing problems might have difficulty with it.

Curriculum Areas
Your child practices the four basic arithmetic operations while making his or her way through mazes of increasing complexity. The program helps develop speed and accuracy in simple math operations while promoting hand-eye coordination.

Arithmetic

- *Concepts*—understanding spatial concepts
- *Fundamental operations*—operating with addition, subtraction, multiplication, and division

Reasoning

- *Gathering information*—taking notes
- *Planning strategies*—making decision

The Program

(Tutor). To play the game, your child moves a fly through a maze to create the answers to math problems. Your child chooses the maze, the operation, and the skill level (for instance, addition with sums up to 10 or addition with sums up to 20). Each game contains 10 math problems.

In *Level 1 (Novice)*, your child moves the fly around the maze, picking up the correct digit(s) to answer a math problem. The problems appear one at a time in the lower left corner of the screen. For instance, for the problem $5 + 5 = $ __ , your child needs to pick up a 1 and a 0 from the digits scattered in the maze.

In *Level 2 (Master)*, your child must avoid a hungry spider while collecting the digits.

In *Level 3 (Expert)*, your child moves the fly around a maze whose walls are invisible.

In *Level 4 (Pro)*, your child must avoid the spider and move around a maze with invisible walls.

The program offers colorful graphics, animation, and sound. The on-screen tutorial is excellent. The game lends itself to playing alone or with a partner. The more advanced levels also promote note taking and use of memory skills.

When your child makes a mistake, the computer beeps and shows the correct answer. When your child answers a problem correctly, he or she earns points. All the games are timed. The faster your child moves through the maze collecting digits, the more bonus points he or she receives. At the end of every 10 problems, the computer shows your child's score and compares it to the high score for that session.

The program offers continuous challenge: Your child can choose from 40 mazes of increasing complexity or can design his or her own mazes. Your child can also choose the facts he or she wants to master at any particular time.

Math Rabbit

4–7 years
Grades PreK–2

The Learning Company, 1986, $39.95

Hardware
Apple II series, 64 KB
- ★ Essential: 3.5-inch or 5.25-inch disk drive
- ☆ Recommended: color monitor, mouse

IBM PC and compatibles, 128 KB
- ★ Essential: 3.5-inch or 5.25-inch disk drive, color graphics card
- ☆ Recommended: color monitor, mouse

ALTERNATIVE VERSION

Talking Math Rabbit
The Learning Company, 1988, $59.95

Hardware
Apple Macintosh, 1 MB
- ★ Essential: 3.5-inch disk drive
- ☆ Recommended: color monitor

Abilities Needed
Your child should know the digits *0* through *9* and be able to count groups of objects before using the program. It is helpful if your child can read words such as *high* and *low* because these are used as clues in the games. A younger child will initially need help your help to understand the games.

This program is appropriate for the learning-disabled child.

Curriculum Areas
The program introduces your child to simple arithmetic skills such as counting and identifying numbers and to the basic operations of addition and subtraction with one- and two-digit numbers. The relationships of "greater than" and "less than," the concepts of *equality* and *inequality*, and the beginning idea of multiplication are introduced. The program also helps develop short-term memory.

Arithmetic

- *Numeration*—matching objects to objects, matching numbers to objects, counting objects, counting sequentially
- *Concepts*—recognizing terms and signs for mathematical operations, understanding relational concepts
- *Fundamental operations*—operating with addition, operating with subtraction

Reasoning

- *Gathering information*—recalling relevant information

The Program

(Tutor). Four intriguing games present a wide array of early math concepts.

In *Clown's Counting Games,* your child creates tunes by moving up and down a 0-to-8 scale on a clown face. Each number chosen is named and sung.

In *Tightrope Game,* your child matches sets of objects, digits, or math problems. For instance, the number *3* appears on a balloon, and your child selects a set of three fish to match the digit.

In *Circus Train Game,* your child answers addition and subtraction problems. For instance, he or she loads a train by filling it up with answers to problems such as *4 – 1 = __.*

In *Mystery Matching Game,* a concentration game, your child matches pairs of objects, numbers, or math problems.

The program is a sound introduction to the world of numbers and math concepts and offers a good selection of beginning math concepts that are well sequenced from easy to hard. It also offers opportunities for an older child to practice his or her skills.

If your child makes a mistake, clear sight and sound cues appear on-screen. The program does not offer specific help for reaching the right answer; it simply displays the answer. At any time during the activities, you or your child can get help by choosing Show Help. A help window then appears that explains how to play the game.

Each time your child completes an activity correctly, he or she is rewarded by appealing animations and sound. For instance, in *Clown's Counting Game*, he or she hears a special song played; in *Tightrope*

Game, Math Rabbit dances a jig; in *Circus Train Game,* the circus train chugs off to the big top. In *Mystery Matching Game,* your child earns prizes for correct matches.

A choice of 30 games options makes this a versatile program. The same games can be played at different levels of difficulty. For instance, younger children (4–5 years) can play the games with objects, and older children (6–7 years) can play them with numbers. The program also allows you to select the speed of the game (slow, medium, or fast), the math operations (addition, subtraction, or both), and the numbers that will be worked with (for instance, 1 through 4 or 1 through 9). You can turn the sound and voice on or off and change the volume settings (soft, medium, or loud).

The manual is well written and clearly explains the many options. There is no way of recording what your child has done.

In the TALKING MATH RABBIT version (available only for the Apple Macintosh, 1 MB) the use of digitized sound allows your child to hear, as well as see, the program activities.

Math Shop

9–14 years
Grades 4–9

Series
Scholastic Family Software, 1986, $32.95

Hardware
Apple II series, 64 KB
Apple Macintosh, 1 MB
  ★ Essential: 3.5-inch or 5.25-inch disk drive
IBM PC and compatibles, 256 KB
  ★ Essential: 3.5-inch or 5.25-inch disk drive, color graphics card

Abilities Needed
To understand the explanations used in this program, your child should be reading at the third-grade level. The instructions are fairly complex, so you might initially need to work with your child. You should encourage him or her to take notes during this program because necessary information is often not repeated.

This program is appropriate for the learning-disabled child, although a child with significant language problems might have difficulty with it.

Curriculum Areas

The program teaches arithmetic by having your child practice math problems in realistic life settings and situations.

Arithmetic

- *Concepts*—understanding relational concepts, understanding equations
- *Fundamental operations*—operating with addition, subtraction, multiplication, and division; applying the operations to fractions, percentages, and decimals
- *Applications*—using estimation, applying measurement to simulated real-life situations
- *Measurement*—using units of money, weight, and length

The Program

(Tutor). The program, set in a colorful shopping mall, features 10 different simulations with hundreds of different problems. Your child takes on the role of the clerk in each of the 10 different stores in the mall, serving customers in different ways by using specific types of math operations.

In the *Boutique Shop,* your child makes change for customers after they have made purchases. Using addition, subtraction, and multiplication with quarters, dimes, nickels, and pennies, your child must make the correct change with as few coins as possible.

In the *Dairy Shop,* your child packs eggs for customers in cartons of uneven sizes. Using addition, your child fills the right number of cartons to make up an order. For instance, if a customer wants 11 eggs, your child fills one carton with 8 eggs and a second carton with 3 eggs.

In the *Donut Shop,* a machine bakes, glazes, and fills donuts. Using addition and fractions, your child sets the machine to fill orders. For instance, an order for 12 plain and 6 glazed donuts equals an order for 18 donuts with one-third of them glazed.

In the *Grocery Store,* your child takes the role of the cashier's assistant. He or she fills bags so that they are of equal weight. For instance, an order with items weighing 17 ounces, 15 ounces, 11 ounces, and 9 ounces can be combined so that one bag contains the 17- and 9-ounce items and the other bag contains the 11- and 15-ounce items.

In the *Health Food Store,* your child mixes precise amounts of oats and bran. Using addition and multiplication, your child combines the ingredients so that they match customers' requests. For instance, the customer wants a cereal mixture containing 42 ounces of oats and 36 ounces of bran. If the oats come in 7-ounce boxes and the bran comes in 6-ounce boxes, your child will need to use six boxes of each.

In the *Jewelry Store,* gold is sold in precise amounts. Using addition of whole numbers and decimals, your child melts bars of gold to meet a customer's order. For instance, if there are 1.5-, 1.8-, 2.3-, and 2.5-ounce bars available, your child determines which of these sizes must be combined to fill an order for 4.8 ounces.

In the *Lumber Store,* your child cuts pieces of lumber to fit customers' requests. Using addition and subtraction, he or she figures out how to cut one piece of wood so that it yields two pieces that differ in length by a precise amount. For instance, he or she might need to cut an 11-foot piece to yield two pieces, one 3 feet longer than the other.

In the *Number Shop,* using concepts such as "greater than," "less than," and "multiples of," your child comes up with numbers that meet a customer's request. For instance, what number is less than 10, greater than 5, and a multiple of 3?

In the *Pharmacy,* your child uses addition with fractions and percentages to come up with the right mixtures of ingredients to fill prescriptions. For instance, the customer needs 80 ounces of Asmedrol; this drug is composed of 15 percent Anadol and 85 percent lysine. Your child decides how many ounces of each ingredient have to be combined to yield the Asmedrol.

In the *Repair Shop,* your child fixes broken computers. These machines need to be reprogrammed with equations so that they function like intact computers. Using addition and multiplication, your child figures out the right equations to feed into the computer. For instance, the computer must output the following numbers; *3, 6, 9,* and *12.* Your child decides what multiple has to be applied to the inputs of *1, 2, 3,* and *4* to get this output.

Within each shop, the problems get progressively more difficult. If your child makes a mistake, the program offers a hint such as "You are using a number that is too low." However, the computer offers only hints, never the answer.

At the end of play in each shop, the program tells your child how many customers he or she served correctly. He or she can select either the "One Shop" game or the "All Shops" game. If your child plays the "All Shops" game, he or she must be aware of the customers waiting for service. If they leave the shop because of delays, your child loses those customers. The game ends when 50 customers have left the shop.

The program offers several options. Your child selects the speed of play and can play against the clock. If the clock is not set, you can vary how long your child spends in each shop by assigning a certain number of problems in that shop.

There are two other programs in this series.

In MATH SHOP, JR. (1989, $32.95), for children 6–9 years old (Grades 1–4), your child practices the basic math operations of addition, subtraction, multiplication, and division in the same kind of shopping-mall simulation. In addition, the program covers odd and even numbers, estimation, and identification of money units. Your child receives "Top Employee" rewards for doing well.

In ALGEBRA SHOP (1987, $32.95), for children 12 years and older (Grades 7 and up), your child practices prealgebra and algebra skills. Factoring, using fractions and decimals, squares and square roots, cube and cube roots, simultaneous equations, and positive and negative numbers are all covered.

MATHTALK

5–11 years
Grades K–6

Series
First Byte / Davidson, 1988, $39.95

Hardware
Apple IIGS, 512 KB
Apple Macintosh, 512 KB
IBM PC and compatibles, 512 KB ($39.95)
   ★ Essential: 3.5-inch disk drive, color monitor, mouse

Abilities Needed

To use this program independently, your child should be reading at the second-grade level.

This program is appropriate for the learning-disabled child.

Curriculum Areas

This program teaches arithmetic by offering a speech-enhanced tutorial that guides your child through the steps needed to master problems in addition, subtraction, multiplication, and division. Your child also learns calculator skills.

Arithmetic

- *Fundamental operations*—operating with addition, subtraction, multiplication, and division
- *Concepts*—understanding equations

The Program

(Tutor/Tool). This program offers a "talking math tutorial." Professor Matt A. Matics is your child's guide. He tutors, challenges, and tests your child's skill in carrying out the four basic math operations. The voice quality is somewhat robotic and artificial, but your child is not likely to be bothered by it. Children who can read can use text pull-down menus; prereaders can use graphic-oriented "picture-box" menus. Five main menu selections are available.

In *Math Book,* you and your child create math pages with up to 24 problems. These individualized pages can be printed, deleted, or saved for later use in the Games segments. The program can accommodate addition problems with up to three 8-digit numbers, subtraction problems with up to two 8-digit numbers, multiplication problems with 4-digit numbers multiplied by 4-digit numbers, and division problems with 3-digit divisors and 4-digit dividends.

In *Whiz,* your child plays two games, *Solve It* (a talking tutorial) and *Scoreboard* (a test simulation).

- In *Solve It,* your child chooses problems in any of the four operations. The Professor coaches your child through each problem with feedback and graphic demonstrations. He might tell your child, for instance, "Now add the ones column."

- In *Scoreboard,* your child is in a testlike situation in which he or she solves problems on each Math Page. The Professor suggests that your child might use paper and pencil in solving the problems but offers no help.

In *Game Room,* two activities, *Table Talk* and *Mystery Number,* help your child test his or her skill in addition, subtraction, multiplication, and division as well as increase speed and accuracy.

- In *Table Talk,* your child works with up to 100 problems in four basic math tables. He or she selects an operation, estimates the time it will take to complete the activity, and enters answers either on the keyboard or on the keypad.

- In *Mystery Number,* your child solves simple math equations with missing numbers. He or she selects the operation and the number of problems (10–100) and estimates the time needed to complete the activity. Answers are entered on the keyboard or keypad. The Professor's special gauges show your child how he or she is doing.

In *Solve It,* your child receives steady help after he or she has made an error. After three mistakes, for example, in trying to solve a two-digit addition problem, the animated Professor might appear and say, "Let me help you with your problem. Here is a picture of your problem. There is one bug plus three bugs. How many bugs are there? Let's count together and see how many bugs we have. I have four bugs in my collection. Enter that number in your problem $(1 + 3 = \underline{\quad})$." For more complex problems, the Professor demonstrates the computational steps on his Chalkboard. Your child can also ask for help from the Professor at any time and can see the demonstration before he or she makes any errors.

In *Scoreboard,* when the test is over, the Professor supplies tools— the Incredible Talking Calculator or the Chalkboard—to help your child correct his or her errors. The Chalkboard demonstrates how to solve the missed problems. The Calculator operates like a regular calculator except that it speaks the answers as well as showing them. When all the problems have been corrected, your child can take the quiz again, change the Math Page, or change the person playing.

In *Table Talk,* an asterisk marks each incorrect answer, and your child tries the missed problems again. At the end of both *Table Talk* and *Mystery Numbers,* a scoreboard appears showing the number of problems tried, the number correct, the percentage correct, and the time your child needed to complete the game.

When your child successfully answers problems, he or she sees and hears messages such as "You're right. You've made the Professor proud" or "Good job. Your answer is correct."

To speed up the program's presentation, you can turn the speech feature off, and you can also adjust the volume setting (0–9).

You can keep track of your child's progress with score cards that include the name of the activity, the title of the Math Page, your child's name, the date, the time taken to complete the activity, the number of problems correct, the number of problems attempted, and the percentage of correct problems.

MATHTALK FRACTIONS (1988, $39.95, 512 KB) is a second program in this series for children aged 8–14 (Grades 3–9). In this program Professor Matt A. Matics helps your child with fractions along with decimals and percentages. Your child can enter his or her own problems and check homework in the Problem Factory.

Mavis Beacon Teaches Typing

8 years and older
Grades 3 and up

The Software Toolworks, 1987, $49.95

Hardware

Apple II series, 64 KB ($39.95)
Commodore 64/128, 64 KB ($39.95)
   ★ Essential: 5.25-inch disk drive (two-disk set)
   ☆ Recommended: printer
Apple IIGS, 1 MB
Apple Macintosh, 800 KB
   ★ Essential: 3.5-inch disk drive (two-disk set)
   ☆ Recommended: printer

IBM PC and compatibles, 512 KB

★ Essential: 3.5-inch disk drive or 5.25-inch disk drive (two-disk set), color graphics card

☆ Recommended: printer

Abilities Needed

Your child should have the finger dexterity necessary for keyboarding.

This program is appropriate for the learning-disabled child.

Curriculum Areas

This program teaches keyboarding through personalized lessons, each created by the computer to fit your child's age and keyboarding performance level.

Writing

■ *The mechanics*—keyboarding

The Program

(Tool). The lessons in this program are constructed from an enormous database. Each time your child uses the program, his or her performance record is updated and the material he or she will face is adapted to the changing skill level. As a result, your child never faces the same lesson twice. The program consists of three segments.

In the *Introduction,* your child is given a guided tour of the features of the program.

In *Help for New Users,* your child sees a demonstration of all the individualized features of the program and learns how to access them during the lessons.

In *Start Lessons,* your child begins the teaching phase of the program. He or she first types in a "biography" that includes age level (under 9 years, 9–14 years, or over 14 years), typing skill level (Novice, Intermediate, or Advanced), and amount of practice time desired (± 30 minutes). Using this data, the program chooses a lesson and a goal speed for your child. The Lessons part of the program has three sections.

■ In *The Chalkboard,* your child sees the teaching plan for the lesson. It shows the focus of the lesson (for instance, how to type the A, S, D, and F keys), the typing problem to be dealt with (for instance, the problem of a novice typist confusing the F and G keys), and the remedy (for instance, introducing the home row). Each lesson focuses on a different kind of text—stories, facts, quotes from history, riddles, rhymes, or jokes.

- In *The Classroom,* your child sees a pair of on-screen "guide hands," poised above a keyboard, ready to type. These hands, which act as the instructors for correct hand placement and finger reach, type the lesson along with your child. As your child types, each key he or she strikes is shown either pressed down on the pictured keyboard or colored (red for the wrong key and black for the correct key).

- In *The Workshop,* your child practices what he or she learned in *The Classroom.* The goal is to increase speed and accuracy. This section displays a clock to time the lesson, a metronome to teach typing in rhythm, and three meters to monitor speed and accuracy.

The program includes a Road Racer Arcade Game in which your child sharpens his or her typing skills by competing against Red Walter. Jet fighter planes blast the typing drills across the top of the screen. If your child types well, he or she leaps forward, and Red Walter is left behind. If he or she makes mistakes, Red Walter begins to creep up, but your child can type quickly, pull ahead, and still win the game.

Extensive Help screens, for beginners to expert typists, can be accessed at any time. These include such options as the Fingers and Keys tutorial that tells your child what key he or she just hit and what finger should have been used.

Customizing features include guide hands, a keyboard, and gadgets such as meters, metronomes, or clocks that can be turned on or off, the choice of either a standard or a Dvorak keyboard, and the choice of whether to display progress charts. You can choose either word processing mode, with wraparound lines, or typewriter mode. A Free Typing option allows your child to type, without a lesson plan, any material he or she chooses.

The program can display up to 19 different graphs that chart your child's performance from Day 1 to the current moment in all typing categories (for example, speed by key, accuracy by letter). If you have a printer, these can be printed out in the form of a report card. As your child's typing improves, the goal speed can be changed in his or her personal file.

An extensive manual offers information on the history of typewriting along with typing fundamentals and samples of different form letters and résumés.

This is a versatile keyboarding program that can grow with your child's abilities. The program's unique design allows it to note consistent error patterns, chart them, and then create corrective drills to increase accuracy and speed.

McGee

2–4 years
Grade PreK

Series
Lawrence Productions, 1990, $39.95

Hardware

Apple IIGS, 512 KB
Apple Macintosh, 1 MB
   ★ Essential: 3.5-inch disk drive (two-disk set), mouse
   ☆ Recommended: color monitor
IBM PC and compatibles, 256 KB
   ★ Essential: 5.25-inch disk drive (two-disk set), mouse
   ☆ Recommended: color monitor

Abilities Needed

This program is part of the *No Words* software series, which uses only pictures, so your prereading child can operate it by himself or herself with little or no help from you. If your child uses the program alone, he or she should know how to work with a mouse.

This program is appropriate for the learning-disabled child.

Curriculum Areas

This program teaches prereading skills and provides an easy way for your child to become familiar with the computer.

Reading

■ *Comprehension skills*—following simple directions, reading stories, identifying sequences of events

The Program

(Tutee). This program offers well-sequenced graphics featuring an appealing character named McGee, who is a young child exploring the sights and sounds of a household. McGee bounces a ball, rides a hobby horse, makes a phone call, and plays with a cat, a dog, and a puppet. By watching McGee carry out such familiar daily activities, your child becomes more aware of the activities he or she does on a regular basis. The character is intentionally drawn so that your child can perceive McGee as either a boy or a girl.

McGee starts by awakening and then explores parts of the house. As McGee reaches each point of exploration, your child sees a room or a section of the house, such as the hall, the garden, or the kitchen. Under each scene are four pictures, each containing a different part of the room. Your child selects one of these, and McGee carries out some relevant action. For instance, in McGee's room the choices are a toy rabbit, a ball, a toy horse, and a door. Depending on your child's choice, McGee might play with the rabbit or leave the room to enter the hallway. Sometimes the choices are accompanied by words (the characters speak to one another) or sounds (McGee splashes in the bathtub).

Your child is free to make as many choices as he or she wishes in any part of the house. There is no opportunity for your child to make a mistake—any choice is fine.

Graphics and animation are well linked to the choices your child makes. For instance, if your child selects the carpet when McGee is in the living room, the following scene shows McGee crawling under the carpet. At the start of the program, your child can set the loudness of the sound.

Although your help is not required, you can sit with your child and easily extend the program by discussing the choices and activities your child makes. The format also includes, on a nonverbal basis, many of the components of storytelling. It provides easy-to-use materials that encourage your child's development in this important area.

McGEE VISITS KATIE'S FARM (1990, $39.95) is the second program in this series. This program requires 1 MB of memory for the Apple IIGS version. McGee explores all the places on the farm: the pond, the barn, the chicken coop, the garden, and the corral. In the chicken coop, your child can have McGee hold one of the fuzzy chicks or help Katie gather eggs. Your child and McGee can go to the corral and choose who will feed the horse a carrot or who will take a ride on the horse.

Memory Castle

9–10 years
Grades 4–5

Sunburst Communications, 1984, $65.00

Hardware

Apple II series, 48 KB

Commodore 64, 64 KB

Tandy 1000, 256 KB

★ Essential: 5.25-inch disk drive, color monitor

IBM PC/PC*jr*, 128 KB

★ Essential: 5.25-inch disk drive, color graphics card, color monitor

Abilities Needed

Your child should be reading at the third-grade level in order to read the on-screen material independently.

This program is appropriate for the learning-disabled child, although a child with significant language or memory problems might have difficulty with it.

Curriculum Areas

This program is designed to teach and strengthen memory skills by having your child recall a series of directions.

Reading

■ *Comprehension skills* — combining sentences, recalling information on topics, identifying sequences of events, following complex directions

Writing

- *The mechanics*—spelling single-syllable words, spelling multisyllable words, using elements of a word processing program

The Program

(Tutor). Your child is a knight who is given a two-part assignment: It directs your child to go to a certain place in the castle and tells him or her what to do after he or she gets to the place. An assignment might be "Go to the shield room and find a shield with a cross on it." The game can be played at three levels of difficulty. At the easy level, your child has 6 items to remember, at the medium level 12, and at the difficult level 20.

The program prompts your child with appropriate questions such as "Where do you have to go?" Your child answers by typing in the correct response on the keyboard. If your child completes the assignment correctly, he or she wins the game. Completing an easy assignment earns a golden goblet, a medium assignment earns the Royal Order of the Torch, and a difficult assignment earns a room full of treasure. If your child forgets part of the assignment, the game ends.

This program offers an interesting and motivating memory game. Recall of details is an important skill. If your child has difficulty with this skill, it is worthwhile for him or her to practice and try to improve performance.

Because the answers are typed in, the room for variation and error is great. To a considerable degree, the program handles this issue quite well. Generally, the program ignores most small typing errors. For example, if your child, in attempting to type *shield*, presses *s*, *h*, and then *e*, the *e* will not appear on the screen. If your child enters a totally unfamiliar word, the program will show a list of places in the castle so that the game can continue. The program might also ask, "What do you mean? Please try again." If this happens three times, the game ends.

Mickey's ABC's: A Day at the Fair

2–5 years
PreK–K

Series
Walt Disney Computer Software, 1990, $49.95

Hardware

IBM PC, PS/2, and compatibles, 512 KB
Tandy 1000, 640 KB

★ Essential: one 3.5-inch disk drive (two-disk set), two 5.25-inch
disk drives (three-disk set), or one 5.25-inch and one hard-disk
drive. The package comes with both 3.5-inch and 5.25-inch disks.

☆ Recommended: The Sound Source ($34.95).

Abilities Needed

Your child will initially need your help to understand the workings of
the program. Once familiar with the format, he or she should be able to
work independently. You will have to be available to enter the copy protection at the beginning of each play session.

This program is appropriate for the learning-disabled child.

Curriculum Areas

This program exposes your child to the alphabet, letter sounds, and the
relationship between letters and words. It is also a good beginning exploration of the computer and the keyboard.

Reading

■ *Decoding skills*—matching and recognizing letters,
linking sounds to letters and words, reading single-
syllable words, matching pictures and words

The Program

(Tutor). The appealing Disney character Mickey Mouse is your child's
guide for learning the ABC's. While visiting Mickey's house and the
country fair, your child sees and hears letters matched with familiar
objects and words. If you have the Sound Source option, the program
speaks all the material and has added sound effects.

The program offers two settings.

In *Mickey's House,* the program begins with Mickey asleep in bed. He wakes up and spends some time doing things around his house. Your child presses a letter key to have Mickey do something in one of the four rooms of his house: the bedroom, the bathroom, the kitchen, or the living room. Each letter of the alphabet is represented in the house by an animation depicting an everyday object or action. If your child presses *T*, for instance, Mickey watches television; if your child presses *C*, Mickey goes to the kitchen to get a cookie. When a letter key is pressed, the letter appears at the upper left corner of the screen. When the animation begins, the word being represented appears at the upper left.

In *Going to the Fair,* Mickey meets his friends Goofy, Minnie, Donald, and Daisy at the Country Fair, where he visits farm animals and engages in contests. Again, pressing a letter key makes something happen. For example, pressing *J* causes Mickey to taste some jelly; pressing *A* causes an airplane to fly over Mickey's head; and pressing *H* causes a horse to whinny.

No errors are possible; each time your child selects a letter key, he or she is rewarded with an animation related to a word beginning with that letter.

The program offers the choice of uppercase or lowercase letters, 10 detailed background screens, and over 80 different animated responses with speech and sound effects. Most letters have more than one animation; which one occurs depends on where Mickey is when the key is pressed. The program is also designed to present randomly a number of surprise animations. If your child presses *H*, for instance, a hot dog might squirt out of its bun and land in the garbage pail. Young children love these kinds of unusual changes in routine.

Your child can turn the sound on or off, control the volume, and activate a Pause Mode so that he or she can take a short rest. When this pause is activated, Mickey sits down and says, "I'll just wait here!"

The program has an unusual copy protection system which, because it is too difficult for a young child to use, requires you to be available to start the program each time your child plays it.

This program is fun for one child alone, for two children as a team, or for you and your child. The manual offers many suggestions for different ways to use and extend the program.

▼

MICKEY'S 1 2 3's : THE BIG SURPRISE PARTY (1990, $49.95) uses a similar format to introduce basic numbers (1–9) and number concepts such as counting. Any number key that your child presses makes something happen. Mickey visits a grocery store, a toy factory, and a post office and then returns home. At each location, he does errands for a party: He shops for food and decorations, makes a gift for the guest of honor, and mails invitations; then he holds a surprise birthday party for a friend.

MICKEY'S COLORS AND SHAPES: THE DAZZLING MAGIC SHOW (1990, $49.95) is an introduction to color and shapes. The program uses a soft plastic overlay that covers part of the keyboard. Your child presses one of the five keys showing basic geometric shapes or one of the eight colored keys to make things happen as Mickey and Minnie go through a three-act magic show. In Act I, Mickey juggles a variety of colorful shapes. In Act II, your child and Mickey create magic pictures that can be printed. In Act III, your child looks behind the shapes to find missing animals. The program offers over 150 animated actions and more than 130 objects that help your child learn to recognize abstract shapes.

Mickey's Crossword Puzzle Maker

5–11 years
Grades K–6

Walt Disney Computer Software, 1990, $39.95

Hardware
Apple II series, 128 KB
- ★ Essential: 3.5-inch disk drive or 5.25-inch disk drive (two-disk set), blank disks for saving new puzzles
- ☆ Recommended: printer, color monitor, mouse

Apple Macintosh, 1 MB
- ★ Essential: 3.5-inch disk drive, blank disks for saving new puzzles
- ☆ Recommended: printer, color monitor, mouse

IBM PC and compatibles, 256 KB ($44.95)

★ Essential: 5.25-inch disk drive (two-disk set), blank disks for saving new puzzles

☆ Recommended: printer, color monitor

Abilities Needed

Your child should be reading at the third-grade level in order to work independently. A younger child will need your help to read the instructions for many of the program's parts.

This program is appropriate for the learning-disabled child, although a child with significant language problems might have difficulty with it.

Curriculum Areas

This program teaches reading and writing by offering a tool for playing, creating, and printing crossword puzzles.

Reading

- *Decoding skills*—analyzing words for their meanings, enlarging vocabulary, defining words
- *Comprehension skills*—playing word games

Writing

- *The process*—creating messages for visual material
- *The mechanics*—spelling single-syllable and multi-syllable words

The Program

(Tutor/Tool). This program lets your child play eight on-disk Disney puzzles, play a surprise puzzle, create original crossword puzzles using word clues or more than 150 picture clues, and print his or her creations with eight colorful Disney backgrounds or two picture borders, in color or in black and white.

The program features easy-to-use picture menus and step-by-step on-screen instructions.

Four main menu choices are available. Each function has a New User Keyboard Help screen that explains how to play or use that function. Your child can also press the question-mark key to see a series of Help screens with information about each function's menu bar and keyboard commands.

In *Play a Puzzle,* your child plays one of his or her previously designed and saved puzzles, a Disney puzzle, or a surprise puzzle. The computer creates the surprise puzzles from a dictionary of over 500 words, divided into three levels of difficulty.

In *Create a Puzzle,* your child makes a new puzzle using his or her own words, picture clues, or the program's built-in dictionary with as many as 500 words. Your child can alter the shape and location on the screen of his or her puzzle as well as add a Disney background (eight pictures and two picture frames).

In *Load a Puzzle,* your child loads either a Disney puzzle or his or her own creation from a saved puzzle disk.

In *Change Program Set-Up,* you or your child changes the printer setup, the music, or the Help screens.

Any child will enjoy the appealing and colorful Disney characters and artwork and the sound of familiar Disney tunes.

In *Play a Puzzle,* your child chooses to play against a Disney character, against a friend, or alone. Your child can choose to play against Goofy, who makes lots of mistakes during his turn; against Donald, who is smarter and makes some mistakes; or against Mickey, who is the smartest and makes few mistakes.

Your child can ask for a hint at any time by selecting the key icon on the top menu bar. One of the letters in the puzzle word he or she selected will be revealed. However, when that turn is over, your child will not receive any points for letters revealed by the hint.

Players receive points for each letter filled in correctly, for each word completed correctly, and for Bonus Squares. The winner of each puzzle game gets bonus points added to his or her total score and an animated fireworks display with a congratulatory message.

You can customize the program by changing the vocabulary level (for the surprise puzzles), the difficulty level of the puzzle, and the type of printout (three formats are available). Level One puzzles include words appropriate for children ages 6–7 years, with 4–8 answers per puzzle. Level Two puzzles include words appropriate for children ages 8–9 years, with 8–20 answers per puzzle. Level Three puzzles include words appropriate for children ages 10–11 years, with 8–20 answers per puzzle. The Mixed Words Level includes words from all three vocabulary levels, with 8–20 answers per puzzle. You can turn off the music, the helper cues, or both.

This is a versatile program, with many options, that lends itself to continued use. Many of the program's functions require your child to handle a lot of information and work through a number of keys and menu screens. At those times, you might need to provide help. The program comes with an extensive manual.

Microtype: The Wonderful World of PAWS

8–14 years
Grades 3–9

South-Western Publishing, 1985, $39.95

Hardware
Apple II series, 48 KB
Apple IIGS, 256 KB
Commodore 64, 64 KB
  ★ Essential: 5.25-inch disk drive
  ☆ Recommended: printer
Apple IIGS, 512 KB
IBM PS/2, 512 KB
  ★ Essential: 3.5-inch disk drive
  ☆ Recommended: printer
IBM PC and compatibles, 128 KB
Tandy 1000, 256 KB
  ★ Essential: 5.25-inch disk drive, color monitor
  ☆ Recommended: printer

Abilities Needed
Your child needs fourth-grade reading skills to use this program independently. Your child should have the finger dexterity necessary for keyboarding. At times you'll have to monitor your child's work to be certain he or she is using correct keyboarding techniques.

This program is appropriate for the learning-disabled child.

Curriculum Areas

This is a step-by-step instructional program that teaches "touch" keyboarding skills.

Writing

■ *The mechanics*—keyboarding, using a word processing program

The Program

(Tool). The program uses PAWS, the cat, as the "presenter of learning." PAWS' animated antics let your child see the correct techniques for typing, including proper hand positioning. Graphics and written instructions guide your child through initial learning, practice, and basic skill building. In the first lesson, for instance, your child sees on the screen both the words "Strike the E with your left pointer finger" and a picture demonstrating this action.

This individualized learning program offers 17 lessons and 2 games. In Lesson One, for instance, your child learns the home keys *ASDF JKL* and *semicolon*, and in Lesson Ten he or she learns *M* and *X*. Your child must work on the lessons in sequence. The menu selections are the same for each lesson.

In *Review Skills,* your child reviews the keys learned in the previous lesson. Practice is offered on two drill lines.

In *New Keys,* your child sees a graphic representation that illustrates the reach to a new key. The emphasis is on which finger is to be used. Practice is offered on two to four drill lines.

In *Build Speed,* your child develops speed with the letters learned in this and all previous lessons. He or she works on four drill lines, one at a time. As your child completes a line, the program analyzes it for the percentage of words typed correctly and for the speed in words per minute. If your child typed fewer than 50 percent of the words correctly, he or she must repeat that line before the program presents a new line.

In *PAWS' Game Run,* your child can play a keyboarding game at the completion of each lesson. PAWS and your child race toward a ball. As your child types a drill line, PAWS' prints move toward the ball.

In *PAWS' Run,* your child earns points through speed and accuracy. These points help PAWS move through a maze, littered with dots and prizes, toward a final treasure.

When your child makes a mistake, PAWS presents a sad face and the correct key is highlighted on the screen keyboard. For correct typing, your child is rewarded both by a smiling PAWS and by a written message such as "Wow, you made it."

The Open Screen option allows your child to enter text from other sources, such as the companion textbook *Computer Keyboarding, an Elementary Course* ($9.75). This option works like a basic word processing program, offering features such as entry, wordwrap, erase, and save. The Apple IIGS version features a Stroke-Call option that allows your child to receive both verbal and visual instruction.

At the end of each lesson, a report includes your child's name, the date, the fastest speed from the *Build Speed* and game lines, the highest point total from *PAWS' Game Run,* a summary lesson code, and a recommendation code, which indicates the lesson your child should do next. These reports can be printed. You or your child can also print copies of material typed using the Open Screen option.

Microzine
Premier Issue

10 years and older
Grades 5 and up

Series
Scholastic Family Software, 1983, $39.95

Hardware
Apple II series, 48 KB (Issues 1–21)
Apple II series, 64 KB (Issues 22–36)
Apple II series, 128 KB (Issues 37–40)
    ★ Essential: 3.5-inch or 5.25-inch disk drive
    ☆ Recommended: color monitor
IBM PC and compatibles, 256 KB
    ★ Essential: 3.5-inch or 5.25-inch disk drive, color graphics card
    ☆ Recommended: color monitor

Abilities Needed

This program is appropriate for the learning-disabled child, although a child with significant language or organizational problems might have difficulty with it.

Curriculum Areas

The program helps develop and strengthen your child's understanding of several types of written language formats.

Reading

- *Comprehension skills*—recalling information on topics, reading stories, following complex directions, reading fictional texts, reading nonfictional texts

Writing

- *The process*—applying supplied messages to visual materials, completing fictional texts, completing non-fictional texts, creating messages for visual materials, using organizational strategies
- *The mechanics*—using elements of a word processing program, using study skills

The Program

(Tutor/Tool/Tutee). The program presents an interactive magazine that your child both reads and creates. The menu, appropriately called "Table of Contents," offers four full-length sections.

In *Twistoplot,* your child directs the flow and outcome of an interactive mystery story titled "Haunted House." Your child makes decisions at various points in the program that change the direction of the story. For instance, he or she can choose whether or not to take a friend along to share the adventure. In addition, your child must type in words at certain points in order to have the story continue.

In *Ask Me,* an interview format, your child interviews and interacts with a well-known figure. For instance, in the original issue (1983) the figure is Robert McNaughton, an actor in the film *E.T.* Your child learns how to interview a person to get information about that person's life and views. Your child asks questions by selecting from phrases that appear at the top of the screen (for instance, "What do," "When was"). When your child selects a phrase, the program adds words that form a complete and meaningful question (for instance, "What do you like to do in your free time?"). The interviewee answers the question and, at times, asks questions of your child. Your child answers these questions by typing in a response of up to 35 letters.

In *Poster,* a construction segment, your child creates posters on the screen, adds sounds, and then saves the productions. Here your child learns to work with programming languages as he or she instructs the computer on how to form the drawings. The instructions involve directions (for instance, *R* for right, *L* for left), and numbers (for instance, typing *10* will result in a shorter line than typing *20*).

In *Secret Files,* your child creates cards similar to index cards, on which he or she enters information such as titles, names, addresses, and phone numbers. The program lets your child manipulate and use the files as he or she learns procedures such as search, erase, and change.

In the segment *Twistoplot,* the program handles your child's errors. The keyboard accepts only the correct word at various points. If your child presses other keys or presses keys in the wrong sequence, nothing appears on the screen, and the story will not continue.

The program offers some nice refinements. In *Twistoplot,* sound and animation accompany the events in the story your child creates. In the *Poster* segment, your child can choose to add color, to change the width of the brushstroke, and to attach a message of up to 26 letters to his or her poster drawing.

The graphics are appealing, and the materials are interesting. The segments are endlessly adaptable to your child's level because so much of what appears on the screen depends on what he or she types into the computer.

The Premier Issue was the first in a long and continuing series put out by Scholastic ($39.95 each). A total of 40 issues are currently available. Each school year, approximately four new issues come out. For the 1990–91 school year, each of the four issues contained four programs with activities in math, science, and social studies, as well as a problem-solving and visual-discrimination activity.

M-SS-NG L-NKS— Young People's Literature

8 years and older
Grades 3 and up

Series
Sunburst Communications, 1987, $65.00

Hardware
Apple II series, 48 KB
Commodore 64, 64 KB
IBM PC and compatibles, 128 KB
IBM PS/2, 256 KB

★ Essential: 5.25-inch disk drive
☆ Recommended: printer

Abilities Needed
Your child should be reading at the fourth-grade level to use the program independently.

This program is appropriate for the learning-disabled child, although a child with significant language problems might have difficulty with it.

Curriculum Areas
This program teaches reading, writing, and reasoning by having your child complete language puzzles.

Reading
- *Decoding skills*—enlarging vocabulary
- *Comprehension skills*—playing word games, reading fictional texts, reading nonfictional texts

Reasoning
- *Analyzing information*—distinguishing relevant from nonrelevant cues, recognizing patterns
- *Developing hypotheses*—making inferences and deductions

Writing

- *The mechanics*—spelling single-syllable words, spelling multisyllable words, using elements of a word processing program, analyzing sentences for grammar, using punctuation

The Program

(Tutor). The Young People's Literature disk offers nine passages taken from such children's classics as *The Wind in the Willows* and *The Secret Garden*.

In all the programs in this series, a passage appears on the screen with some letters or words missing. For instance, in a passage from *The Wind in the Willows* by Kenneth Grahame, your child sees the following on the screen: "When they got home, the Rat made a bright fire in the parlour, and planted Mole in an arm-chair in front of it, having fetch-d -o-n- d-e-s-n- g-w- a-d -l-p-e-s -o- h-m, -n- t-l- h-m -i-e-s-o-i-s -i-l -u-p-r." Your child reconstructs the original passage by filling in letters or words one at a time, making educated guesses based on his or her knowledge of word structure and spelling, grammar, meaning in context, and sense of literary style. Your child fills in the missing letters in as few guesses as possible. He or she is given five tries to complete each word.

The pattern of missing letters and words varies, with nine formats available, each progressively more difficult: only consonants and no vowels; only vowels and no consonants; only the first letter of each word; every other letter; only the first and last letters of each word; only the first word in each sentence; whole words missing every second to eighth word; only the number of letters for each word; only the name of the passage. Each program provides more than 500 different puzzles.

In the Apple version of the program, an Editor allows you or your child to create your own customized pattern of missing letters and words for the puzzles. You can also vary the number of players (1–4), the topic and passage, the format, the number of guesses (1–5) before the computer gives your child the right answer, and the maximum number of guesses each player may have per turn. If a printer is available, you can print out passages and score screens to help assess your child's progress.

In the Apple version, a Spanish Editor is also available (1987, $75.00). In the IBM versions, German, Spanish, and French Editors are available (1987, $75.00 each).

MICROENCYCLOPEDIA; CLASSICS: OLD AND NEW; SCIENCE DISK; and ENGLISH EDITOR are the four other programs available in the series.

MICROENCYCLOPEDIA (1986, $65.00) for children 11 years and older (Grades 6 and up), offers a variety of passages on subjects of interest to children. There are seven topics (ice cream, bicycles, baseball, whales and sharks, elephants, airplanes, and inventions), with a choice of eight passages about each.

CLASSICS: OLD AND NEW (1986, $65.00) for children 13 years and older (Grades 8 and up), offers 81 passages (9 passages on each of 9 topics) from literature by such authors as Hemingway, Twain, Shakespeare, Flaubert, Melville, and A.A. Milne. Topics covered are the sea (*Moby Dick, The Old Man and the Sea*), unreal worlds (*Gulliver's Travels*), humor, food (*Winnie-the-Pooh*), sounds (*Loon Lake*), memories of childhood (*Growing Up*), limericks, mysteries, and the human condition (*Madame Bovary*).

SCIENCE DISK (1986, $65.00) for children 8 years and older (Grades 3 and up), is available only for the Apple II series. It presents passages about elementary science topics such as animal life, health and anatomy, earth science, and astronomy.

ENGLISH EDITOR (1986, $75.00) allows you or your child to enter up to 72 passages of your own, at any difficulty level.

Muppet Slate

5–7 years
Grades K–2

Series
Sunburst Communications, 1989, $75.00

Hardware
Apple II series, 64 KB
- ★ Essential: 3.5-inch or 5.25-inch disk drive (two-disk set includes a teacher/parent disk and a student disk), printer
- ☆ Recommended: Muppet Learning Keyboard or regular Apple keyboard

Abilities Needed
Your child will need your help in the first several sessions to understand and use the various operations. After that, he or she should be able to work independently.

This program is appropriate for the learning-disabled child.

Curriculum Areas
This program teaches writing by offering young children a beginning word processor that includes pictures.

Writing
- ■ *The mechanics*—using elements of a word processing program
- ■ *The process*—creating simple written messages, creating messages for visual materials

The Program
(Tool). This is a simple first word processing program. Your child can write any message he or she chooses. The letters appear in large size on the screen. At any one time, your child will be able to see four lines of text, with three to four words on each line. The program is not set up to handle long stories.

A special feature of the program is the availability of pictures. Your child can choose from 126 pictures of Muppets, bugs, vehicles, animals, and so on. To get a picture, your child types the first letter of the word for that picture. To see a telephone, for example, he or she types the letter *T*. Several pictures appear under each letter (for example, top, toy, train); your child has to repeatedly press the letter key until the picture he or she wants appears on the screen.

The pictures also allow your child to write rebuses, in which letters and pictures combine to "spell" words. For example, your child can take the icon for rain and combine it with the letters *B*, *O*, *W* to form the rebus "rainbow." The end result of the process is a written product that is far more colorful and attractive than words alone.

The menu appears in both pictures and words to let your child make selections with a minimum of reading. The menu offers six choices. With New, your child clears the screen and calls up a blank screen. In Load, your child calls up a file that has been saved. In Write, your child writes messages on the screen. In Save, your child saves a piece of writing. In Print, your child prints a file. In Quit, your child leaves the program.

The screen offers appealing Muppet characters, and its general appearance is inviting. The program lets you write in partnership with your child, which can be an enjoyable experience.

This program is the first in a four-part word processing series from Sunburst. MAGIC SLATE II, a more advanced program, is available in three versions. It requires 128 KB of memory on your Apple II.

MAGIC SLATE II: 20 COLUMN (1989, $75.00) is a word processing program designed for grades K–3. It does not have the rebus feature, but it does use large print. It has an easy-to-use picture menu and offers features such as delete, insert, replace, underline, and three different type styles.

MAGIC SLATE II: 40 COLUMN (1989, $75.00) is a word processing program designed for grades 4–7. It has all the features of the 20-column version, but uses smaller letters, although the letters are still larger than those adults are accustomed to, so fewer words at a time can be seen on the screen. Additional features include block commands, vertical spacing, submargins, and many customizing options.

MAGIC SLATE II: 80 COLUMN (1989, $75.00) is a sophisticated word processing program for junior and senior high school students as well as adults. It offers standard-size letters.

Muppets on Stage

3–5 years
Grades PreK–K

Sunburst Communications, 1987, $65.00

Hardware

Apple II series, 128 KB

  ★ Essential: 3.5-inch or 5.25-inch disk drive

  ☆ Recommended: Muppet Learning Keys, color monitor

Commodore 64, 64 KB

IBM PC and compatibles, 128 KB

  ★ Essential: 5.25-inch disk drive

  ☆ Recommended: Muppet Learning Keys, color monitor

Abilities Needed

The program requires minimal reading, and you can easily teach your child the game formats. After becoming familiar with the format, he or she should be able to work independently.

    This program is appropriate for the learning-disabled child.

Curriculum Areas

The program provides practice in letters, numbers, picture recognition, and color recognition.

Reading

  ■ *Decoding skills*—matching and recognizing letters, linking sounds with letters

  ■ *Comprehension skills*—following simple directions

Arithmetic

  ■ *Numeration*—matching numbers to objects, counting objects, counting sequentially

The Program

(Tutor). The program covers all the letters of the alphabet and the numbers *1* through *9*. It is divided into three activities.

    In *Discovery,* your child is free to press, on the keyboard, any letter or number. When he or she presses a letter, that letter appears on the screen with a picture of an object that starts with the sound of that letter. For instance, if your child presses *N*, a nose appears. If he or she then presses *4*, three more noses will appear—four in all.

In *Letters,* a letter appears on the screen and your child presses that same letter on the keyboard.

In *Numbers,* objects appear on the screen along with the written question "How many?" Your child presses the number on the keyboard that corresponds to the number of objects on the screen.

Graphics, sound, color, and animation are appealing, and the program is easy to use. Some of the pictures, such as a nose that appears by itself, might initially be difficult for your child to identify, making it difficult for him or her to connect the letter with the sound it makes in the word.

Music and movement show your child when his or her answer is correct; beeps indicate a wrong response. The program does not offer hints on how to get a correct answer.

You can vary the program in several ways. For instance, if you want your child to deal with only 10 letters at a time, rather than all 26, you can set the program accordingly. Similarly, you can limit the number of numerals so that your child does not have to deal with all 9. You can choose whether you want the letters presented randomly or in alphabetic sequence and whether you want them to appear in uppercase or lowercase.

Muppetville

3–6 years
Grades PreK–1

Sunburst Communications, 1986, $65.00

Hardware
Apple II series, 64 KB
- ★ Essential: 3.5-inch or 5.25-inch disk drive, color monitor
- ☆ Recommended: Touch Window or Muppet Learning Keys

Abilities Needed
Your child should be able to recognize letters, numbers, basic shapes, and colors. He or she should also understand the concepts *same* and *different*.

This program is appropriate for the learning-disabled child.

Curriculum Areas

The program teaches the beginning reading and arithmetic skills of letter and word recognition, number recognition, color recognition, symbols, and addition.

Reading

- *Decoding skills*—matching and recognizing letters, matching pictures and words

Arithmetic

- *Numeration*—matching objects to objects, matching numbers to objects
- *Concepts*—understanding spatial concepts
- *Fundamental operations*—operating with addition

The Program

(Tutor). Kermit the Frog, riding a unicycle, guides your child through Muppetville. Six buildings along Main Street feature Muppet characters. Each offers your child a different activity, providing practice in visual discrimination, memory, matching, and beginning addition skills.

In *Animal's Apartment House,* your child matches songs, random notes, or note patterns in a concentration game. A house appears with six closed windows, behind which are hidden different choices. Your child selects matching pairs of windows.

In *Sam the Eagle's School,* your child opens and closes 12 windows, labeled with letters, to match a numeral with a die that has a corresponding number of dots. For instance, your child presses the letter *M* and a die with two dots appears; then he or she presses the letter *U* and the numeral *6* appears. Because that is not a match, your child continues to look among the windows for a match.

In *Muppet Factory,* your child helps Beaker solve simple addition problems that Bunsen creates. This game has two levels of difficulty: The easy level contains problems whose sums range from 2 to 10, and the hard level contains problems whose sums range from 2 to 18. Your child types in the correct answers. The program offers hints; for instance, in the problem *1 + 4 = How many?*, one small square appears below the *1* and four squares below the *4*.

In *The Statler-Waldorf Hotel,* your child plays a concentration game in which he or she matches objects, either by shape alone or by shape and color.

In *Gonzo's Zoo,* your child helps Gonzo identify which beast is shaped differently from three other beasts. This game has three levels (easy, hard, and a random mix of easy and hard).

In *Muppet Movie,* your child takes part in a discovery activity. Your child presses any letter on the keyboard, and a corresponding picture appears on Miss Piggy's movie screen. For instance, when your child presses *H,* a picture of a hat appears along with the word *HAT.*

The graphics, sound, and Muppet characters make this an appealing program.

Mistakes are clearly highlighted with visual cues: The characters shake their heads, letters blink, and so on. Correct choices are rewarded by clear responses from the characters and other visual cues or by pleasant sound effects.

The program offers several options. You can turn the sound on or off and change the focus of the games. For example, in *Animal's Apartment House,* you can use songs, random notes, or random sound patterns. In *The Statler-Waldorf Hotel, Gonzo's Zoo,* and *Muppet Factory,* you can change the level of play.

As in all Sunburst programs, which are designed for school as well as home use, an extensive manual provides additional materials that correlate with kindergarten curricula. Twenty-four lesson plans are included.

Muppet Word Book

3–6 years
Grades PreK–1

Sunburst Communications, 1986, $65.00

Hardware
Apple II series, 64 KB
- ★ Essential: 3.5-inch or 5.25-inch disk drive
- ☆ Recommended: color monitor, printer, mouse, Touch Window or Muppet Learning Keys

Abilities Needed

To use this program, your child should be familiar with both uppercase and lowercase letters of the alphabet.

This program is appropriate for the learning-disabled child.

Curriculum Areas

This program introduces your child to beginning reading skills.

Reading

- *Decoding skills*—matching and recognizing letters, linking sounds to letters and words, matching pictures and words

Writing

- *The mechanics*—using elements of a word processing program

The Program

(Tutor/Tool). The program uses five progressive games plus a beginning word processing program to introduce your child to letters, words, and simple text writing. The engaging graphics feature the Muppet characters as guides.

In *Parking Lot,* your child distinguishes letters from nonletters. He or she has to send letters to one parking lot and nonletters (symbols, signs, shapes, and numbers) to a different lot.

In *Elevator,* your child matches lowercase consonants with their uppercase partners and matches a picture with the beginning letter of a word.

In *Pigs in Space,* your child is offered an open-ended exploration of initial letters in words and their sounds. By typing in a letter, your child sees 1 of 55 vocabulary words with a matching picture.

In *Circus,* your child selects a beginning consonant to combine with a word ending in order to create a complete word. For instance, -*et* appears on the screen and your child selects from the letters *n, f,* and *z* displayed below.

In *Muppet Labs,* your child has to recognize the word endings that combine with beginning consonant letters to form words. The two zany Muppet scientists, Bunsen and Beaker, help in this endeavor.

Muppet Words is a very simple first word processing program. It appears on the screen as an old-fashioned writing slate. Your child can experiment with uppercase and lowercase letters, words, punctuation marks, numbers, spacing, and so on, and can also save and print his or her work.

The antics of the Muppet characters and the engaging graphics make this an appealing program. Materials are presented in varied ways so that your child will not become bored.

Visual cues highlight mistakes. Your child can then make a second selection. If he or she makes a second error, the program offers the correct choice. Your child can always ask for help if he or she is having difficulty selecting the right answer.

Clear but amusing actions reward correct answers—for example, Gonzo shoots out of a cannon or beakers bubble in the Muppet laboratory. Special rewards are offered after your child gives six correct answers in any one game.

Several change options allow you to vary the program. For instance, in *Elevator* you can change the focus of the game from letters to pictures, and in *Parking Lot* you can preselect any of five different kinds of discriminations.

Your child can print and save his or her work with the word processing program, but there is no way to keep a record of work accomplished in the other games.

As with many programs designed for both home and school use, there is an extensive manual. Besides offering instructions for program use, it also contains additional materials that correlate with many kindergarten curricula (for example, vocabulary lists with rhyming words) and 26 classroom lesson plans.

Music Construction Set

7 years and older
Grades 2 and up

Electronic Arts, 1984, $14.95

Hardware

Apple II series, 48 KB
Apple IIGS, 512 KB ($19.95)

★ Essential: 5.25-inch disk drive, mouse or joystick
☆ Recommended: a soundboard such as Cricket, Echo,
   Mockingboard, Sound II synthesizer, or Apple sound speaker

Commodore 64, 64 KB
IBM PC and compatibles, 128 KB

★ Essential: 5.25-inch disk drive, mouse or joystick
☆ Recommended: printer, blank disks for saving music

Abilities Needed

Unless your child has some familiarity with musical notation, he or she will need your help in using this program.

This program is appropriate for the learning-disabled child, although a child who has significant visual-spatial or timing problems might have difficulty with it.

Curriculum Areas

The program lets your child explore and play with the world of music.

Reasoning

■ *Analyzing information*—organizing or sequencing
   details, recognizing patterns

The Program

(Tool). This program turns the building blocks of music (notes, rests, sharps, and flats) into pictures, which your child assembles into a piece of music. The computer then plays it back. Your child selects easy-to-use picture icons (a scissors for cutting, a paste jar for pasting, and a piano for composing new music) by simply pointing and clicking the mouse. The main menu offers two major segments.

In *Play Music,* your child plays 12 selections that are already on the disk. Each piece demonstrates a different musical form, period, or type, such as canon, scherzo, traditional, ragtime, or baroque.

In *Create Your Own,* your child creates his or her own compositions. He or she selects notes and other elements on the screen and, using an on-screen hand, places them on a composition sheet that shows the top and bottom staffs. By clicking on the piano icon, your child can instruct the computer to play back his or her composition. He or she can also print the composition.

The program offers five note values and five corresponding rests to work with as well as dots, accidentals, and two clef symbols. Your child can set the time signature (2/4, 3/4, 4/4, or 6/8) and can also transpose musical compositions into another key. He or she can control the speed, volume, and sound quality of the playback. Eight different instrument sounds are available: piano, harpsichord, tam-tam, accordion, flute, snare, organ, and banjo.

The program will appeal to either a child or an adult interested in music and music theory. It can be used for serious music instruction or by a computer user who wants to experiment with music making. If your child is a music novice, you should supplement the program with a basic music instruction book.

My Grand Piano

3–8 years
Grades PreK–3

Fisher-Price / GameTek / IJE, 1988, $14.95

Hardware
Apple II series, 128 KB
Apple IIGS, 512 KB
   ★ Essential: 5.25-inch disk drive, color monitor
IBM PC and compatibles, 256 KB
   ★ Essential: 3.5-inch ($16.95) or 5.25-inch disk drive, color monitor

Abilities Needed
If your child is a preschooler or a prereader, he or she will initially need your help to learn how to use the program. Your child should be reading

at approximately the second-grade level in order to use this program independently.

This program is appropriate for the learning-disabled child.

Curriculum Areas

This is a music program to introduce your child to the theory of the piano, but it also provides an easy introduction to the computer keyboard. Your child needs to be familiar with only the Spacebar, the Tab key, and the X, C, V, B, N, M, <, and > keys to operate the program.

Reasoning

- *Analyzing information* — recognizing patterns

The Program

(Tutor/Tool). Your child can play 33 familiar songs and also create original ones that can be stored and played back. There are seven parts to the program.

In *Grand Piano,* your child can play any song or notes on the piano keyboard.

In *Record Music,* your child can record any notes played on the keyboard. The notes are shown, on sheet music appearing above the piano, in colors matching the keyboard.

In *Play Music,* your child hears the song he or she recorded in *Record Music.* The notes are shown in colors matching the keyboard. As the song is played, the notes change to black.

In *Select Song,* your child selects a favorite tune from an alphabetic jukebox listing ("Farmer in the Dell," "Frère Jacques," "Mulberry Tree," and so on).

In *Play Song,* your child can play the tune selected from the jukebox on the piano keyboard. As each note is played, its color changes from the keyboard color to black.

In *Teach Song,* the computer teaches your child how to play the song chosen from the jukebox by making each key on the keyboard flash in turn. When your child presses the correct key, the note color changes to black and the next key flashes.

In *Sheet Music,* your child sees the sheet music of the song chosen from the jukebox. Your child can read the sheet music and play the song.

Generally, when your child makes an error and presses the wrong key, the notes will not sound or change color. In *Sheet Music,* each key makes its musical sound when pressed, but the notes on the sheet music will not advance until the correct key is pressed.

The program also includes visual cues consisting of a different animal face for each note of the scale, with the corresponding syllable (*do, re, mi,* and so on) displayed beneath it.

At any time, your child can access help in the form of simple written instructions by pressing the > key.

Mystery Objects

8–10 years
Grades 3–5

Series
MECC, 1988, $59.00

Hardware
Apple II series, 128 KB
  ★ Essential: 3.5-inch or 5.25-inch disk drive
  ☆ Recommended: color monitor

Abilities Needed
If your child is reading at the third-grade level, he or she will need your help initially to read the instructions. Once your child is familiar with the format, he or she should be able to run the program independently.

Curriculum Areas
The program uses a problem-solving format. Your child systematically collects information and then puts that information together to solve the problem presented.

Reasoning
  ■ *Gathering information*—recalling relevant information, seeking information in reference and available sources, taking notes
  ■ *Analyzing information*—organizing details
  ■ *Developing hypotheses*—making inferences and deductions, eliminating alternatives

Reading
  ■ *Comprehension skills*—recalling information on topics, playing word games

The Program

(Tutor). The program uses a game format in which your child guesses the identity of an object using clues obtained from the computer. The program presents six objects at the beginning, using both words and pictures. They might be a bird's nest, a button, a coat hanger, a bicycle, a chicken, and a pencil. One of the six is the "mystery object." Six helpers (Data Snoopers) allow your child to get clues about the object. The Funny Feeler tests for texture, the Size Upper tests for size, the Super Sniffer tests for smell, the See Shaper tests for shape, the Color Seeker tests for color, and the Heavy Holder tests for weight. For instance, if the mystery object is a button, the Funny Feeler might say that the object feels hard and smooth, with curved edges.

The game menu has three segments:

In *Information,* your child learns how the game is played.

In *Practice Sessions,* your child can practice playing the game.

In *On Your Own,* your child actually plays the game.

Your child must work systematically through the material. First he or she uses the Getting Hints cue to ask one or more of the helpers for information. Then he or she asks to view the objects and determines which ones fit the information so far received. When your child thinks he or she knows the answer, he or she names the mystery object.

When your child makes a mistake in naming the object, the computer offers the written message "NO, it is not the mystery object...." The program then tells your child to go back to the helpers and get additional information. Your child keeps choosing and testing objects until he or she gets the right one. (Because of this design feature, an impulsive child might not work well with this program or the related ones in the series.) When your child chooses the correct object, the program confirms that he or she is right.

The program lets you vary the level of difficulty for the objects (easy, medium, or hard) and turn the sound on or off. If you have a monochrome monitor, you can remove the Color Seeker snooper. After he or she completes play, your child sees a summary chart of his or her performance.

▼

This program is part of MECC's *Science Inquiry Collection* ($59.00 each). MYSTERY OBJECTS involves the easiest level of concepts. The other 10 programs are for older children (grades 5 and up).

In MYSTERY MATTER (1988), your child uses animated testing tools to identify the properties of an unknown substance. This is done by testing its reactions to such things as water, heat, cold, and a magnet as well as such properties as its pH and its electrical conductivity.

In MINER'S CAVE (1988), your child searches for lost treasure using concepts of physics. Your child enters any of eight caves to look for and retrieve lost treasure. To do this, he or she must determine which of five machines (ramp, lever, pulley, wheel, or axle) will work in the space available and must provide maximal use of the force available for each machine.

In INVISIBLE BUGS (1989), your child learns the rules of genetics and how to apply them to practical situations. These principles include how traits are passed on from parent to offspring and how dominant and recessive genes influence traits. Then your child puts these concepts to work by creating a population of bugs that are invisible to the eye of a predator.

In LUNAR GREENHOUSE (1989), your child works with the concepts of biology. Your child investigates the influence of four variables—light, temperature, water, and plant food—on the germination, growth, and yield of plants. Once your child has grasped these principles, he or she uses them to determine the best set of variable conditions needed to produce a crop of vegetables.

In WEEDS TO TREES (1989), your child learns how a plant community changes over time. Beginning with a plowed tract of land, your child selects and places nine different kinds of plants in the field and observes the changes over a simulated year. As the plants grow and reproduce, your child discovers the principles of plant succession. Then he or she creates a plan to manage the land from year to year, keeping certain plants on the land for a given period of time.

In BACKYARD BIRDS (1989), your child learns to identify birds by collecting information about each bird's characteristics and comparing it to the online field guide. Your child sends out an "observer," who describes the features of the mystery bird. By recording data, he or she narrows the list of possibilities, identifies the bird, and adds it to the Backyard Bird Life List. The program includes a database of North American birds, indexed by name or by family, and an online glossary.

In FOSSIL HUNTER (1990), your child learns the concepts of paleontology. Your child explores a site from one of the various geological periods, finds and identifies fossils, and then identifies the period itself. This program involves the use of timelines.

In MURPHY'S MINERALS (1990), your child digs through mazelike fields trying to locate minerals. Once a mineral is discovered, your child conducts a variety of tests on the unknown mineral to learn about its physical properties and then to identify it. The test results have to be recorded so that your child can evaluate his or her findings.

In FIVE-STAR FORECAST (1990), your child acts as a meteorologist conducting weather research in different climatic regions. Working with variables such as wind direction, wind speed, temperature, air pressure, and humidity, your child studies the weather in cities surrounding his or her home station. Then he or she uses that information to predict and forecast the weather at the home station.

In SUN AND SEASONS (1990), your child learns about the regular and predictable events happening in the daytime skies as the seasons change. Its goal is to have your child use the concepts of place (latitude and longitude), time (month of the year and hour of the day), and motion (of Earth relative to the Sun) to figure out the "reasons for the seasons" and to understand the changes seen in the daytime sky. The program offers two perspectives, "Backyard View" (a close-to-home view) and "Space View" (a point in space high above the North Pole), from which to observe astronomical phenomena.

The first program in the series, MYSTERY OBJECTS, might appeal to almost any child. The others in the series demand knowledge of particular areas of science. If your child is taking courses in chemistry, physics, biology, astronomy, or earth science, the programs will be useful in helping to consolidate classroom teaching. If your child has a keen interest in and love of science, he or she will have fun with these programs.

Mystery Sentences

11 years and older
Grades 6 and up

Scholastic Family Software, 1984, $59.95

Hardware

Apple II series, 48 KB

★ Essential: 5.25-inch disk drive

☆ Recommended: printer, blank disks for saving original work

Curriculum Areas

This program teaches writing and reading by giving your child practice in grammar, sentence structure, and reading for meaning.

Writing

■ *The mechanics* — analyzing sentences for grammar

Reading

■ *Decoding skills* — reading words in text, analyzing words for their meanings

■ *Comprehension skills* — reading fictional and nonfictional texts

The Program

(Tutor). At the start of each game, your child sees a mystery sentence on the screen. Only the vowels in each word and the number of words in the sentence are revealed. For instance, --e --i-e -e--- i- --e --oo-.... A label beneath each word tells your child what part of speech it is (adverb, adjective, noun, preposition, and so on).

By trading points for letters, words, and clues, your child tries to guess the sentence in as few moves as possible. Your child types in his or her choices on the keyboard. The game can be played alone or with one to four partners.

Your child can ask for three kinds of help from the computer: Reveal a Letter (letters of each word, one at a time), Guess a Word (words, one at a time), or Get a Clue (clues to the sentence's meaning). A clue for a sentence on the human body might be "These are the body's soldiers that destroy germs."

All players begin play with 250 points. Each move your child makes costs him or her points. If he or she uses a clue, 15 points are deducted; if he or she guesses a single word, 10 points are deducted; if he or she asks the computer for a single letter, 5 points are deducted. In order to win, your child needs to plan a strategy for guessing the sentence. He or she earns bonus points for guessing the sentence in the fewest moves.

The program is a bit cumbersome to use. Each move requires your child to press several keys to access the feature he or she wants to select.

If your child makes an error in guessing a word, the message "Sorry. That wasn't it" appears on the screen and the game continues. If your child makes errors in guessing the entire sentence, he or she sees a message such as "You got 8 words out of 11 correct."

For each correct guess of a word, your child sees a message like the following: "Good work, Dave." When he or she guesses the entire sentence correctly, your child sees a message such as "Well done, Mary. You guessed this sentence in 18 moves. You earned 260 points."

The disk contains nine sample files, each covering a different topic. There are sentences on common sayings, astronomy, U.S. history, mystery questions, animal facts, world geography, the human body, song lines, and famous inventions.

The program offers three progressive levels of play: Reveal Every Other Word (easiest), Reveal Only the Vowels (intermediate), and Reveal Blanks Only (hardest). It also offers two playing options, Standard and Secret Screens. In Standard play, each team or player gets a different sentence selected randomly by the computer. At the end of three rounds of play, the team with the highest score wins. In Secret Screens, all teams or players work on the same sentence. The winner is the team that guesses the sentence in the fewest moves.

You can turn the sound on or off. The program also lets you or your child create, edit, and store original sentence files on blank, initialized disks and print out any file.

The New Oregon Trail

10 years and older
Grades 5 and up

MECC, 1988, $39.95

Hardware

Apple II series, 64 KB

IBM PC and compatibles, 256 KB

★ Essential: 3.5-inch or 5.25-inch disk drive

Abilities Needed

Your child should be reading at the fourth-grade level to use this program independently.

This program is appropriate for the learning-disabled child, although a child with significant language or organizational problems might have difficulty with it.

Curriculum Areas

The program teaches reasoning by having your child plan a trip across the United States during the early part of the century. Your child also learns about an important phase of American history.

Reasoning

- *Gathering information*—recalling relevant information, taking notes
- *Analyzing information*—organizing details
- *Planning strategies*—making decisions, selecting relevant information to create a plan of action, managing resources

Reading

- *Decoding skills*—enlarging vocabulary

The Program

(Tutee). Your child takes the role of a trailblazer who must plan a trek across the United States to Oregon by covered wagon in 1848. The trip has to be completed before money or provisions run out, the oxen die, the endurance of the travelers gives out, or severe weather begins.

Before beginning travel, your child must make decisions on such questions as "What supplies should be taken?" "How should the money available be spent?" "What time of year is best for such a journey?" "Which paths should be followed?" and "How many oxen should be bought?"

Along the way, your child has to make effective use of the information and resources available on the 2000-mile trip (for example, talking to people he or she meets on the trail, hunting for food when supplies run low). He or she must keep notes on the information gathered along the way or the information is likely to be lost. Throughout the game, the program defines words to enhance your child's vocabulary (for instance, to *ford* a river, to *caulk* a wagon).

Your child receives points if all pioneers arrive safely; more points are awarded for each traveler arriving in good health and each supply item still available at the journey's end.

The difficulty level depends on the person your child chooses to be at the start of the game (for example, carpenter, banker, farmer); more points are awarded for a choice that makes the trip more difficult.

The New Print Shop

6 years and older
Grades 1 and up

Series
Broderbund Software, 1988/89, $49.95

Hardware

Apple II series, 128 KB
IBM PC and compatibles, 512 KB (640 KB for color printing, $59.95)
★ Essential: 3.5-inch or 5.25-inch disk drive, color monitor, printer
☆ Recommended: color printer, mouse

Abilities Needed

Your child should be reading at the third-grade level to use this program independently. A younger child can profitably use and enjoy the program but will need your help.

The Apple IIGS version of this program is the most sophisticated and is recommended for children 9 years and older (grades 4 and up).

This program is appropriate for the learning-disabled child.

ALTERNATIVE VERSION

The Print Shop
Broderbund Software, 1986/87, $59.95

Hardware
Apple IIGS, 512 KB
- ★ Essential: 3.5-inch disk drive, printer
- ☆ Recommended: color printer, mouse

Apple Macintosh, 1 MB
- ★ Essential: 3.5-inch disk drive, color monitor, printer
- ☆ Recommended: color printer, mouse

Commodore 64, 64 KB ($54.95)
- ★ Essential: 5.25-inch disk drive, color monitor, printer
- ☆ Recommended: color printer, joystick or Koala Pad

Curriculum Areas
The program teaches writing by having your child create and print personalized greeting cards, signs (for parties, garage sales, meetings), letterheads (for school or business) and stationery, invitations and announcements, certificates, and banners.

Writing
- ■ *The process*—creating simple written messages, creating messages for visual material
- ■ *The mechanics*—using elements of a word processing program, keyboarding, proofreading

Arithmetic
- ■ *Measurement*—using units of time

The Program
(Tool). This program allows your child to create a drawing, write an accompanying message, and then print the graphics and text. The program automatically centers text for greeting cards; the graphic designs can be placed wherever your child wants them on the page.

The program features easy-to-read menus, 8 type styles with a choice of solid, outline, or "3-D" type in 3 sizes (small, medium, or large), 12 fonts, 9 border designs, and 100 pictures and symbols. Multicolor graphics as well as full-panel graphics allow your child to create certificates and awards. Both text and graphics can be shrunk, enlarged, or centered. A "what you see is what you get" preview feature offers versatility.

Your child can select ready-made designs for printing holiday cards, birthdays cards, invitations, thank-you notes, and notepaper, or he or she can create personalized logos and pictures with the Graphics Editor. The new greeting-card feature produces both side-fold and top-fold cards in many different sizes. In addition, the new Customize option allows your child to flip graphics and text and also place multiple multicolor graphics and fonts on a single page.

A calendar feature allows your child to create personalized calendars in daily, weekly, monthly, and yearly formats and in various sizes. Your child can design and make giant posters and signs up to 9' by 6' 5" in both tall and wide formats; double-wide banners up to 28" (if a wide-carriage printer is available); or tiny place cards and gift tags. The program can also print designs either full size or reduced.

THE NEW PRINT SHOP COMPANION (1990) is available for the Apple II series (128 KB, $39.95) and the IBM PC and compatibles (512 KB, $49.95). It expands the capability of THE NEW PRINT SHOP with features such as Page Publisher, Envelope Maker, and Utilities. Your child can choose from over 50 professionally designed templates for reports, flyers, newsletters, and handouts. Your child simply adds the text and graphics. The Envelope Maker can create envelopes for greeting cards and stationery. The new Graphics, Border, and Font Editors are full paint programs allowing true custom designs with special drawing tools such as mirror imaging and flood-fill patterns. There is also a utility that catalogs all your child's Print Shop graphics, borders, and fonts and another that permits your child to import favorite paint-program drawings.

The NEW PRINT SHOP GRAPHICS LIBRARY: SAMPLER EDITION (1990) and PARTY EDITION (1990) for the Apple II series (128 KB, $24.95), the Apple IIGS (512 KB, $34.95), and the IBM PC and compatibles (512 KB, $34.95) can be used with either THE NEW PRINT SHOP or THE NEW PRINT SHOP COMPANION. These disks have hundreds of extra graphics, borders, and fonts and cover themes such as traditional holidays, special occasions, sports and games, animals, hobbies, jobs, zodiac signs, seasons, and myth and fantasy.

Number Farm

3–6 years
Grades PreK–1

DLM Software, 1984, $32.95

Hardware

Apple II series, 48 KB

Commodore 64/128, 64 KB

   ★ Essential: 5.25-inch disk drive

   ☆ Recommended: color monitor

IBM PC and compatibles, 256 KB

   ★ Essential: 3.5-inch or 5.25-inch disk drive, color graphics card

   ☆ Recommended: color monitor

Abilities Needed

Your child will initially need your help to read the on-screen instructions. Once familiar with the format, he or she should be able to work independently.

This program is appropriate for the learning-disabled child.

Curriculum Areas

The program teaches arithmetic and writing by having your child work with number concepts, recognition of numerals, and number words.

Arithmetic

   ■ *Numeration*—matching numbers to objects, counting objects, counting sequentially

   ■ *Concepts*—understanding relational concepts

Writing

   ■ *The mechanics*—using elements of a word processing program, keyboarding

The Program

(Tutor). The program offers six activities for teaching and reviewing number concepts.

In *Number Farm,* the numbers *1* through *9* appear at the top of the screen. A farmer invites your child to press any number on the keyboard. The appropriate number blinks on the screen, and the screen fills with that number of animals. For instance, if you child presses *8,* eight pigs appear on the screen.

In *Old MacDonald,* the classic song of the same name is played. When the song stops, your child presses the numeral that matches the number of animals he or she sees on the screen.

In *Crop Count,* a timed activity, your child counts the number of fruits and vegetables on the screen and then presses that number on the keyboard. Your child keeps adding as quickly as possible, until the sun sets and the game is over.

In *Hen House,* two players take turns guessing the number of eggs in the hen house. There are nine hens, but not all have eggs under them. After each guess, the program gives a clue—either "more than" or "less than." For instance, if your child has selected *5,* the clue might say that the number of eggs is fewer than five. With each guess, the numbers that are eliminated are crossed off the top of the screen, which helps your child narrow his or her choices. For instance, in the example just given, *5* and all the numbers above it would be crossed off.

In *Animal Quacker,* your child listens to the number of times an animal makes a sound. Then he or she presses the number key that matches the number of sounds heard. By pressing the letter *A,* your child can hear the sounds again.

In *Horseshoes,* the farmer's son is assigned a number of horseshoes to throw. Your child directs the son's actions so that he throws the right number of horseshoes.

The graphics and sound are attractive, and the formats of the six activities are varied enough to hold your child's interest. All the activities except the introductory one, *Number Farm,* are in game formats in which your child must meet a goal. If your child makes a mistake, cues guide the next two choices. For instance, in *Horseshoes,* the farmer displays the message, "Too many, try again" or "To few. Try again" after the first incorrect choice. After the second incorrect choice, the farmer shows your child the correct number of horshoes, and the game continues. There is no feedback or guidance of your child's performance in the *Number Farm* activity.

At times, the rewards that are given might be confusing to a young child, particularly if he or she is not adept at number concepts. For instance, in the *Animal Quacker* activity, two milk bottles are awarded for each correct answer on a first try and one bottle for each correct answer on a second try.

With the exception of *Number Farm,* the program keeps a record of your child's performance. He or she sees the results after a set number of trials or at the end of the game.

Number Munchers

8 years and older
Grades 3 and up

Series
MECC, 1986, $39.95

Hardware
Apple II series, 64 KB
IBM PC and compatibles, 512 KB ($49.95)
★ Essential: 3.5-inch or 5.25-inch disk drive
Apple Macintosh, 1 MB ($49.95)
★ Essential: 3.5-inch disk drive

Abilities Needed
This program is appropriate for the learning-disabled child, although a child with significant visual-spatial or timing problems might have difficulty with it.

Curriculum Areas
This program teaches arithmetic by having your child work with numeric concepts such as multiples, factors, primes, equalities, and inequalities.

Arithmetic
- *Concepts*—understanding relational concepts
- *Fundamental operations*—operating with addition, subtraction, multiplication, and division

The Program

(Tutor). In five fast-paced Pac-Man–type arcade games, your child directs the hungry Muncher through a grid, having him "eat" all the numbers that meet a given criterion. In each game, Muncher must eat the numbers or math problems without being caught by a Troggle.

In *Multiples,* the numbers to be eaten are multiples of a displayed value (for instance, "Find multiples of 6").

In *Factors,* the numbers to be eaten are those that can be evenly divided into a displayed value (for instance, "Find factors of 8").

In *Primes,* only prime numbers must be eaten. (A prime number is a number greater than 1 that can be divided only by itself or by 1, such as *3, 7,* or *19.*)

In *Equality,* the numbers to be eaten are expressions (simple math problems) that result in a number equal to a displayed value. For example, if the displayed value is 150, problems such as 75×2 and $300 \div 2$ would be eaten.

In *Inequality,* the numbers to be eaten are simple math problems that result in a number that does not equal a displayed value. For example, if the displayed value is 100, problems such as 50×3 and $100 \div 4$ would be eaten.

When your child makes a mistake, the program explains why the answer was incorrect. For example, in *Multiples,* your child might see "17 is not a multiple of 2."

When your child has mastered one level, the computer moves to the next higher level. Your child wins points each time Muncher eats a correct number. High scores earn a place in the Hall of Fame.

You can customize the program somewhat to your child's level of ability. Two additional features, Time Out (an unlimited pause) and Safe Zones (Munchers may enter, Troggles may not), provide your child with an opportunity to take a rest during these fast-moving games. However, he or she loses points by choosing either option.

FRACTION MUNCHERS (1987, $39.95), available for the Apple II series (128 KB), is another program in the Muncher series by MECC that uses the same game format. The four activities offer practice in fraction types, equivalent fractions, comparing fractions, and fraction expressions.

Ollie and Seymour

3–6 years
Grades PreK–1

Hartley Courseware, 1987, $49.95

Hardware

Apple II series, 48 KB

★ Essential: 3.5-inch or 5.25-inch disk drive
☆ Recommended: color monitor

Abilities Needed

This program is appropriate for the learning-disabled child.

Curriculum Areas

Using the theme of the activities in a community park and a neighbor-hood, the program enables your child to practice a range of early learn-ing skills, such as matching shapes and colors, counting to ten, and following directions.

Arithmetic

- *Numeration*—matching numbers to objects, counting objects, counting sequentially
- *Concepts*—understanding spatial concepts
- *Applications*—using visual representations

Reading

- *Comprehension skills*—following simple directions, recalling information on topics

Reasoning

- *Gathering information*—recalling relevant information
- *Planning strategies*—making decisions

The Program

(Tutor). The program opens with a picture menu. Ollie, the balloon man, is in a park. In the center of the park is a fountain with four radiating paths. By walking Ollie down a path, your child gets to work with one of the four games.

In *Ship Shapes,* your child plays a memory or concentration game. A grid of 16 boxes appears on the screen, and he or she has to find pairs of shapes in the grid that match. Each time a match is found, pieces of a picture of a ship fill the two boxes that match. By the end of the game, your child sees the completed picture of the ship.

In *Shape Playground,* your child gets the monkey, Seymour, to pick up blocks of different shapes. Your child then has to position the monkey so that he places the shapes one on top of another. Your child is able to stack up to 10 blocks. If the placement is stable, the stack will grow; if it is unstable, the stack will fall. Your child then counts the number of blocks in the stack and types that number on the keyboard.

In *Monkey Hunt,* the most complex of the games, your child practices traffic safety. He or she guides a child on the screen who is looking for his pet monkey. The monkey has left the park, and the on-screen child has to cross streets in the town during the search. Your child must make the on-screen child follow pedestrian rules—for example, the child can cross streets only at corners and must look both ways before crossing. A map in the manual offers a layout of the town.

In *Ollie's Balloons,* Ollie moves close to a balloon cart. A balloon then begins to blow up. A series of colors appears at the bottom of the screen, and your child selects the color that matches the balloon. Your child cannot play this game until he or she has successfully completed *Monkey Hunt.*

The graphics are appealing, and the games are designed so that reading is not needed. This program was originally designed for the learning-disabled, so the pacing of the games is totally under the control of the child in order to eliminate any pressure for speed—a useful feature for most young children.

In *Ship Shapes,* when your child makes an error, the program does not offer a correction. In *Monkey Hunt,* the on-screen child does not move unless your child's selections follow the pedestrian rules. In the other segments, the computer makes a sound that tells your child when he or she has made an error.

Monkey Hunt, the most complex game, will be interesting and relevant to 6-year-olds. In this game, your child might need your help to see the correspondence between the map in the manual and the city streets he or she sees on the screen. This segment, however, is a good way of introducing and reinforcing pedestrian safety rules. The other three games are geared for preschoolers and kindergartners.

The extensive manual offers a number of related activities that you might like to carry out with your child.

Once upon a Time

6–12 years
Grades 1–7

Volume I
CompuTeach Educational Software, 1987, $49.95
Volume II
CompuTeach Educational Software, 1988, $49.95
Volume III
CompuTeach Educational Software, 1990, $49.95

Hardware

Apple II series, 128 KB

  ★ Essential: 5.25-inch disk drive (two-disk set), printer

IBM PC and compatibles, 256 KB

  ★ Essential: 3.5-inch or 5.25-inch disk drive (two-disk set), color
   graphics card, printer, mouse or joystick

ALTERNATIVE VERSION

Talking Once upon a Time

CompuTeach Educational Software, 1988, $59.95

Hardware

Apple IIGS, 1 MB
Apple Macintosh, 1 MB

  ★ Essential: 3.5-inch disk drive (two-disk set), printer

IBM PC and compatibles, 384 KB

  ★ Essential: 3.5-inch or 5.25-inch disk drive (two-disk set),
   printer

Abilities Needed

If your child is in the early grades, he or she will need your help in reading the instructions and learning how to operate this program. Your
child has to do a substantial amount of shifting between the master
disk and the story disk when he or she prints out a storybook.

This program is appropriate for the learning-disabled child,
although a child with significant problems in visual-motor or language
skills might have difficulty with it.

Curriculum Areas

This interactive program lets your child design and print his or her own illustrated storybooks. It provides an early experience with simple desktop publishing.

Writing

- *The process*—creating fictional texts, editing texts
- *The mechanics*—spelling single-syllable words, spelling multisyllable words, using elements of a word processing program, constructing phrases and sentences, keyboarding

Reading

- *Decoding skills*—enlarging vocabulary

The Program

(Tool). Your child learns concepts of story creation, illustration skills, and editing methods to refine simple text. In building the pictures, your child learns to deal with perspective and other spatial relationships.

Your child creates pictures on the computer by selecting graphics from the master disk. Volume I, "Passport To Discovery," offers hundreds of familiar objects; themes are *Along Main Street, The Farm,* and *On Safari.* Volume II, "Worlds of Enchantment," uses scenes related to *Underwater, Dinosaurs,* and *Forest.* Volume III, "Journey Through Time," has pictures related to *Space Travel, Medieval Times,* and the *Wild West.*

The program allows your child to draw a picture by selecting objects from a menu. For instance, in *The Farm,* your child can select such graphics as a horse, a maple tree, a girl, or a fence by typing the name of the object on the keyboard. Then your child decides where on the page to place the picture by enlisting the help of Ruby the Robot. Some objects are available in three sizes to allow the use of perspective.

Your child can add up to three lines of text to any picture. At any point in the process, your child has the option to draw, write, move, erase, save, or print. All three volumes come with a Text Page option that allows your child to create and print pages with both text and graphics or pages with text alone.

Your child can display his or her work on the screen or print the work out as an illustrated book. The program comes with a set of eight colored crayons.

Paint with Words

5–6 years
Grades K–1

MECC, 1984, $39.95

Hardware

Apple II, 64 KB

★ Essential: 5.25-inch disk drive, color monitor

☆ Recommended: printer, mouse or joystick, Jostens Ufonic
   Voice System

Abilities Needed

Your child is likely to need your help in the first few sessions until he or she becomes familiar with the program and with some of the written material that it contains. In order to make maximal use of this program, it will be important for you to work along with your child.

This program is appropriate for the learning-disabled child.

Curriculum Areas

The program allows your child to select common words and convert them into pictures that he or she can use for activities such as story writing, decoration, and sign making.

Reading

■ *Decoding skills* — reading single-syllable words, matching pictures and words, reading multisyllable words

Writing

■ *The process* — creating messages for visual materials
■ *The mechanics* — using elements of a word processing program

The Program

(Tool). The program contains 128 common words, with corresponding pictures. The words, grouped into units of 8, are nouns from categories such as Street, Rooms, School, Winter, and Lake. In the group called Lake, for example, your child sees the words *cloud, deer, duck, fish, frog, sun, swan,* and *turtle* at the bottom of the screen. He or she can then move any of these words anywhere on the screen. When your child has placed a word in position, he or she changes the word into its corresponding picture by pressing a key. At any point, your child can change the picture back to its word so that it is possible to have both words and pictures in the "painting" he or she is creating.

The graphics are attractive and clear, and the program is an excellent one for encouraging your child, while still in the earliest stages of writing, to create materials that are individualized and appealing. At the same time, he or she gets valuable practice in reading basic primary-grade words. After a few sessions, your child can probably work the program independently. However, he or she is likely to get the greatest benefit by having your input. You might, for example, show him or her how to create a game in which words in one column have to be matched with pictures in another, or a game that puts down a row containing, for example, three animals and one tree and asks, "Which one does not belong?"

Your child can also add an appropriate background to any of the pictures he or she paints; the background for Rooms, for example, shows the outline of a room. (Backgrounds have to be added before the words are selected; otherwise, they will erase the existing words.) Your child can print out the picture he or she has created and can also save up to seven pictures in a section of the program called *Word Art Show*.

You can create up to 12 word lists or categories, tailored to fit your child's interests and the words he or she is learning in school.

Path Tactics

5–11 years
Grades K–6

MECC, 1986, $59.00

Hardware
Apple II series, 48 KB
  ★ Essential: 5.25-inch disk drive
  ☆ Recommended: color monitor
IBM PC and compatibles, 256 KB
  ★ Essential: 5.25-inch disk drive
  ☆ Recommended: color monitor

Abilities Needed
Nonreaders or beginning readers will initially need your help to read the instructions. Your child should be reading at the fourth-grade level

to work independently. After becoming familiar with the format, your child should be able to work independently.

This program is appropriate for the learning-disabled child, although a child with significant visual-spatial problems might have difficulty with it.

Curriculum Areas

The program teaches arithmetic and reasoning by offering your child practice in using the basic operations (addition, subtraction, multiplication, and division) with whole numbers from 0 through 9. It also challenges his or her problem-solving abilities in using strategies to move a robot on a game board.

Arithmetic

- *Fundamental operations*—operating with addition, subtraction, multiplication, and division

Reasoning

- *Planning strategies*—selecting relevant information to create a plan of action

The Program

(Tutor). Your child can play this game either against the computer or with a friend. Your child tries to outsmart his or her opponent and help his or her robot to reach the finish line first. He or she is rewarded by winning the game and earning the title of "Path Master."

At each of seven levels of play, your child sees a set of three numbers. By using the math skills selected and positioning the numbers, your child controls the actions of his or her robot on the game board. For instance, in Level 2 (addition), your child sees:

Your child chooses one number and types it into the first space. He or she then chooses another number and types it into the MOVE box. After adding the two numbers, your child types the answer in the last space. If the answer is correct, your child moves his or her robot ahead the number of spaces indicated in the MOVE box. Your child must plan how to manipulate the numbers in the problem boxes to his or her best advantage. Game strategies allow your child to bump another player back or drop through a trapdoor to get ahead. The trapdoor is indicated by a space with an X on it. If your child's robot ends its move on another robot's space, the first robot is bumped back 10 spaces.

When your child makes a mistake, the computer crosses out the incorrect answer and offers the right answer. Your child's robot does not move on that turn.

The seven levels of play are counting, adding, subtracting, adding and subtracting, multiplying, dividing, and subtracting with negative results allowed. You can select the operations, allowing your child to focus his or her attention on a single operation. In the higher levels of play (4–7), you can choose how the spaces will be counted on the board: Your child can either watch the motion of the robots as the spaces are counted slowly or can see the spaces counted quickly. You can also turn the sound on or off and delete or add names to the Winner's List. The Winner's List keeps a record of the number of moves each of the top 10 Path Masters needed to win at each level.

Patterns

5–6 years
Grades K–1

MECC, 1988, $39.95

Hardware
Apple II series, 128 KB
★ Essential: 3.5-inch or 5.25-inch disk drive

Abilities Needed
Your child will initially need your help to read the on-screen instructions. After becoming familiar with the format, he or she should be able to work independently. It is helpful if your child is familiar with basic attributes of objects, such as size and color, before using the program.

This program is appropriate for the learning-disabled child, although a child with significant problems in memory skills might have difficulty with some of the games.

Curriculum Areas

The program helps your child recognize visual and auditory patterns, extend those patterns, and create original patterns. It also helps sharpen your child's analysis of visual details and use of memory skills.

Reasoning

■ *Gathering information*—recalling relevant information, seeking information in available sources

■ *Analyzing information*—distinguishing relevant from nonrelevant cues, sequencing details, recognizing patterns

■ *Developing hypotheses*—making inferences and deductions, eliminating alternatives

Arithmetic

■ *Concepts*—understanding spatial concepts

The Program

(Tutor). This is a four-part program with an outer-space theme that enhances your child's understanding of patterns.

In *Space Objects,* your child sees a variety of space objects that vary in shape, color, design, and height. He or she sees several of the objects in a row. Together, they create a particular pattern—for example, figure 1, figure 2, figure 1 again, and a blank space. Your child extends, or completes, the pattern by adding another figure 2 so that the pattern is A B A B. He or she makes a choice by selecting one of four objects at the bottom of the screen.

In *Moon Walker,* your child sees and extends patterns that are similar to the ones in *Space Objects.* However, in this game, the objects perform different actions, and it is the different actions that create the sequence. Again, your child selects the object that correctly completes the pattern. This game places more demands on your child's memory, but he or she can always press a key to see the actions repeated.

In *Astro Sounds,* your child deals with auditory patterns. Here the objects create patterns with the different pitches of the sounds they produce. For instance, any object can make a high note, a midrange note, or a low note. Because the sounds rapidly fade, your child has to rely significantly on memory to work effectively with this game.

In *Cosmic Creator,* your child creates patterns by working with choices the computer offers. He or she sees a variety of selections at the bottom of the screen. When he or she makes a selection, the choice moves into place on the screen. Your child can easily erase and change the pattern while working on it. When your child chooses Stop, the pattern is complete and he or she then sees the whole screen filled with the pattern created. If your child is attentive, he or she can learn a lot about pattern construction by watching the way in which the pattern emerges. However, an impulsive child might not recognize the underlying pattern that determines the arrangement of the objects.

The graphics and sound are appealing, and the formats of the four segments are varied enough to hold your child's interest. All of the segments except *Cosmic Creator* are in game formats in which your child has to meet a goal.

When your child makes a mistake, sophisticated corrections guide him or her to the right answer. In *Space Objects* and *Moon Walker,* the computer analyzes the error to determine whether your child has failed to figure out the pattern or has failed to notice details of the objects. Then the computer offers whatever hint is appropriate. Your child continues to make choices until he or she makes the correct selection. Because only four choices are possible, three errors at most are possible on any trial. If, however, your child is maintaining a high level of error over too many of the trials, it means that the program is too difficult for him or her at that time.

After each correct choice, a figure appears and moves in an animated way that shows it is pleased and that your child has been successful. In the first three games, after each set of five trials, a summary of your child's performance is shown on a rocket ship.

The program offers a wide range of variable features including the difficulty level of the problems, the range of patterns, and the types of figures in the patterns. For instance, in *Astro Sounds,* you can alter the difficulty level greatly by setting the number of notes per element (from one to three) and the number of different pitches for each note (either two or three).

Peanuts Maze Marathon

4–9 years
Grades PreK–4

Random House/American School Publishers, 1984, $29.95

Hardware
Apple II series, 64 KB
- ★ Essential: 5.25-inch disk drive
- ☆ Recommended: color monitor, joystick

ALTERNATIVE VERSION

Talking Peanuts Maze Marathon
Random House/American School Publishers, 1990, $39.95

Hardware
Apple IIGS, 1 MB
IBM PC and compatibles, 1 MB
- ★ Essential: 3.5-inch disk drive
- ☆ Recommended: color monitor, joystick, printer

Abilities Needed
If your child is younger than 6, he or she will probably require your help for a few sessions before being able to use the program independently.

The program is appropriate for a learning-disabled child, although a child with significant visual-spatial problems might have difficulty with it.

Curriculum Areas
The program teaches reasoning by having your child solve mazes at different levels of complexity. Your child strengthens hand-eye coordination and decision-making strategies.

Reasoning
- *Analyzing information*—distinguishing relevant from nonrelevant cues
- *Developing hypotheses*—eliminating alternatives
- *Planning strategies*—making decisions

The Program

(Tutor). This delightful program features the irresistible Peanuts characters, who enlist your child's help in solving a series of mazes to get them out of various situations (for instance, getting Charlie Brown's kite out of a tree, helping Linus find his blanket, or having Marcie find the water to go swimming). Your child's goal is to move the dot from the starting point through the maze to the X that marks the way out. If he or she completes the maze in the set time, the Peanuts characters complete their adventures.

The program offers appealing graphics as well as an activity that children love to do.

Each time your child plays the mazes they change, so the program is endlessly variable. Side 1 of the disk offers simple mazes for younger children, and side 2 contains more complex mazes. You or your child can choose a preset time limit (two, three, or four minutes or no time limit) or set your own time limit (in seconds or minutes). If you choose a time limit, a time bar on the screen shows how much time is left for your child to race out of the maze. You can also turn the sound on or off.

The newer version of the program, TALKING PEANUTS MAZE MARATHON, offers a talking component. The voice of Charlie Brown speaks the instructions and offers verbal praise to your child for good work. In addition, there are four progressive levels of play, an editing component that allows you to change the Peanuts characters in each picture, a printout of the maze screens, and an Award Certificate, which can also be printed.

Peanuts Picture Puzzler

4–8 years
Grades PreK–3

Random House / American School Publishers, 1984, $29.95

Hardware

Apple II series, 64 KB

★ Essential: 5.25-inch disk drive

☆ Recommended: color monitor

ALTERNATIVE VERSION

Talking Peanuts Picture Puzzler
Random House / American School Publishers, 1990, $39.95

Hardware

Apple IIGS, 1 MB
- ★ Essential: 3.5-inch disk drive
- ☆ Recommended: color monitor, printer

IBM PC and compatibles, 1 MB
- ★ Essential: 5.25-inch disk drive
- ☆ Recommended: color monitor, printer

Abilities Needed

If your child is younger than 6, he or she will likely require your help for several sessions before being able to use the program independently.

This program is appropriate for a learning-disabled child, although a child with significant visual-spatial problems might have difficulty with it.

Curriculum Areas

The program teaches arithmetic and reasoning by offering your child on-screen jigsaw puzzles that he or she has to put together. Puzzles on the computer screen place greater demands on memory than do traditional jigsaw puzzles because the entire model and your child's work are never on the screen at the same time.

Reasoning
- *Gathering information*—recalling relevant information
- *Analyzing information*—organizing or sequencing details, recognizing patterns
- *Planning strategies*—making decisions

Arithmetic
- *Concepts*—understanding spatial concepts

The Program

(Tutor/Tool). Your child sees on the screen a scene that contains one or more of the 11 familiar Peanuts characters, such as Charlie Brown, Linus, and Snoopy. The picture then disappears and your child sees a screen containing blank rectangles. He or she also sees one piece from the original picture. The task is to place that piece in the correct rectangle. If the placement is correct, the piece will enter the rectangle. When all the pieces have been placed correctly, the original picture is once again complete.

The program is easy to operate in that it involves only a few basic moves. Moving the arrow keys changes the piece of the puzzle that is currently on the screen, and pressing the Spacebar moves the puzzle piece to the different rectangles. Your child can always press the Escape key to see the original puzzle and thereby get help in fitting the pieces correctly.

If the choice of placement is not correct, the program beeps, and the piece will not move. If your child exceeds the set time limit, the puzzle disappears, and he or she sees the message "Sorry, time is up."

The program offers a wide range of options. You can select the number of pieces you want the puzzle to be divided into (4, 8, or 16) and also the characters that you want to have in the puzzle. You can select a preset time limit (30 seconds, 2 minutes, 5 minutes, or no limit) or set your own limit. You can set the program for the number of problems you want your child to have in any session (from 1 to 20). The program keeps score on each player's performance.

The Peanuts characters are irresistible, and this, along with the available options, makes the program highly attractive. The program can grow with your child: The 4-piece puzzles can be a pleasant introduction to computer jigsaw puzzles for your preschooler, and the 8- and 16-piece puzzles can be a challenge when he or she gets a bit older.

The newer version, TALKING PEANUTS PICTURE PUZZLER, offers a talking component. Your child hears the voice of Charlie Brown throughout the program, speaking the program instructions as well as offering verbal praise and encouragement. In addition, there are 4 levels of play with 60 puzzle combinations, plus the ability to print out a Puzzle Solver Certificate for work well done.

Perplexing Puzzles

9 years and older
Grades 4 and up

Hartley Courseware, 1985, $39.95

Hardware
Apple II series, 48 KB
- ★ Essential: 5.25-inch disk drive (two-disk set)
- ☆ Recommended: printer

Abilities Needed
This program requires a great deal of reading, particularly of on-screen step-by-step instructions. In order to use the program independently, your child should be reading above the fourth-grade level.

This program is appropriate for the learning-disabled child, although a child who has significant language problems might have difficulty with it.

Curriculum Areas
This program encourages the growth of your child's logical thinking and deductive reasoning skills. It teaches a step-by-step approach to developing problem-solving strategies.

Reasoning
- *Analyzing information*—distinguishing relevant from nonrelevant cues, comparing facts and categories
- *Developing hypotheses*—making inferences and deductions

The Program
(Tutor/Tutee). The first disk contains a five-step tutorial.

In the *Introduction,* your child learns how to make well-reasoned deductions from clues.

In *Practice,* your child practices reading clues and making deductions from them.

In *Explanation,* your child reads an explanation of the process of elimination and is taught how to find information presented indirectly or hidden in clues. For instance, the program offers two clues: (1) Lima is the capital city of Peru, and (2) Peru is in South America. Your child needs to select the correct logical deduction from among four choices— in this case, the deduction that Lima is in South America.

In *Demonstrations,* your child learns how to use a grid or matrix to eliminate wrong answers and identify right ones.

In *Solve a Puzzle,* your child sees the steps he or she must use to solve a deduction puzzle.

The second disk contains 30 deduction puzzles for your child to solve. One easy puzzle has to do with three different foods. Your child is told that kibbe, ratatouille, and sauerbraten are made with eggplant, beef, and lamb, and must use the clues to find out which is the main ingredient of which dish. Before he or she begins the puzzles, two sample problems demonstrate the step-by-step method for solving the reasoning problems. Each time your child boots up this disk, the same two samples appear; thus the program features both teaching and review.

You or your child can modify the program. Each puzzle can have a varied number of clues—as many as nine. The puzzles increase in level of difficulty, and you can change the amount of help the computer offers your child.

You can create as many as 10 new or edited puzzles and add them to the disk. You can print out puzzles for later review or paper-and-pencil solving. The program reports the number of puzzles your child has correctly solved.

Picture Chompers

4–6 years
Grades PreK–1

MECC, 1990, $59.00

Hardware
Apple II series, 128 KB
- ★ Essential: 3.5-inch or 5.25-inch disk drive, color monitor
- ☆ Recommended: joystick

Abilities Needed
Your child should be reading at the first-grade level to read the directions. You will initially need to explain the game if he or she is a prereader. After becoming familiar with the format, your child should be able to work independently.

This program is appropriate for the learning-disabled child.

Curriculum Areas

Your child selects objects that can be classified according to different concepts. The program uses a range of categories suitable for young children, such as shape, color, and size.

Reading

■ *Comprehension skills*—following simple directions, recalling information on topics

Arithmetic

■ *Concepts*—understanding spatial concepts

Reasoning

■ *Analyzing information*—distinguishing relevant from nonrelevant cues

The Program

(Tutor). The program uses a game format to help your child work with six categories of concepts. The categories are color, size, shape, design (for instance, dots or stripes), class (for instance, clothes or furniture), and use (for instance, cooking or writing).

Once your child selects a category, a 4-by-4 grid of 16 boxes appears, each containing an object. Your child has to move the "chomper" (a set of huge-looking teeth) to find all the objects that fit that category. For instance, in the category of use, your child might have to find all the objects that are used for cooking; in the category of shape, he or she might need to locate all the triangles.

If a choice is correct, it is chomped up and disappears from the screen. If the choice is incorrect, your child hears a beep. On the second incorrect try, the computer puts a large X on the incorrect choice.

At the end of the game, a little figure appears who jumps and dances to show its pleasure at your child's success.

The game can be played with a variety of options. You can set the number of screens that each game will contain. You or your child can also select the difficulty level of the game (easy, medium, or hard). As difficulty increases, your child has to deal with more complex cues. For example, he or she might be looking for a particular design, such as stripes, but the objects might also vary in shape and size.

You and your child can decide whether or not to have time limits on each game. For timed games, a high enough score allows your child to be entered into the Chompers Club. As in all MECC programs, which are designed for school as well as home use, there is room for several names to be entered into the program. This option might be helpful for those times when your child plays with a partner. You can turn the sound on or off.

The Playroom

3–6 years
Grades PreK–1

Broderbund Software, 1989, $49.95

Hardware
Apple II series, 128 KB ($39.95)
IBM PC and compatibles, 512 KB ($44.95)
  ★ Essential: 3.5-inch disk drive or 5.25-inch disk drive (two-disk set)
  ☆ Recommended: color monitor, printer, mouse or joystick
Apple Macintosh, 1 MB
  ★ Essential: 3.5-inch disk drive (two-disk set)
  ☆ Recommended: color monitor, printer, mouse

Abilities Needed
Although reading is not required, the program presents a somewhat complicated format, and you will probably have to explain the program to your child and initially play it with him or her. Once your child is familiar with the format, he or she should be able to play without your guidance.

The program is appropriate for the learning-disabled child.

Curriculum Areas
Your child learns about numbers, letters, and time. He or she also begins to develop computer and thinking skills.

Arithmetic
  ■ *Numeration*—matching numbers to objects, counting objects
  ■ *Measurement*—using units of time

Reading

- *Decoding skills*—matching and recognizing letters, matching pictures and words
- *Comprehension skills*—following simple directions

Writing

- *The mechanics*—using elements of a word processing program

Reasoning

- *Analyzing information*—distinguishing relevant from nonrelevant cues

The Program

(Tutor). The program features a white mouse, Pepper, who lives in the Playroom and accompanies your child through the seven activities. A mouse or joystick is highly recommended because using the program with the keyboard is quite cumbersome.

The *Playroom,* a graphic representation of a playroom, serves as the introduction to the activity. Your child selects various objects. Some of them become animated when chosen (for instance, a songbird sings, windows open, a radio plays music, a goldfish does flip-flops); others (the Clock, the Mousehole, the ABC Book, the Computer, the Mixed-Up Toy, and the Spinner Toy) are the gateways to the six games.

In the *Clock,* your child sets the clock's hands to a time on the clock face, and Pepper then performs a time-appropriate task, such as brushing his teeth in the morning or taking a bath at bedtime. A bird sings out the correct number of musical notes to match the time, and the notes are shown above the clock. The time is also displayed in a window, both in digital form (*5:00*) and in words (*five o'clock*).

In the *Computer,* two modes are available, either free play or structured. In the simpler free play, your child selects a letter on the keyboard and the lowercase letter appears on the screen. In the more difficult structured mode, your child selects a "gift" from 11 choices shown on the screen and then spells out its name with help from Pepper (for instance, a frog jumps out of a box and your child types *Frog*).

In the *Mixed-Up Toy,* your child experiments with changing each of the three body parts (head, torso, legs) of a toy by selecting exchangeable parts. Your child creates a new combination each time he or she selects a different body part from the choices.

In the *Mousehole,* your child plays a counting board game, either against the computer or with a partner. There are three different levels of play: counting to 4, to 6, or to 9. Your child must count forward and backward in the process of playing the game.

In the *ABC Book,* your child places any of 52 stickers of animals, people, and objects on one of two background pictures. He or she chooses a picture by pressing the letter on the keyboard that is the first letter in the object's name.

In the *Spinner Toy,* two modes, free play and structured, are available. In the free-play mode, your child chooses a number from one spinner and an object from the other spinner (for instance, the number *3* and a hat). The two combine so that, for example, three hats appear on the screen. In the structured mode, your child must count the number of objects on the screen. For instance, three faucets appear; your child counts them and then moves the spinner to the number *3.* When the answer is correct, the objects become animated.

The graphics, animation, sound, and color are very appealing. The program is well designed for prereaders: There is no text, the on-screen prompts are intuitively clear, and an exit door appears for easy navigation between games. The *Clock* might be somewhat confusing because it uses both a 12-hour and a 24-hour time frame.

When your child makes a mistake, Pepper guides him or her to the right answer. For instance, in the *Computer* activity, if your child selects an incorrect letter, Pepper shows the right letter by highlighting it on the on-screen keyboard.

The program offers several options: different levels of play in the *Mousehole, Spinner,* and *Computer* games; the ability to change backgrounds and pictures; and a choice of uppercase or lowercase letters in the *ABC Book.* In the *Computer* activity, you can change the words that appear in the "gift" panel, and you can limit the words to a maximum number of letters. In the *Spinner* game, you can set the maximum number to be shown on the dial.

If a printer is available, your child can print out the different *Mixed-Up Toys* and the pictures from the *ABC Book* that he or she creates. The manual offers additional follow-up games and activities for each program segment.

Power Drill

8 years and older
Grades 3 and up

Sunburst Communications, 1986, $65.00

Hardware
Apple II series, 48 KB
Commodore 64, 64 KB
IBM PS/2, 256 KB
Tandy 1000, 256 KB
   ★ Essential: 5.25-inch disk drive
IBM PC and compatibles, 128 KB
   ★ Essential: 5.25-inch disk drive, color graphics card

Abilities Needed
Your child should be reading at the third-grade level to be able to deal with the instructions independently.

This program is appropriate for the learning-disabled child, although a child with significant organizational problems or visual-spatial problems might have difficulty with it.

Curriculum Areas
The program teaches arithmetic and reasoning by having your child use estimation to solve equations involving the four fundamental operations of addition, subtraction, multiplication, and division.

Arithmetic
- *Concepts*—understanding equations
- *Fundamental operations*—operating with addition, subtraction, multiplication, and division
- *Applications*—using estimation

Reasoning
- *Analyzing information*—recognizing patterns
- *Developing hypotheses*—eliminating alternatives
- *Planning strategies*—making decisions

The Program
(Tutor). The program is designed both to teach and to strengthen your child's skills in using estimation to help solve arithmetic problems. The menu has four major segments.

In *Altogether,* your child solves problems involving addition.

In *What's the Difference?* your child solves problems involving subtraction.

In *Easy Times, Hard Times,* your child solves problems involving multiplication.

In *The Great Divide,* your child solves problems involving division.

In each segment, there are three difficulty levels. At Level 1, the largest number your child sees is between 100 and 999; at Level 2, it is between 1000 and 9999; at Level 3, it is between 10,000 and 99,999. The difficulty levels are designed to allow the program to grow with your child. Level 1 is designed for grades 3–4, Level 2 for grades 4–5, and Level 3 for grades 5–6.

In all segments of the program, your child sees the same basic format. In *Altogether,* for instance, the problem on the screen might be:

```
4776 + ___ = 4985
```

Your child then enters a number that he or she thinks is close to the correct answer. The computer shows your child a running record of each entry and its effect on the problem. If, for example, he or she has entered the number *200,* the screen will show the following:

```
4776 + 200 = 4976
4776 + ___ = 4985
```

At this point, your child might be ready to enter the number *209.*

If your child's guesstimate is far above or below the number that is needed, the computer will come up with the message that the number is "way too big" or "way too small." But the computer does more than that. With estimates that are way off the mark, the computer will come up with a rounded number that is close to the number that your child needs. It might, for example, show your child that by adding 200, he or she would get close to the answer.

At the end of each problem, the computer tells your child that the answer is correct and also shows the number of trials he or she used to reach the exact answer.

The program is well designed to teach an arithmetic skill that will serve your child throughout his or her life. It is quite demanding and will appeal primarily to children who enjoy working with numbers and who are motivated to find fast, accurate answers. No appealing graphics accompany the problems, but graphics are not essential to this type of program. The material on the screen is clearly and effectively presented.

Professor Al's Sequencing Labs

5–7 years
Grades K–2

Micrograms Publishing, 1990, $39.95

Hardware
Apple II series, 64 KB
- ★ Essential: 5.25-inch disk drive (two-disk set)
- ☆ Recommended: color monitor

Abilities Needed
The reading section of this program will be difficult for a nonreader or a beginning reader. Therefore, you should be prepared to do this section with your child.

This program is appropriate for the learning-disabled child.

Curriculum Areas
This program teaches reading by offering practice in sequencing of pictures and in reading and understanding the events in a short story.

Reading
- *Decoding skills*—dealing with sequence and direction, reading words in text
- *Comprehension skills*—following simple directions, reading stories, identifying sequences of events

The Program
(Tutor). Using the character of Professor Al, who helps your child through the activities, the program offers two levels of difficulty.

In *Sequencing Pictures* (disk 1), your child sees four pictures in a mixed-up order. He or she uses the clues within the pictures to rearrange them into a logically sequenced order for that activity. One such set might show a mouse eating breakfast, awakening to an alarm clock, leaving the house, and getting out of bed. The 20 sequences include making an apple pie, going shopping, planting a garden, going to the library, and making a snowman.

In *Sequencing Story Events* (disk 2), your child practices understanding events in short stories. After reading the story on the screen, your child must recall details in order to arrange three events from the story in proper sequence. He or she sees on the screen the question "What happened first?" and, below that, three sentences from the story. Your child must choose the correct sentence. Then your child sees "What happened second?" and finally "What happened third?" The set has a total of 40 stories. Your child can refer to the story for another look before answering any question.

If your child makes a mistake, the words "Try again" appear on the screen, and your child must either resequence the whole set of pictures (in *Sequencing Pictures*) or choose another sentence (in *Sequencing Story Events*). If he or she makes a second mistake, Professor Al offers extra help—for example, he blinks the number of the first picture.

Rewards for correct choices include various kinds of animation. After three sets of pictures or sentences are correctly sequenced, Professor Al does a funny activity, such as turning off a light bulb, making shadow puppets on the screen, or making silly pictures appear on his TV monitor, accompanied by crazy sounds. Each time your child sequences a set of four pictures correctly, Professor Al says "Right," and a row of lights under the professor's TV monitor light up.

Several options allow you to tailor the program to your child's needs. In *Sequencing Pictures,* you can vary the number of picture sets (1–5) in each exercise and also select the step (1–3) at which help will be offered. In *Sequencing Story Events,* you can vary the number of stories in each exercise (1–5), determine whether or not your child can refer to the story at any time, and specify on which attempt (1–3) extra help will be given. You can turn the sound on or off.

Punctuation Put-On: Elementary Level

8–11 years
Grades 3–6

Sunburst Communications, 1985, $75.00

Hardware
Apple II series, 48 KB
   ★ Essential: 5.25-inch disk drive (two-disk set)
IBM PC and compatibles, 128 KB
   ★ Essential: 5.25-inch disk drive (two-disk set), color monitor

---

OTHER LEVELS

Punctuation Put-On: Junior High School
11–14 years, Grades 6–9
Sunburst Communications, 1985, $75.00

Punctuation Put-On: Senior High School
14 years and older, Grades 9 and up
Sunburst Communications, 1985, $75.00

Abilities Needed
Your child should be reading at the third-grade level in order to use and benefit from the program. Initially, you might have to help your child learn how to enter new text selections, but after one or two demonstrations he or she should be able to do this independently.

This program is appropriate for the learning-disabled child, although a child with significant visual-spatial or language problems might have difficulty with it.

Curriculum Areas
The program offers your child practice in using the following forms of punctuation: periods, exclamation points, quotation marks, colons, semicolons, hyphens, dashes, ellipses, parentheses, and apostrophes.

   #### Writing
   ■ *The mechanics*—using punctuation, using elements of a
      word processing program

The Program

(Tutor). The program does not teach the rules of punctuation but assumes that your child has had some beginning instruction in them. It provides a range of opportunities for your child to practice the rules.

The disk contains 15 segments of writing. Each selection appears on the screen, and your child can take as much time as he or she needs to look it over. Then, when your child is ready and presses a key, all the punctuation marks disappear from the selection, leaving only the text. The cursor then moves along the text, and your child has to enter the correct punctuation at each point indicated by the cursor. The possible choices are at the bottom of the screen, and your child can either select one of the choices or enter the punctuation by using the appropriate key on the keyboard.

For most children, punctuation is not an exciting skill to practice, but the program makes the activity as clear and pleasant as possible. The texts are well written and call for the use of important, common punctuation rules. Your child can easily work on the program with a partner.

The program is well designed from an instructional point of view. In addition to showing the correct model at the start, it keeps good track of your child's performance. When he or she has made the right selection, the program enters the punctuation and moves on to the next point in the text; when your child is wrong, the program indicates the correct answer and he or she then has to enter it into the text.

In addition to the 15 segments on the disk, you can add new selections and also alter them. This allows your child to use the program repeatedly without its becoming stale.

A summary page after each selection indicates your child's performance on that selection, and a score page indicates how he or she has done on all the selections. Finally a progress table tells your child how well he or she has done with each kind of punctuation.

The Puzzle Storybook

3–8 years
Grades PreK–3

First Byte / Davidson, 1989, $39.95

Hardware

Apple Macintosh, 512 KB

★ Essential: 3.5-inch disk drive, printer

☆ Recommended: mouse

IBM PC and compatibles, 512 KB

★ Essential: 3.5-inch disk drive or 5.25-inch disk drive (two-disk set), color monitor, color graphics card, printer

☆ Recommended: mouse

Although not essential for operation, several speech accessories (ranging from $50.00 to $150.00) made by Covox (503-342-1271), Hearsay, Inc. (718-232-7266), and Street Electronics Corp. (805-684-4593) are compatible with the program. These accessories provide a crisper and more natural-sounding voice.

Abilities Needed

If your child is a prereader, he or she will initially need your help to follow the instructions. Once familiar with the format, he or she should be able to work most of the program independently. Prereaders will also need your help in the segment of the program that deals with writing stories to accompany illustrations.

This program is appropriate for the learning-disabled child, although a child with significant visual-spatial problems might have difficulty with it.

Curriculum Areas

This program offers a speech-enhanced tool, with easy-to-use picture icons, for creating pictures, writing accompanying stories, and changing the pictures into jigsawlike puzzles.

Reasoning

- *Gathering information*—recalling relevant information
- *Analyzing information*—organizing details, recognizing patterns
- *Planning strategies*—making decisions

Reading

- *Comprehension skills*—combining words into sentences, combining sentences, reading stories

Writing

- *The process*—creating simple written messages, creating fictional texts, editing texts
- *The mechanics*—using elements of a word processing program, constructing phrases and sentences, keyboarding, proofreading

Arithmetic

- *Concepts*—understanding spatial concepts

The Program

(Tool/Tutor). Zug, the talking Megasaurus, guides your child through a series of activities that combine language and visual discrimination skills. Your child begins by building pictures from a library of graphic icons. He or she can also choose to construct a picture and use it to illustrate a story he or she writes. The program has three segments.

In *Picture,* your child creates colorful scenes by clicking the mouse on different picture icons or by pressing the directional arrow keys. He or she selects a setting (park, street, beach, hills), characters, buildings, and other objects (such as vehicles) from Zug's Picture Library. After your child completes the picture, he or she can print it, store it in his or her library, turn it into a puzzle, or use it as an illustration for an original story.

In *Puzzle,* your child selects a picture, either one just created or one stored in the library, and changes it into one of two kinds of puzzles.

- In *Shape Puzzle,* one missing shape is highlighted in the picture puzzle, and six geometric shapes (oval, circle, triangle, square, rectangle, and parallelogram) are displayed on the right side of the screen. Your child selects the matching shape to replace the missing piece. Your child can change the color of the shapes by using one of the 12 choices in the crayon box. There are two levels of difficulty. In the Easy Level, the missing piece is outlined, and your child hears a spoken cue such as "Find the circle." In the Hard Level, the missing shape is outlined but no spoken prompt is offered.

- In *Tile Puzzle,* the picture is broken into tile squares that appear in a mixed-up pattern on the right side of the screen. The left side of the screen displays empty squares. Your child has to select the correct tile to fill a target square (indicated by a question mark). As he or she uses the tiles, they disappear from the screen. There are two levels of difficulty: In the Easy Level, the picture is broken into six tiles; and in the Hard Level, it is broken into nine tiles. At any point, your child can select Show Me and get a look at the completed puzzle as a clue. The Move Box keeps track of how many moves a player made to solve the puzzle.

In *Story,* your child uses a new picture he or she created, or one stored in the library, as an illustration for an original story. The picture appears on the left side of the screen, and your child types in the accompanying story on the right side. The stories can be spoken as they are created. Your child can edit the stories after writing them.

This is an especially appealing program, with excellent multicolor graphics and sound. The voice speaks all the instructions and words, including menu choices, story sentences, and individual words.

The program offers additional options: You can turn the sound on or off or change the volume, and you can enter your child's name at the beginning so that the program repeats it throughout as a reward for good work. The program can be set to speak the stories letter by letter, word by word, or sentence by sentence. If a printer is available, your child can print out all pictures and stories.

The program has potential to grow with your child through the early childhood years. The youngest children can easily use the picture icons to create pictures and play the puzzles. As your child grows and learns to read and write, he or she will enjoy writing original text to go with the illustrations.

Read and Rhyme

5–8 years
Grades K–3

Unicorn, 1986, $39.95

Hardware
Apple II series, 48 KB
> ★ Essential: 5.25-inch disk drive

Apple IIGS, 768 KB ($49.95)
> ★ Essential: 3.5-inch disk drive

Abilities Needed
This program is appropriate for the learning-disabled child, although a child with significant language problems might have difficulty with it.

Curriculum Areas
The program teaches reading and writing skills through games in vocabulary building, rhyming, and word discrimination.

Reading
- *Decoding skills*—rhyming words, dealing with sequence
- *Comprehension skills*—playing word games

Writing
- *The mechanics*—using study skills

The Program
(Tutor). This program offers four games in which your child practices language-arts skills.

In *Rhyming Rockets,* your child selects from three words the one that does not rhyme. For example, your child sees three rockets on the screen, each containing a word (dank, rank, and wham). Your child moves the smiling face on the rocket to the correct choice.

In *Alpha Blast,* your child alphabetizes lists of 10 words. The program offers cues, such as "Which word comes first?" "Which comes next?" and so on.

In *Flying Saucer,* your child chooses the word that best completes the sentence appearing at the bottom of the screen.

In *Rhyming Challenge,* the program provides a word, and two players challenge each other to see how many words each player can make that rhyme with it. Each player selects one of three levels that establish the number of words he or she will rhyme.

When your child makes an error, the program does not offer hints. The computer gives him or her a second try and the message "Sorry. Try again" appears on the screen. After the second mistake, the computer supplies the right answer.

The program rewards correct responses with animated sequences, including rocket blast-offs, spaceship launches, and responses from friendly aliens.

Reader Rabbit and His Fabulous Word Factory
4–7 years
Grades PreK–2

The Learning Company, 1984, $39.95

Hardware
Apple II series, 64 KB
Commodore 64, 64 KB
   ★ Essential: 5.25-inch disk drive
   ☆ Recommended: color monitor, mouse
IBM PC and compatibles, 256 KB ($49.95)
Tandy 1000, 256 KB
   ★ Essential: 3.5-inch or 5.25-inch disk drive, color graphics card
   ☆ Recommended: color monitor, mouse

ALTERNATIVE VERSION

Talking Reader Rabbit
The Learning Company, 1987, $59.95

Hardware
Apple IIGS, 256 KB
Apple Macintosh, 1 MB
   ★ Essential: 3.5-inch disk drive
   ☆ Recommended: color monitor, mouse

Abilities Needed

To use this program, your child should know most of the letters in the alphabet, and it would be helpful if he or she knew the sounds of at least 8 to 10 letters. A very young child might initially need your help to understand the games.

This program is appropriate for the learning-disabled child.

Curriculum Areas

This program teaches reading by helping your child acquire beginning reading-readiness skills. It also helps your child develop memory and concentration.

Reading

- *Decoding skills*—matching and recognizing letters, linking sounds to letters and words, reading single-syllable words, matching pictures and words
- *Comprehension skills*—following simple directions

Writing

- *The mechanics*—spelling single-syllable words

Reasoning

- *Gathering information*—recalling relevant information

The Program

(Tutor). The program offers four different games in which your child works with 200 three-letter words and pictures for 70 of the words.

In *Sorter,* your child looks for words that contain certain letters. For example, all words ending with *M* go in a box; all others are left out.

In *Labeler,* your child spells words to match pictures. For example, your child sees a picture of a bus and has to find the letters that spell that word.

In *Word Train,* your child recognizes words that differ by one letter—for instance, *bat, bag,* and *ban.*

In *Matchup,* a Concentration-type memory game, your child matches pairs of words or pictures.

The program offers no specific help when your child makes mistakes. Your child must rely on trial and error if he or she does not know the right answer. At any time during the games, you or your child can choose Help, and a list of instructions appears.

The games are sequenced from easy to hard, which steadily helps your child to handle the material. Eye-catching formats present the information, and the program rewards every correct answer with a cute rabbit that dances a jig.

The program offers several options that alter the games to match your child's level of ability. You can turn the sound on or off and adjust the volume (quiet, medium, or loud). In *Sorter,* you can adjust the speed (slow, medium, or fast), change the position in the word of the displayed letter (first, middle, last, or random), and change the letters to be presented. In *Labeler,* you can change the picture sets shown. Finally, in *Matchup,* you can vary whether your child matches pictures to pictures, pictures to words, words to words, or pictures to letters.

The program does not keep a record of what your child accomplishes in any session. You must keep notes on his or her progress, or that information is lost.

In TALKING READER RABBIT, a digitized voice allows your child to hear, as well as see, the material.

Reading and Me

4–7 years
Grades PreK–2

Davidson, 1987, $39.95

Hardware
Apple II series, 128 KB
   ★ Essential: 3.5-inch or 5.25-inch disk drive
   ☆ Recommended: color monitor, printer, mouse
IBM PC and compatibles and IBM PS/2, 256 KB
   ★ Essential: 3.5-inch or 5.25-inch disk drive, color graphics card
   ☆ Recommended: color monitor, printer, mouse

Abilities Needed
Your child should be able to read simple single words, such as *hat, can,* and *drum,* in order to play the more difficult games, such as *Phonics* and *Words.*

This program is appropriate for the learning-disabled child.

ALTERNATIVE VERSION

Talking Reading and Me
Davidson, 1988, $49.95

Hardware
Apple IIGS, 512 KB
★ Essential: 3.5-inch or 5.25-inch disk drive
☆ Recommended: printer
IBM PC and compatibles, 512 KB
★ Essential: 3.5-inch or 5.25-inch disk drive, color graphics card
☆ Recommended: printer

Curriculum Areas
The program teaches reading by having your child practice reading-readiness skills and then apply them to beginning reading tasks.

Reading
- *Decoding skills*—matching and recognizing letters, linking sounds to letters and words, reading single-syllable words, dealing with sequence and direction, matching pictures and words, rhyming words
- *Comprehension skills*—combining words into sentences, playing word games

The Program
(Tutor). The program covers four areas: readiness, the alphabet, phonics, and words. Each area offers three different games consisting of 10 items each, and each game builds systematically from easy to more difficult tasks.

In *Readiness Games,* the program introduces your child to the concepts of *same* and *different* by having him or her classify objects by category. For example, in a category such as toys, clothing, or furniture, your child must identify the object that does not belong.

In *Alphabet Games,* the program introduces your child to the letters of the alphabet by asking him or her to match initial letters with representative pictures and words, match uppercase and lowercase letters, and sequence letters.

In *Phonics Games,* your child learns initial consonants by matching a picture and corresponding word with initial consonants, matching ending consonants, and matching words that rhyme. In this game, your child can either select the correct letters or type them on the keyboard.

In *Word Games,* your child learns to recognize individual letters and their sounds and then to read words and complete simple sentences—for example, "The [a picture of a car] is blue."

The program offers essential early reading skills in an entertaining manner, making use of lively animation, sound (familiar melodies), and excellent color graphics.

When your child makes a mistake, the program gives him or her a second chance. If he or she repeats the error, the program supplies the correct answer. Although the material is well designed, a very young child will need your help in the first few sessions to understand the cues and learn where they appear. For example, "Try again" appears at the top of the screen. In the talking version, however, the program reads many of the written cues aloud, which eliminates the need for you to be at the computer with your prereading child.

When your child answers correctly, each of the games rewards him or her with a different animated character, such as a clown who pops up or a magician who pulls letters from his hat.

After completion of an activity, you or your child can print out a certificate featuring your child's name and a clown illustration that he or she can color.

Reading Magic Library *3–6 years*
Grades PreK–1
Jack and the Beanstalk

Series
Tom Snyder Productions, 1988, $44.95

Hardware
Apple II series, 64 KB
IBM PC and compatibles, 256 KB
★ Essential: 3.5-inch or 5.25-inch disk drive
☆ Recommended: color monitor

Apple IIGS, 512 KB

  ★ Essential: 3.5-inch disk drive

  ☆ Recommended: color monitor

Abilities Needed

Before using the program, your child should be familiar with the letters of the alphabet. He or she will need your sustained help to complete each story.

    This program is appropriate for the learning-disabled child.

Curriculum Areas

The program offers an opportunity for you and your child to share a reading experience that helps him or her become familiar with written text and develops decision-making skills.

Reading

    ■ *Decoding skills*—matching and recognizing letters

    ■ *Comprehension skills*—reading and listening to stories

Reasoning

    ■ *Planning strategies*—making decisions

The Program

(Tutee). In this interactive fiction program, you and your child work together at the computer, sharing the storytelling of an up-to-date version of "Jack and the Beanstalk." You and your child view a series of graphics while you read the story aloud. At various points, the program asks you and your child to step into the hero's shoes and choose what will happen next in the story. For instance, Jack must decide either to go straight home or to stop off at the zoo after selling his pet, Robocow, for the magic beans. At this point, flashing lights appear on the screen, together with the following message: "Let's choose a letter together. (H) go straight home. (Z) go to the zoo." The team makes a choice by pressing one of the letters, and Jack follows the course you and your child determine. The pictures illustrate the text in a clear and amusing fashion, and all the graphics are attractive and designed to maintain the interest of a young child. Because of the unique decision-making format, the story is versatile, and your child will enjoy it over many viewings.

    The time needed to complete each story, 10 to 15 minutes, is appropriately geared to the attention span of your young child.

READING MAGIC LIBRARY: FLODD, THE BAD GUY (1989, $44.95), the second program in this series, is a fable about an ill-tempered chap who's making life difficult for the hero, King Alex, and his dog, Ollie. Together with your child, you help decide how to use the three wishes from the magic lamp to save the kingdom from Flodd.

As in JACK AND THE BEANSTALK, you and your child make decisions at various points in the story, pressing letters to determine the course it takes.

Read 'N Roll

9 years and older
Grades 4 and up

Davidson, 1987, $49.95

Hardware
Apple II series, 128 KB
- ★ Essential: 3.5-inch or 5.25-inch disk drive
- ☆ Recommended: printer

IBM PC and compatibles, 512 KB
- ★ Essential: 3.5-inch or 5.25-inch disk drive, color graphics card
- ☆ Recommended: printer

Abilities Needed
A young child will need your help to understand the demands of each activity.

This program is appropriate for the learning-disabled child, although a child with significant language problems might have difficulty with it.

Curriculum Areas
The program helps to improve reading comprehension by having your child read stories and answer questions about them.

Reading
- *Comprehension skills*—recalling information on topics, recalling details from stories, reading stories, identifying sequences of events, identifying main ideas, reading fictional texts

■ *Decoding skills*—enlarging vocabulary

The Program

(Tutor). This program is one of the few reading comprehension programs available. In it, your child can work with 320 short paragraphs. They encompass 4 different ability levels, with 80 passages at each level. Every level contains 20 passages covering each of the following skill areas: identifying the main idea, identifying relevant facts, identifying sequences of events, and making inferences. In all of the four main activities, your child must read the passage and select the correct answer from among four choices.

An additional arcadelike bowling game, *Strike and Spare,* helps your child build a better reading vocabulary by requiring him or her to define 320 words in context. The words are drawn from the passages in the four main activities. The program presents a sentence in which one word is highlighted, and your child selects a synonym from among four choices. For example, the sentence might be "Ted *convinced* him to go." The choices might be: (a) persuaded, (b). wanted, (c) invited, and (d) allowed. When your child answers correctly, an animated bowler releases his ball, and your child collects points.

The program gives your child two chances to select the right answer, and it offers hints to help him or her make the right choices. If your child answers incorrectly a second time, the program supplies the right answer.

For activities in which your child has given five or more correct answers, he or she can print out a Certificate of Excellence with colorful graphics. The program also offers a record-keeping feature, which you can either maintain on disk or print out.

The bowling simulation is fun, and the stories are generally interesting. However, the program is limited in that it asks only one question per passage, which results in a small payoff for the amount of reading done. In addition, the text is displayed in colored print, which might be distracting.

Remember!

12 years and older
Grades 7 and up

DesignWare Plus/Britannica Software, 1985, $49.95

Hardware

Apple II series, 64 KB

Commodore 64, 64 KB

IBM PC and compatibles, 128 KB

★ Essential: 5.25-inch disk drive

☆ Recommended: printer

Abilities Needed

Your child needs basic keyboarding skills to take best advantage the program.

Curriculum Areas

The program teaches writing and reading skills by helping your child to organize information on any topic to make recall easier. It also teaches a system to aid in memorizing information.

Writing

■ *The process* —learning organizational strategies

Reading

■ *Comprehension skills*—recalling information on topics, reading nonfictional texts

The Program

(Tool). Your child enters information on any subject—for example, vocabulary words, foreign-language word lists, chemistry facts, or history dates. The program presents this material in a variety of formats and provides your child with tools to help him or her make appropriate associations. Each "lesson" can have up to 28 questions and answers.

The program lets your child set up the material in four ways: *Review, Study, Practice,* and *Test.* He or she can also choose any one of four formats to test recall of information:

■ In *Question to Answer,* your child sees questions in the following form: "What is the Spanish word for *tomorrow?*"

- In *Answer to Question,* questions take this form: "*Mañana* means what?"

- In *Multiple Choice,* your child selects the correct answer from among three choices.

- In *List,* your child elects to have the information presented either in the sequence in which it was entered or at random.

The program also offers your child the ability to create mnemonic hints in three modes (visual, auditory, or written) that will help him or her form associations. For example, for the question "What is the capital of Wyoming?" your child can draw an outline of the state, enter a short tune that helps him or her recall the answer, or type in a written hint.

When your child makes a mistake in *Practice,* he or she can ask for hints to recall the information. Missed problems are recycled in this format. In *Test,* the program does not offer hints, and your child cannot retake missed questions.

The program has character sets for French, German, Italian, and Spanish. It can also provide chemistry symbols, subscripts, and superscripts for physics and advanced math. If a printer is available, your child can print out study lessons for review away from the computer.

An SAT Study Disk (for vocabulary and math skills), a French Vocabulary Disk, and a Spanish Vocabulary Disk are also available for use with the master disk ($19.95 each).

Sailing Through Story Problems

9–13 years
Grades 4–8

DLM Software, 1987, $46.00

Hardware
Apple II series, 64 KB
- ★ Essential: 5.25-inch disk drive (two-disk set)
- ☆ Recommended: printer

Abilities Needed

Your child should be reading at the fourth-grade level to use this program independently. He or she should also have basic computational skills in addition, subtraction, multiplication, and division as well as a basic knowledge of the ways in which amounts of money are expressed—for example, $46 or $46.00.

This program is appropriate for the learning-disabled child, although a child with significant memory problems might have difficulty with it.

Curriculum Areas

The program teaches arithmetic by having your child solve one- and two-step word problems involving the operations of addition, subtraction, multiplication, and division. Your child also practices reading maps, gathering information from charts, and working with units of money.

Arithmetic

- *Concepts*—recognizing terms and signs for mathematical operations
- *Fundamental operations*—operating with addition, subtraction, multiplication, and division
- *Applications*—analyzing word problems with single and multiple operations, using visual representations
- *Measurement*—using units of money

Reading

- *Comprehension skills*—combining sentences, following complex directions

The Program

(Tutor). The program is organized around a pirate theme. Your child works through a series of word problems divided into 12 levels of increasing difficulty. Each level requires that he or she use a different kind of process—for example, your child needs to find the information; use addition, subtraction, multiplication, or division; solve two-question problems; and choose which basic operation needs to be done in Step 1 of a two-step problem.

In *Levels 1–5,* your child solves single-step word problems by using a specific process. For example, if the process is find the information, the problem might be "The cook made 14 pots of stew. He used 735 onions, 961 carrots, and 85 eggs. He cooked it for 14 hours. How many carrots did he use?"

In *Level 6,* your child solves single-step problems by using a different operation for each problem.

In *Level 7,* the program introduces your child to two-step problems by asking two separate questions. For example, the program supplies a chart with all the necessary information and then offers the following: "A jug of cider costs more than 5 glasses of punch. What's the cost of 5 glasses of punch? How much more does a jug of cider cost than 5 glasses of punch?"

In *Levels 8–11,* your child solves two-step problems by using a specific operation in the first step.

In *Level 12,* your child practices selecting operations needed to solve two-step problems. For example, the problem might be "These pirates have been with me for a long time. What is the average length of service for these three pirates?" A chart supplies the information needed, and your child must identify and perform the operations necessary to solve the problem—in this case, addition and division.

When your child makes a mistake, the computer offers progressive hints for solving the problem. For example, in the Level 1 problem "How many carrots did the cook use?" the hints would be "Select a label to work in" (pounds, carrots, dozens), and then "Find carrots" and "Read the amount." After your child makes three unsuccessful attempts, the computer gives the correct answer.

Your child earns points for solving problems correctly, earning the most points for solving them on the first try. The program uses the points to award gold bars from the pirates' treasure chest.

The program allows you to vary the number of problems offered in each game (5 to 10) and the percentage of correct answers required for advancement (70, 80, 90 or 100 percent). The mastery level you set determines whether your child advances to the next content level, remains on level, or returns to the previous level, depending on his or her performance. He or she can use an on-screen calculator at any time for help in computation.

If a printer is available, you can save and print out game analysis records. The program records all the problems your child missed in the last game and his or her specific error pattern.

School Bus Driver

3–7 years
Grades PreK–2

Fisher-Price / GameTek / IJE, 1988, $14.95

Hardware

Apple II series, 128 KB
Apple IIGS, 512 KB

★ Essential: 5.25-inch disk drive
☆ Recommended: color monitor, joystick

IBM PC and compatibles, 256 KB

★ Essential: 3.5-inch disk drive ($16.95) or 5.25-inch disk drive
☆ Recommended: color monitor, joystick

Abilities Needed

If your child is a preschooler or a prereader, he or she will initially need your help in learning how to use the program. To use the program independently, your child should be reading at about the second-grade level.

This program is appropriate for the learning-disabled child, although a child with significant problems in memory skills might have difficulty with it.

Curriculum Areas

The program teaches reasoning through a game in which your child maneuvers a school bus through a series of mazes. The game offers practice in hand-eye coordination, recall of details, and navigation.

Reasoning

- *Gathering information*—recalling relevant information
- *Planning strategies*—making decisions, selecting relevant information to create a plan of action

The Program

(Tutor). Your child assumes the role of a school bus driver who must pick up children at their bus stops and take them to school. There are six children and six stops. Your child maneuvers the bus along the road, using either a joystick or the four direction (arrow) keys. When all six children have been dropped off at school, the game is over. The program offers four progressive levels of play.

In *Level 1,* all six children are at their own bus stops waiting for the driver. There is no time limit, and no obstacles are in the road.

In *Level 2,* the six children are randomly placed at the bus stops. Your child has to find out at which of the stops a child is waiting. There is no time limit, and no obstacles are in the road.

In *Level 3* (which can be played only when Level 2 has been completed), the children are randomly placed, and your child is given a 5-minute time limit in which to finish the game. If time runs out before all six children are picked up, the game ends.

In *Level 4* (which can be played only when Level 3 is completed), the children are randomly placed, your child is given a 5-minute time limit, and he or she must avoid obstacles in the road, such as cows and fallen trees.

As the bus travels along the roads, the program makes a continuous beeping sound, which could be distracting to some children. You can turn off this sound at any time.

See the USA

8 years and older
Grades 3 and up

CompuTeach Educational Software, 1986, $49.95

Hardware

Apple II series, 64 KB
   ★ Essential: two 5.25-inch disk drives (four-disk set), blank disks for saving questions
   ☆ Recommended: color monitor
Apple II series, 128 KB
   ★ Essential: one 5.25-inch disk drive (four-disk set), blank disks for saving questions
   ☆ Recommended: color monitor
IBM PC and compatibles, 256 KB
   ★ Essential: 3.5-inch or 5.25-inch disk drive, blank disks for saving questions
   ☆ Recommended: color monitor

Abilities Needed

Your child should be reading at the fourth-grade level to use the program independently.

This program is appropriate for the learning-disabled child.

Curriculum Areas

The program teaches geography by helping your child learn states and their capitals.

Reading

- *Comprehension skills*—recalling information on topics, following complex directions

Writing

- *The mechanics*—spelling multisyllable words, using elements of a word processing program, keyboarding

Reasoning

- *Gathering information*—recalling relevant information, seeking information in reference and available sources, taking notes
- *Planning strategies*—selecting relevant information to create a plan of action, managing resources

The Program

(Tutor/Tool). Your child makes a series of cross-country trips by car, travelling through various states and planning each route carefully in order to reach a destination in a certain amount of time. Along the way, your child learns the names of the states and their capitals that he or she has passed through. The main menu offers five choices:

In *Practice States,* your child moves from state to state while the program displays the names of the states on a map of the United States.

In *Play States,* your child drives across the United States (or takes a boat to and from Alaska and Hawaii). The program gives him or her a starting state and a destination state. If you have activated the timer, he or she is also given a deadline for arrival. In meeting the deadline, he or she must take time zone differences into account. Your child moves from state to state by typing in the names of states. As the car travels, a red path indicates where the trip has taken him or her. In addition, the time is displayed at the top of the screen.

In *Practice Capitals,* your child moves from state to state while the program displays the names of state capitals.

In *Play Capitals,* your child plays the same game as in *Play States,* except that he or she types in the names of the state capitals as he or she advances across the country.

In *Play Quiz Game,* your child chooses a set of 20 questions to answer. He or she answers the questions by moving to the correct state or capital. The categories include questions about famous places, famous people, general facts, state flowers, state birds, and state mottos. A sample question might be, "In what state capital is the Mark Twain House?" The program offers hints, if your child needs them, such as "It's in New England."

The program comes with five region disks that display maps of different areas of the United States: Northeast, East Central, South, West Central, and Far West. The package also includes a large wall map of the United States. If your child reads all the on-screen information, he or she can learn a great deal of geography and many state facts. When your child reaches a destination state, a picture shows a special feature of that state; when he or she reaches a destination capital, the program gives a state fact. Over 100 colorful screens offer this information.

The program offers several cues that help your child achieve success. He or she has more than one chance to spell the place name; if the spelling is incorrect but close, the program gives the correct spelling and asks your child if this was the intended spelling. If your child cannot remember the name of a state, he or she types in *help*, and the program offers the name of the state he or she is currently in, as well as the names of all the bordering states. In the Quiz section, the program offers hints that point your child to the correct answer.

Several options allow you to adjust the program to your child's needs. You can activate the timer or not and turn the sound on or off. In the Quiz section, an editing tool allows you or your child to create, delete, copy, or edit questions to test knowledge on any topic related to states and capitals. You can customize the questions as well as the computer's response to each player's answers. For example, you can program helping hints and praise for correct answers.

The games in this program nicely complement schoolwork in geography. The program also affords opportunities for you and your child to play together.

Snoopy Writer

6–9 years
Grades 1–4

Random House/American School Publishers, 1985, $39.95

Hardware
Apple II series, 64 KB
- ★ Essential: 5.25-inch disk drive, printer, blank disks for saving work
- ☆ Recommended: color monitor, second disk drive, mouse or joystick

Abilities Needed
Your child should be reading at the second-grade level to use the program independently.

This program is appropriate for the learning-disabled child.

Curriculum Areas
The program teaches writing and word processing by offering your child the opportunity to use an extremely simple word processor.

Writing
- *The process* — creating simple written messages, creating messages for visual material, editing texts
- *The mechanics* — using a word processing program

The Program
(Tool). Using this very simple word processor, your child can write stories, change them, print them, erase them, or save them in Snoopy's file cabinet. Snoopy and the other Peanuts characters act as on-screen tutors, guiding your child through the various steps of writing, editing, and printing. The main menu offers the following choices:

Write allows your child to create text. The computer first asks your child whether he or she wants to create a picture or write a story. If your child elects to do a picture first, he or she chooses one of four settings (beach, camp, stage, or party) and a cast of Peanuts characters to create a full-color picture. Then he or she writes a story to go with the picture. At any point in the writing, your child can go back and look at the picture again.

File allows your child to read, change, erase, store, and print the stories he or she creates in *Write*.

Customize allows you to set the program for the number of disk drives you are using and for the card slot your printer is plugged into.

Quit allows your child to exit the program at any time.

The program offers a unique feature called Story Starter that is particularly helpful for beginning writers. When your child selects this option, the program furnishes a sentence or two that relates to the picture he or she has created, and your child finishes the story in his or her own words. Sometimes the starter ends with an incomplete sentence, and your child must use his or her imagination to finish both the sentence and the story. For example, if your child has chosen the party background and the characters Linus and Franklin, the following message might appear on the screen: " 'I'm not the Little Green Giant,' said a disappointed Linus. 'Couldn't you tell, I'm...' "

Easy-to-use menus feature both words and pictures, and directions are simple and clear. The program displays every key that your child needs to use on the screen. This kind of program can provide a good way to introduce your child to using the computer as a tool for writing.

Speedway Math

6–11 years
Grades 1–6

MECC, 1986, $59.00

Hardware

Apple II series, 64 KB

★ Essential: 3.5-inch or 5.25-inch disk drive

☆ Recommended: color monitor, printer

Abilities Needed

Your child should be reading at the third-grade level to use this program independently. A younger child will initially need your help to read the instructions. After becoming familiar with the format, he or she should be able to work alone.

This program is appropriate for the learning-disabled child, although a child who has significant problems in memory skills or in working with time limits might have difficulty with it.

Curriculum Areas

The program teaches arithmetic by offering practice in quick recall of basic math facts in addition, subtraction, multiplication, and division.

Arithmetic

- *Fundamental operations*—operating with addition, subtraction, multiplication, and division

The Program

(Tutor). The program offers three activities, all with a racing theme. Your child can play alone or against other players. Competition with others will encourage your child to increase his or her speed and commit basic math facts to memory.

In *Tune-Up Time,* your child works with a set of electronic flash cards. He or she defines the type of operation to be used and the range of the problems (addition with sums up to 18, subtraction with minuends up to 18, multiplication with factors up to 12, and division with divisors up to 12). He or she determines the number of problems presented (1–50). This activity is not timed, and your child can review missed facts.

In *Practice Laps,* a timed activity, your child practices on a set of 10 problems (one lap). At the end of each lap, the program displays a score and a time and then combines these two factors to give a lap speed expressed in miles per hour. Your child can select from any of the operations and complete as many laps as desired.

In the *Big Race,* a timed activity, your child works as quickly as possible on an entire set of basic math facts. You or your child define the set of facts to be used. The program records his or her time, score, and speed. If he or she finishes within a certain time limit or achieves a perfect score, your child can record his or her name in "car clubs."

In *Tune-Up Time,* if your child makes a mistake, the message "No, try again" appears on the screen. In *Practice Laps,* each error your child makes reduces his or her lap speed. In the *Big Race,* your child can opt to take up to two pit stops (rest periods); however, each rest taken adds 5 seconds to his or her time.

Rewards for performance depend on time and accuracy. In *Practice Laps,* the program reports your child's speed at the end of each lap. In the *Big Race,* the reward for either a fast time or a perfect score is permission to join a special car club. You define the club requirements. For instance, you can specify that membership in the Time Club requires a total time of 4 minutes or less. When your child completes the *Big Race,* a scorecard appears on the screen. The program then adds his or her name to one of the clubs, and a supporting message appears: "Nice race, Laura. Your name has been added to the Hall of Fame."

The program can be varied. In *Tune-Up Time* and *Practice Laps,* you can choose which operation to use. In *Practice Laps,* you can also select mixed problems and change the problem formats (vertical presentation, horizontal presentation, or mixed presentation). In the *Big Race,* you can modify the number of problems presented (10–100) and choose the operation (addition, subtraction, multiplication, division, or mixed operations). You can also set up optional car clubs with specific requirements for membership.

As in most MECC programs, this program can save records for several individuals. The total number of tries, the best time, and the best score are saved on a scoreboard. After each set of problems in *Practice Laps* and the *Big Race,* your child sees a scorecard that tells him or her the number of problems tried, the number answered correctly, the time, and the speed.

This program lends itself nicely to team play. If the players select a long race (100 problems), two or three children can form "racing teams." The team members can switch off after every set of 20 problems or so.

Spellicopter

6–10 years
Grades 1–5

DesignWare / Britannica Software, 1983, $39.95

Hardware
Apple II series, 64 KB
Commodore 64, 64 KB ($29.95)
- ★ Essential: 5.25-inch disk drive
- ☆ Recommended: joystick

IBM PC and compatibles, 256 KB ($14.95)
- ★ Essential: 5.25-inch disk drive, color graphics card
- ☆ Recommended: joystick

ALTERNATIVE VERSION

Super Spellicopter
DesignWare / Britannica Software, 1990, $34.95

Hardware
IBM PC and compatibles, 512 KB
  ★ Essential: 5.25-inch disk drive
  ☆ Recommended: joystick

Abilities Needed

To use this program independently, your child should be reading at the second-grade level. Initially, you might have to explain how to operate the program.

This program is appropriate for the learning-disabled child, although a child who has significant problems in visual-spatial and timing skills might have difficulty with it.

Curriculum Areas

The program offers your child practice in spelling skills by having him or her play an action-oriented game.

Writing

- *The mechanics* — spelling single-syllable words, spelling multisyllable words, using elements of a word processing program

The Program

(Tutor). Your child practices spelling while piloting a spellicopter on various missions. Your child maneuvers the chopper over mountainous terrain, through skies crowded with obstacles, to the letter field. Here your child must pick up letters, in the right order, to spell a target word. Then your child flies back to the landing field with the cargo and refuels for the next mission.

The program includes 400 words divided into 40 lists of 10 words each. The lists are grouped into Basic, Intermediate, and Advanced levels. Your child can select the level and also choose one of three levels of piloting expertise (Pilot, Captain, and Ace).

Your child selects a list and views the 10 words. A screen displays an altimeter, a fuel gauge, and score and cargo areas. Then a context sentence or sentences appear in which the word to be spelled is missing. For example, "A cat is small. A horse is ___." Your child then flies to the letter field to pick up the letters of the target word. En route, he or she must avoid obstacles such as lightning bolts, storm clouds, high mountains, and UFOs.

For each word spelled correctly and each safe trip completed with enough fuel to return to the landing field, your child earns 20 points.

Your child loses points if any of the following events occur: the chopper hits an obstacle and explodes, your child misspells a word, or your child takes too much time to spell the word and fuel runs out. If your child misspells a word, the correct spelling flashes in the cargo window on the screen, the letters are scattered again on the letter field, and your child gets another chance.

The program offers an editor, which lets you create, edit, delete, store, and print your own word lists.

Other options you can vary include: turning the sound on or off, using a keyboard or a joystick, requesting context sentences for clues, and setting the skill level of the pilot. For example, at the Pilot level, only a few obstacles appear and there are no UFOs on the letter field. At the Captain and Ace levels, UFOs land on the letter field and the skies are crowded with obstacles.

SUPER SPELLICOPTER is designed for children 7–14 years old (Grades 2–9). This version offers enhanced graphics and sound, which results in a very realistic flying game.

Spell It Plus!

10 years and older
Grades 5 and up

Davidson, 1989, $49.95

Hardware
Apple II series, 128 KB
Apple IIGS, 512 KB

    ★ Essential: 3.5-inch or 5.25-inch disk drive
    ☆ Recommended: printer, mouse or joystick

Apple Macintosh, 1 MB ($49.95)

★ Essential: 3.5-inch disk drive

IBM PC and compatibles, 512 KB

★ Essential: 3.5-inch or 5.25-inch disk drive, color graphics card

☆ Recommended: printer, mouse or joystick

ALTERNATIVE VERSION

Spell It!
Davidson, 1986, $49.95

Hardware
Apple II series, 48 KB

Commodore 64/128, 64 KB ($29.95)

★ Essential: 5.25-inch disk drive

☆ Recommended: printer, mouse or joystick

IBM PC and compatibles, 128 KB

★ Essential: 3.5-inch or 5.25-inch disk drive, color graphics card

---

Abilities Needed
This program is appropriate for the learning-disabled child.

Curriculum Areas
The program helps develop and improve spelling skills by presenting 1000 of the most commonly misspelled words.

Writing
- *The process*—editing texts
- *The mechanics*—spelling single-syllable words, spelling multisyllable words, using elements of a word processing program, keyboarding, proofreading

Reading
- *Decoding skills*—analyzing words for their elements

The Program
(Tutor). The program consists of five activities, which move progressively from easy to hard. It presents 1000 words divided into 50 lists, with 12 presentations of each word. There are five levels of difficulty, from Novice to Grand Master.

In *Study It,* your child sees the applicable spelling rule for the list of words he or she is working on. For example, he or she might see "In number words, the spelling of the root might change when the number changes: *four* becomes *forty* and *five* becomes *fifty*." Then the program displays a word (for example, *five*) and a sentence with a blank space for the altered word (for example, "There are ____ singers in the chorus"). Your child types the correct word (in this example, *fifty*) when he or she feels ready.

In *Decode It,* your child practices spelling words as he or she completes a mystery message shown on the screen. The message is composed of list words, each with a missing letter. As your child types in the missing letters, they are entered into the mystery message to help decode it.

In *Correct It,* your child edits text to correct misspelled words. He or she can use either the Edit option (in which the misspelled word is underlined) or the Search and Edit option (in which no cues are offered).

In *Unscramble It,* your child plays a spelling version of tic-tac-toe in which scrambled list words are hidden behind a grid. Your child chooses a box and has to unscramble the word in the box. The goal is to complete a row. Two players can compete in this activity, or your child can compete against the computer.

In *Spell It,* your child plays a fast-paced arcade-style game in which a frog identifies and gobbles up either all the correctly spelled words or all the incorrectly spelled words. The format requires judgment and fast reaction to material your child has learned in the other parts of the program.

When your child makes a mistake, the program offers the cue "Try again" before repeating the word display. The program also provides support through Help cues, which are available at any time. Your child can select

- How To, which reviews the instructions for each activity
- Rule, which offers the spelling rule for the current work
- Words, which offers the complete list of words for that segment

You can vary the difficulty level, the rate at which words are presented, and the word lists (by using the editor to make the words easier or harder). The easy-to-use editor allows you or your child to add your own word lists—in four languages (English, French, Spanish, and German)—to any of the five activities. In addition, a printing option permits you to print lists of words for review away from the computer. You can also print an All Star Speller Certificate, for those who score 100 percent in any activity, and cumulative records and scoreboards, which allow you to easily assess your child's progress.

SPELL IT PLUS! data disks ($19.95 each), designed for specific grade levels from 1 through 6, are also available.

States and Traits

9 years and older
Grades 4 and up

Series
DesignWare/Britannica, 1984, $39.95

Hardware

Apple II series, 64 KB
Commodore 64 KB ($29.95)
IBM PC and compatibles, 64 KB
★ Essential: 5.25-inch disk drive, color monitor

Curriculum Areas

The program offers a "tool kit" for reviewing, in a game format, a broad range of information about the United States. Topics include: geography (location of each state and all bordering states), historical facts, names of capitals, current state facts, and locations of major landforms and bodies of water.

Reading

■ *Comprehension skills*—following simple and complex directions, recalling information on topics

Arithmetic

■ *Concepts*—understanding spatial concepts
■ *Applications*—using visual representations

The Program

(Tutor). The program consists of over 250 questions, available in two game formats. Your child can play at two levels, easy and expert. The levels vary the number of cues that appear for help in answering the questions. For example, at the easy level, the name of the state appears above the outline of the state; at the expert level, only the outline appears. Your child can work either with a map of the entire United States or with one of four regional maps. He or she can also vary the amount of information on the maps so that they show all the state borders or only rivers and mountains.

In *Place the States,* your child moves states to their correct positions on the map by using a screen pointer. He or she answers questions about that state that combine categories of information—for example, "In which state was there a Confederate and a Union capital in the last year of the Civil War?"

In *Match States and Traits,* your child answers questions about different states on different topics—for example, Landforms: "In which state are the Rocky Mountains, the Colorado River, and the Great Salt Lake?" Historical Fact: "In which state were the famous Lincoln-Douglas debates of 1858?"

When your child makes a mistake, the computer offers the correct answer immediately, giving both the state and its location.

The games are timed; your child earns extra points for answering quickly, but he or she is not penalized for slower responses.

The program is somewhat restricted in that the answers to all questions are either the name of a state or its location. However, by using the Editor, you or your child can design original cues based on new information. In addition, the manual offers reproducible maps.

This program is a good complement to the school curriculum in United States history, geography, and recent events. If your child needs to learn this material, the program is useful in consolidating classroom teaching.

EUROPEAN NATIONS AND LOCATIONS (1985, $39.95) is the second program in this series. Using the same game format as in STATES AND TRAITS, your child learns about important European nations and capitals, neighboring countries, landmarks, and historical events. Again, if your child needs to learn this material, the program is useful in consolidating classroom teaching.

Stickybear Math

6–9 years
Grades 1–4

Series
Weekly Reader Software / Optimum Resource, 1984, $39.95

Hardware

Apple II series, 64 KB
   ★ Essential: 3.5-inch or 5.25-inch disk drive
Commodore 64/128, 64 KB
   ★ Essential: 5.25-inch disk drive
IBM PC and compatibles, 128 KB
   ★ Essential: 3.5-inch or 5.25-inch disk drive, color graphics card, color monitor

Abilities Needed

You will need to be available to set the difficulty level before your child begins play. A younger child will initially need your help to understand the playing instructions.

This program is appropriate for the learning-disabled child.

Curriculum Areas

The program teaches arithmetic by offering your child drill and practice in the operations of addition and subtraction.

Arithmetic

■ *Concepts*—recognizing terms and signs for mathematical operations
■ *Fundamental operations*—operating with addition, operating with subtraction

The Program

(Tutor). The program offers sets of problems in addition (with single digits and digits of up to four places, with carrying) and subtraction (with single digits and digits of up to four places, with carrying and borrowing).

A unique feature of the program is that it automatically adjusts the difficulty level, depending on your child's performance. For example, if your child is correctly answering a sufficient number of problems at a particular level, the program will increase the level of difficulty. But even at the higher level, the program continues to present some problems from the preceding level for positive reinforcement and to reduce frustration.

After your child gives a set of correct answers, he or she is rewarded by the opportunity to help Stickybear out of 10 different "sticky" situations.

The graphics in this program are not as appealing as in some. However, the ability to customize features goes a long way in meeting the individual needs of your child. You can vary the number of tries allowed (one to four) before the correct answer is offered, the level of difficulty (20 levels), the type of problem (addition, subtraction, or a mixture of both), and the format of the problems (for example, missing addends, column addition and subtraction, and multiple addends).

The program offers you the ability to compile and store records of levels reached, scores, and types of problems completed, which helps you keep track of your child's progress.

STICKYBEAR MATH 2 (1986, $39.95) is designed for children 7 years and older (Grades 2 and up). It offers practice in the math operations of multiplication (with factors of up to three digits) and division (divisors of up to two digits, and a three-digit quotient).

Stickybear Music

8 years and older
Grades 3 and up

Weekly Reader Software / Optimum Resource, 1986, $49.95

Hardware
Apple II series, 48 KB
   ★ Essential: 5.25-inch disk drive
   ☆ Recommended: printer

Abilities Needed
Your child should be reading at least at the third-grade level to use this program. A younger child will initially need your help in learning to use this tool.

This program is appropriate for the learning-disabled child, although a child who has significant language problems might have difficulty with it.

Curriculum Areas

This program teaches fundamentals of music notation and composition by having your child compose and play a piece of music.

Reasoning

- *Analyzing information*—organizing details, recognizing patterns

The Program

(Tutor/Tool). With this music "word processor," your child can create, edit, save, and replay songs. As your child creates musical pieces, he or she can change the music as many times as desired. The program allows him or her to vary time signatures (4/4, 3/4, 2/4); sharps, flats, and accidentals; and tempo (six choices). If a printer is available, your child can print the compositions.

The program also contains nine familiar songs—for example, "Bach Minuet," "Over the Rainbow," and "Clementine." Your child can play these songs and see the notes light up on a sheet of music displayed on the screen.

Besides music-writing capability, the program offers a section entitled *What Is Music?* which presents exercises that teach musical terminology. Your child can learn about sharps, flats, rests, measures, time signatures, tempo, rhythms, pitch, and octaves. At the end of the section, exercises show how to use all the components to create a song.

Stickybear Reading

5–8 years
Grades K–3

Weekly Reader Software / Optimum Resource, 1984, $39.95

Hardware

Apple II series, 48 KB

- ★ Essential: 3.5-inch disk drive (64 KB) or 5.25-inch disk drive
- ☆ Recommended: mouse or joystick

Commodore 64, 64 KB
> ★ Essential: 5.25-inch disk drive

IBM PC and compatibles, 256 KB
> ★ Essential: 3.5-inch or 5.25-inch disk drive, color monitor, color
> graphics card
>
> ☆ Recommended: mouse or joystick

Abilities Needed

Your child should know the letters and sounds of the alphabet and be able to read familiar words before using this program. You will have to work with your child in order to get maximum benefit from the program.

This program is appropriate for the learning-disabled child.

Curriculum Areas

The program teaches reading by having your child build vocabulary, practice word-recognition skills, and focus on simple sentences.

Reading

> ■ *Decoding skills*—linking sounds with letters and
> words, reading single-syllable words, matching pic-
> tures and words
> ■ *Comprehension Skills*—combining words into sentences

The Program

(Tutor). The program consists of three simple games.

In *Match the Word,* your child builds word-recognition vocabulary by working with familiar word-picture sets. He or she sees three pictures (for example, a tractor, a chair, and a chicken) and three matching words. Your child draws a line between the matching picture and word.

In *Find the Word,* your child turns words into animated graphics. The program presents a sentence with a missing word (for instance, "The ___ jumps over Stickybear") and shows a picture illustrating the correct sentence. From a choice of three words, your child selects one that will complete the sentence so that it matches the picture. When your child selects the correct word, the sentence becomes animated.

In *Build a Sentence,* your child sees a choice of three phrases for each part of a sentence. For example, he or she sees the following noun phrases: The cow, A turtle, A skunk (each accompanied by a picture);

the following verb phrases: walks behind, runs behind, runs past; and the following objects: a chair, Bumper the Bear, the blocks (each accompanied by a picture). Your child combines choices from the three sections to produce a sentence, which is then illustrated in animated graphics.

This is a visually appealing program that children love. Working together with your child on the exercises offers the opportunity to review basic words and sentences.

The program is, however, limited in teaching new skills. If your child makes a mistake, the program offers no on-screen help but only beeps to indicate that an error has occurred. In addition, it does not control the number of incorrect choices your child can make. Consequently, your child might not be highly motivated to seek the correct answer and might simply choose at random.

Stickybear Reading Comprehension

7–9 years
Grades 2–4

Weekly Reader Software / Optimum Resource, 1986, $49.95

Hardware

Apple II series, 48 KB

★ Essential: 3.5-inch disk drive (64 KB) or 5.25-inch disk drive

☆ Recommended: color monitor, printer

Commodore 64/128, 64 KB

★ Essential: 5.25-inch disk drive

☆ Recommended: color monitor, printer

IBM PC and compatibles, 256 KB

★ Essential: 3.5-inch or 5.25-inch disk drive, color graphics card

☆ Recommended: color monitor, printer

Abilities Needed

Your child should be reading at the second-grade level in order to read the stories at Levels 1 and 2 independently.

This program is appropriate for the learning-disabled child.

Curriculum Areas

This program offers practice in reading comprehension.

Reading

- *Comprehension skills*—recalling information on topics, recalling details from stories, reading stories

The Program

(Tutor). This is a multilevel reading-comprehension program containing 30 stories. Your child reads a story and then answers several questions about the story. The stories are divided into seven levels: Levels 1 and 2 require second-grade reading ability, Levels 3 and 4 require third-grade reading ability, and Levels 5 and 6 require fourth-grade reading ability. Level 7 lets you add customized stories for your child.

After reading a Level 1 story called "A Dog Named Tiny," consisting of three short paragraphs, your child completes multiple-choice questions such as the following: "Grandpa gave Paul a (a) cat, (b) puppy, (c) goldfish." He or she then types in the letter of the correct answer.

After reading a Level 6 story about being President of the United States, consisting of 10 or so paragraphs, your child completes items such as the following: "Which is something that a President does not do? (a) command the Army, (b) stop bills from becoming law, (c) make laws."

If your child makes a mistake, the program beeps but does not offer hints or cues. Your child gets a second chance to choose the right answer before the computer offers the response. When your child is correct, he or she is rewarded with music.

The program automatically adjusts the difficulty level, depending on your child's performance. Your child can either progress at his or her own rate, or follow the automatic adjustments of the program. The program keeps track of your child's previous work and starts him or her at the appropriate level in the next session. Your child can move forward or backward through the stories at any time, so review is always possible. This is particularly helpful if your child has difficulty remembering information.

The program offers several options. You can turn the sound on or off, select the level of difficulty (1–7), and specify the number of tries your child can make before the computer offers the answer (1–4). If a printer is available, you can print out the program's exercises. When using Level 7, you can add, delete, or print your own exercises.

The program keeps a record of your child's work after each session and saves starting level, current level, questions answered, number correct, and overall score. In addition, it shows information about the current exercise, such as the questions answered, the number correct, and the current score.

Stickybear Town Builder
6–9 years
Grades 1–4

Weekly Reader Software / Optimum Resource, 1985, $49.95

Hardware
Apple II series, 48 KB
Commodore 64, 64 KB
 ★ Essential: 5.25-inch disk drive
 ☆ Recommended: color monitor, joystick

Abilities Needed
If second-grade reading poses no problems for your child, this is an easy game for him or her to use. Your child might initially need your help to become accustomed to the aerial perspective in the display of the town.

This program is appropriate for the learning-disabled child, although a child with significant visual-spatial problems might have difficulty with it.

Curriculum Areas
This program introduces your child to map-reading skills. He or she learns about map symbols, aerial perspectives, distances, direction (up, down, left, right), cardinal directions (north, south, east, west) and concepts of relative distance.

Reasoning
 - *Gathering information* —recalling relevant information
 - *Planning strategies* —making decisions, managing resources

Arithmetic
 - *Concepts* —understanding spatial concepts
 - *Applications* —creating and using visual representations

The Program

(Tutor/Tutee). The program offers three games.

In *Build a Town*, your child constructs a town by placing, one at a time, his or her choices from 30 available buildings on an empty map. He or she can build and store up to 20 towns on the disk, complete with roads, parks, buildings, and bridges.

In *Take a Drive*, your child's original map serves as the guide he or she uses to drive a car through the town. Your child completes as many stops as possible before running out of gas.

In *Find the Keys*, a hide-and-seek activity, your child's goal is to locate 12 mystery keys randomly hidden in the town. Again, your child works against the threat of running out of gas before he or she can complete the game.

Although the graphics are not as captivating as those in more recent programs, the program effectively teaches, in a simple format, the important skill of map design. This skill is necessary in both arithmetic and social studies.

Stickybear Word Problems

7–10 years
Grades 2–5

Weekly Reader Software / Optimum Resource, 1987 $49.95

Hardware

Apple II series, 48 KB

   ★ Essential: 3.5-inch or 5.25-inch disk drive

   ☆ Recommended: color monitor, printer

IBM PC and compatibles and P/S 2, 256 KB

   ★ Essential: 3.5-inch or 5.25-inch disk drive, color graphics card

   ☆ Recommended: color monitor, printer

Abilities Needed

Your child should be reading at the second-grade level to read the word problems independently. In addition, he or she should be familiar with the digits 0 through 9 and be able to enter his or her name. You will probably need to explain how to solve problems that require more than one operation.

This program is appropriate for the learning-disabled child, although a child who has significant language problems might have difficulty with it.

Curriculum Areas

The program provides practice in solving simple mathematical word problems in addition, subtraction, and multiplication.

Arithmetic

- *Concepts*—recognizing terms and signs for mathematical operations
- *Fundamental operations*—operating with addition, subtraction, and multiplication
- *Applications*—analyzing word problems with single and multiple operations

Reading

- *Comprehension skills*—following simple directions, combining sentences

The Program

(Tutor). The program presents hundreds of problems, related to everyday situations, at six levels of difficulty. Your child must determine the basic math operations needed to solve the problems as well as calculate the solutions. Each of the problems requires one or two steps for solution. For example, at Level 1, your child solves a single-step addition problem such as "Betsy found 3 pennies in one pocket and 2 pennies in another pocket. How many pennies did Betsy find?" At Level 4, he or she might encounter a two-step problem requiring one addition step and one subtraction step, such as "John had 5 rabbits. He bought 5 more. Then he sold 4. How many rabbits does John have now?"

A unique feature of the program is that it automatically adjusts the difficulty level of subsequent problems based on your child's performance. For example, if your child is correctly answering a sufficient number of problems at a particular level, the program will increase the level of difficulty. However, it continues to present some problems from the previous level for positive reinforcement and to reduce frustration.

You can expand the program by adding new problems of your own. You can also print out problems to create traditional paper worksheets. And the program has a record-keeping feature that allows you to assess progress easily.

The program does not explain how to solve two-step problems. Therefore, it is best used for practice of skills already learned rather than for instruction in new skills. You can control the pacing of the program by specifying the number of attempts (1–5) your child can make to solve a problem before the correct answer is offered. However, when your child does make mistakes, the program does not effectively explain how to reach the correct solution.

In addition, the graphics that are used as rewards for correct answers are not particularly appealing.

Although the program has drawbacks, it is one of the few available for young children that presents word problems.

Super Story Tree

9–13 years
Grades 4–8

Scholastic Family Software, 1989, $79.95

Hardware
Apple II series, 128 KB
IBM PC and compatibles, 256 KB
　★ Essential: 3.5-inch or 5.25-inch disk drive (two-disk set)
　☆ Recommended: printer, color monitor, mouse

Abilities Needed
Your child should be reading at the fourth-grade level to use this program independently. You will need to provide only initial help in working the program. If your child is an inexperienced writer, he or she might have difficulty mapping out choices and thus might require your sustained help.

This program is appropriate for the learning-disabled child, although a child who has significant language and memory problems might have difficulty with it.

Curriculum Areas

The program teaches reading and writing through a novel approach that involves interactive branching.

Reading

- *Comprehension skills*—reading stories, following complex directions, reading fictional texts

Writing

- *The process*—completing fictional texts
- *The mechanics*—using a word processing program

Reasoning

- *Planning strategies*—making decisions

The Program

(Tutor/Tutee). Your child creates stories by linking plots in interesting ways. The program consists of two parts, the *Story Tree Program* and the *Story Tree Stories*.

Three story categories—Mysteries, Science Fiction, and Animal Stories—are available; each contains six stories. Your child chooses the way a story unfolds, page by page. For example, in a story about a haunted house, your child can choose one of two doors to open. Behind one door, your child meets a ghost; behind the other door, he or she finds a long-lost treasure.

The stories branch out from one beginning to many possible endings as your child selects the page-linking features. A Continue link takes your child to the next page. A Choice link gives your child as many as eight paths to follow. A Chance link randomly sends your child to one of two different pages. For example, your child selects a story about bigfoot. At one point in the story, your child chooses from the following four branching paths: footprint sightings, reported sightings of bigfoot, what Native Americans and Tibetans say about bigfoot, or what scientists say about bigfoot.

The program features a large collection of graphics that your child can add to any story. It also contains a large library of sounds, music, and sound effects. Your child can use drawing tools such as brushes, pen line, oval, and floodfill to create original artwork and can use different text fonts to print the stories. He or she can also use a special-effects page to create interesting scene changes.

The program offers a built-in editor and word processor that permit your child to write his or her own branching stories and easily edit, revise, reorganize, and save them. In addition, your child can change the sample stories that the program provides. If a printer is available, your child can save and print his or her own stories and artwork.

Switchboard

8 years and older
Grades 3 and up

Sunburst Communications, 1988, $65.00

Hardware

Apple II series, 64 KB
IBM PC and compatibles, 128 KB
Tandy 1000, 256 KB
   ★ Essential: 5.25-inch disk drive

Abilities Needed

Because the instructions are complicated, your child is initially likely to require your guidance in using the program.

Curriculum Areas

The program teaches writing and reasoning by having your child unscramble out-of-order sentences to make them grammatically correct. The program encourages your child to think about the organization of language and about how to formulate sentences that are clear and well organized.

Writing

- *The process*—editing texts
- *The mechanics*—using elements of a word processing program, analyzing sentences for grammar

Reasoning

- *Analyzing information*—organizing and sequencing details
- *Developing hypotheses*—making inferences and deductions
- *Planning strategies*—making decisions, selecting relevant information to create a plan of action

The Program

(Tutor/Tool). The program consists of a game in which your child makes sentences from rows of scrambled words. For example, he or she might see

the	rain	go	grey
rain	clouds	are	away

There are three levels of play.

In the *Easy Level,* the words stay in their columns and can move only up or down from one row to the next.

In the *Intermediate Level,* the first and last words of each row are fixed. However, your child can freely move all the other words both within rows and across rows.

In the *Hard Level,* your child plays with no constraints and can move all words to any place in any row.

The object of the game is to create complete, correct sentences with as few switches as possible. When your child feels that the game is complete, he or she presses a key, which reveals whether the decision was correct. Many of the sentences have more than one solution. For instance, the sentences "She wrote down the number" and "She wrote the number down" are both correct although the word order is different in each one.

Feedback is in the form of written messages that appear on the screen. If the answer is not valid, the computer asks your child to try again. This pattern continues until he or she gives a correct answer. The program also offers hints that your child can use. In the *Hard Level,* for example, your child can get a start by asking to see the first word in the sentence.

Options make the game endlessly variable. Your child can select the number of words in the sentences (from four to eight words) as well as the number of sentences (from 2 to 10). As you might imagine, changing 10 sentences, each made up of eight words, can pose quite a challenge. Your child can select, from a wide range of themes, the topics he or she wants the sentences to be about (such as weather, music, or noises). If your child selects topics from literature, the sentences will be from a well-known book, such as *Huckleberry Finn.* Before your child begins working on the changes, the program tells him or her the name of the book from which the sentences are drawn.

Your child also has the opportunity to add to the game. The program has room for 40 new answers for each topic. A Sentence Editor option allows him or her to review the sentences that have been added, add a new topic, delete a topic that he or she has added, and edit sentences.

This is an excellent game to play with a partner. The material is challenging enough to appeal to adults as well as to children.

Talking Money

5–9 years
Grades K–4

Orange Cherry Software, 1989, $59.00

Hardware
Apple IIGS, 512 KB
★ Essential: 3.5-inch disk drive, mouse

Abilities Needed
This program is appropriate for the learning-disabled child.

Curriculum Areas
The program teaches your child the names and values of common units of currency and provides practice in adding and subtracting these units.

Arithmetic
- *Measurement*—using units of money
- *Applications*—applying measurement to simulated real-life situations

The Program
(Tutor). The program consists of five segments.

In *Money Talks,* your child sees various coins and bills on the screen. When he or she clicks a mouse on one of the items, the program tells him or her the name of the item.

In *Money Values,* your child sees a unit of money and, at the bottom of the screen, an equivalent value made up of smaller currency or coins. For example, your child might see a dime and, below, a nickel and five pennies.

In *Adding Coins,* your child sees several coins, and he or she has to add up their values. At the bottom of the screen, your child sees three choices and has to select the one that represents the correct amount.

In *Adding Coins and Bills,* your child works with a format similar to the one in *Adding Coins,* except that the units include dollar bills.

In *Cash Register,* your child sees, at the top of the screen, a picture of an item and the amount of money it costs. For instance, he or she might see a pencil that costs 18 cents. Below, he or she sees the amount that was given to the cashier. Your child must select which of two choices at the bottom of the screen represents the correct amount of change that he or she should receive.

The attractive graphics and clear speech of this program make it a good one for helping your child learn about money. The speech component of the program is used well, both to give your child information about units of money and to provide feedback about the correctness of his or her answers.

When your child is correct, the program offers a range of spoken responses, such as "Congratulations" and "That's right." When your child is wrong, the program tells him or her that the answer was incorrect; at the same time, the correct answer blinks on the screen. Unfortunately, the program misses the opportunity to show your child how to arrive at the correct answer. At the end of 10 problems, your child sees a summary of his or her performance.

The design of this program is such that you'll probably want to use it over several years. If your child is, for example, in kindergarten or first grade, he or she will likely benefit from learning about the names and values of units of money. In contrast, the *Cash Register* segment will probably not be useful until your child is in the second or third grade. This is also the sort of program that provides the opportunity for you to work with your child, discussing the problems and showing him or her actual units of currency.

Teasers by Tobbs with Whole Numbers

9 years and older
Grades 4 and up

Series
WINGS for learning, a Sunburst Company; 1989; $65.00

Hardware

Apple II series, 64 KB
★ Essential: 3.5-inch or 5.25-inch disk drive
Commodore 64, 64 KB
IBM PS/2, 256 KB
Tandy 1000, 256 KB
★ Essential: 5.25-inch disk drive
IBM PC and compatibles, 128 KB
★ Essential: 5.25-inch disk drive, color graphics card

Abilities Needed

The program assumes your child has mastered the basic drill-and-practice skills of addition and multiplication.

This program is appropriate for the learning-disabled child, but a child with significant visual-spatial or organizational problems might have difficulty with it.

Curriculum Areas

The program teaches arithmetic and reasoning by using a matrix to help your child think logically about addition and multiplication and flexibly apply these skills.

Arithmetic
- *Concepts*—understanding relational concepts, under-standing equations
- *Fundamental operations*—operating with addition, operating with multiplication

Reasoning
- *Analyzing information*—distinguishing relevant from nonrelevant cues

- *Developing hypotheses*—making inferences and deductions, eliminating alternatives

The Program

(Tutor). The program presents problems in addition and multiplication. Each problem appears in a 2-by-2 matrix. For example, an addition problem might look like the following:

	2	5
4	6	9
6	8	

A little character called Tobbs appears in the empty box and asks your child to enter the missing number, which in this case is *11*. For both addition and multiplication, your child can select problems from one of six levels of difficulty. The easier problems have only a single correct answer. In the problem above, for instance, the only possible answer is *11*. The more difficult problems involve more complex numbers and have more empty boxes, requiring your child to enter a range of answers in the matrix. Consequently, your child must think carefully to complete these problems because he or she must differentiate between answers that must be, answers that might be, and answers that cannot be. Each game contains four to five problems, and there is no time limit for any of the levels.

At the outset of the program, your child learns step by step how a matrix is formed and how to work with it. The program also sets out the rules that your child must follow. One rule, for example, is that all entries must be within the range 0 through 99; no other numbers can be entered.

When your child's answer is correct, Tobbs responds with a merry dance and your child earns one point. When his or her answer is incorrect, Tobbs shakes his head and asks for another try. Your child must keep trying until he or she enters a correct answer. However, your child can turn to a Help option, which gives answers that he or she can enter and thereby continue working.

Options allow your child to select the difficulty level of the problems, specify where Tobbs appears in the more complex matrices, and set the number of players per game (from one through four). The program includes a scratch pad for computations and calculator results so that answers can be entered in equation form.

The other programs in this series require 64 KB of memory and are available only for the Apple II series (3.5-inch or 5.25-inch disk drive).

MORE TEASERS FROM TOBBS: DECIMALS AND FRACTIONS (1988, $65.00) is designed for children age 10 and older (Grades 5 and up). In this program, your child again works with math problems in grids with missing numbers but must add and multiply fractions and decimals to solve the puzzles. The program helps develop mental arithmetic and estimation skills.

TEASERS BY TOBBS WITH INTEGERS: (1989, $65.00) is designed for children age 7 and older (Grades 2 and up). Your child solves the same kind of grid puzzles as in TEASERS BY TOBBS WITH WHOLE NUMBERS, but uses integers instead.

TOBBS LEARNS ALGEBRA: PUZZLES AND PROBLEM SOLVING (1983, $65.00), for children age 13 and older (Grades 8 and up), is an extension of TEASERS BY TOBBS. In this program, your child gets practice in algebraic thinking, making and testing hypotheses, and problem solving.

Teddy Bear-rels of Fun

5 years and older
Grades K and up

DLM Software, 1987, $39.95

Hardware
Apple II·series, 64 KB
Commodore 64, 64 KB
> ★ Essential: 5.25-inch disk drive (two-disk set), color monitor, printer, blank disks for saving work

Abilities Needed

Your child should be reading at the second-grade level to use this program independently. If your child is a nonreader, you will initially need to help him or her read the on-screen instructions. After becoming familiar with the format, he or she should be able to work independently.

This program is appropriate for the learning-disabled child.

Curriculum Areas

The program teaches writing by allowing your child to design custom artwork, create captions or stories to accompany it, and print out the results.

Writing

- *The process*—creating messages for visual material
- *The mechanics*—using elements of a word processing program

The Program

(Tool). This easy-to-use program contains two disks, *Teddy's Art Shop* and *Teddy's Library*. *Teddy's Art Shop* includes over 250 pieces of artwork that your child can use to design and produce stories, pictures, posters (from one to four pages), labels, stickers, and cards. The artwork includes 50 bears in three sizes (small, medium, and large), 8 general and seasonal backgrounds (the four seasons, windy day, beach, lake, and picnic), and scenes and props (pieces of "stick-on" art that can be moved around the screen). Your child selects from the pull-down menu one of the following instructions: See Picture, Get Background, Get Stick-Ons, Teddy's Library, Special Artwork, Data Disk (for saving up to 10 pictures), or Print. Selecting Special Artwork allows your child to use his or her original backgrounds or artwork in the Teddy Bear program.

Teddy's Library graphics disk allows your child to dress his or her bears in different clothing and to select 10 different decorative borders and 9 additional backgrounds. This disk also offers an easy word processing component that permits your child to create personal messages, stories, and captions to go with his or her artwork. He or she can choose from three typefaces (small, medium, and large).

You will need separate, blank initialized disks in order to save your child's creations for future use. You can print out work in both black and white or color. The program also comes with an Activities booklet that contains over 100 related activities that you can do with your child.

Tetris: The Soviet Challenge

8 years and older
Grades 3 and up

Series
Spectrum Holobyte, 1987, $34.95

Hardware
Apple II series, 48 KB
IBM PC and compatibles, 128 KB
★ Essential: 5.25-inch disk drive
Apple IIGS, 512 KB
Apple Macintosh, 512 KB
★ Essential: 3.5-inch disk drive

Abilities Needed
Your child should be reading at the third-grade level to use this program independently.

This program is appropriate for the learning-disabled child, although a child with significant visual-spatial problems might have difficulty with it.

Curriculum Areas
The program teaches reasoning and arithmetic by having your child apply visual-spatial skills to the construction of patterns. It provides practice in hand-eye coordination and fine-motor skills.

Reasoning
- *Analyzing information*—organizing or sequencing details, recognizing patterns
- *Planning strategies*—making decisions, formulating solutions

Arithmetic
- *Concepts*—understanding spatial concepts

The Program

(Tutee). In this game, designed by a Soviet programmer, sets of square pieces attached to each other in a variety of zigzag configurations gradually float down from the top of the screen. As the shapes move downward, your child must manipulate them (move them left or right, or rotate them on their axes) so that they fit in columns that form complete rows with no blank spaces. The faster the pieces come to rest in the columns, the more points your child accrues. As your child completes the rows, they disappear from the screen. After 10 rows have been successfully completed and removed, your child advances to a higher level, and the pieces begin to fall at a faster rate. There are 10 levels of difficulty (0–9). Rows with spaces do not accrue points, but new layers continue to form above earlier ones. If the rows reach the top of the screen, the game is over.

Two features allow your child to control the difficulty of the game: He or she can vary the speed of play and can also vary the number of rows in place when play begins (0–13). If your child selects 7, for instance, 7 randomly filled layers are already in place when play begins. The higher the number of starting layers in the pit, the more points your child receives for rows he or she completes.

Other options available are Advanced Mode, which doubles the speed at all levels of play; Tournament Play, which allows up to four players to compete; Help Screen, which leaves the directions on-screen at all times; Pause, which allows a rest period; and Next Shape, which permits advanced planning by displaying the next piece that will fall. (Use of this option reduces the score by 25 percent, however.)

Because the game is different each time it is played, this program offers endless variety.

Two other programs are available in this series.

WELLTRIS, the second program in this series (1989, $34.95), for children 9 years and older (Grades 4 and up), is a three-dimensional game available for the IBM PC and compatibles (256 KB of memory) and the Apple Macintosh (1 MB of memory). Your child positions shapes in a four-sided well with gridlike walls and floor. He or she rotates the falling pieces within each wall, as well as around the four outer walls (in a clockwise or counter-clockwise direction), while they fall deeper into the pit. Unlike TETRIS, your child has to remove columns as well as rows. The program offers three levels of difficulty with five speeds in each. As the level of difficulty increases, the falling pieces also become more complex in shape.

FACES, the third program in the series (1990, $39.95), for children 7 years and older (Grades 2 and up), is available for the IBM PC and compatibles (512 KB of memory) and the Apple Macintosh (1 MB of memory). It uses the same concept, but in this game, the falling blocks have pieces of famous and not-so-famous faces that must be stacked in the proper order to form complete faces. Your child must swap the pieces, flip them, and drop them into place. The program offers 10 levels of play and a tournament mode for up to 10 players. There is also a mode called Head-to-Head. In this mode, when your child creates a perfect face, the program dumps a stack of face pieces on his or her opponent's screen. The program includes 60 faces of familiar people, holiday characters, monsters, and so on.

Text Tiger

8 years and older
Grades 3 and up

Mindplay, 1986, $39.99

Hardware
Apple II series, 48 KB
> ★ Essential: 5.25-inch disk drive, blank disks for saving work
> ☆ Recommended: printer

Abilities Needed
Your child should be reading at the third-grade level to be able to follow the instructions and use this program independently.

This program is appropriate for the learning-disabled child, although a child with significant problems in timed activities might have difficulty with it.

Curriculum Areas
The program teaches keyboarding through a series of games and offers an introductory word processor.

Writing

- *The process*—creating simple written messages, creating fictional texts, creating nonfictional texts, editing texts
- *The mechanics*—constructing phrases and sentences, keyboarding, using a word processing program, proofreading

The Program

(Tutor/Tool). This program contains a word processor and four games to help beginners learn word processing and keyboarding skills. The main menu has five segments.

In *Keyboard Quest,* your child learns typing skills by pressing the letters on the keyboard to match letters that appear continually on the screen. Your child earns points for each correct key press. The goal is to earn as many points as possible before time runs out. There are nine lessons, each covering different letters. Lesson 1, for example, covers the home keys (*A, S, D, F, J, K, L,* and *semicolon*); Lesson 5 covers the letters *Y, M,* and *G;* and Lesson 9 covers the digits *1* through *0*.

In *Tiffy Text,* your child practices keyboarding and using different parts of speech. He or she types in specific kinds of words as the program asks him or her to enter a noun, verb, adjective, or adverb. When your child has entered all the words the program has asked for, a story appears with your child's selections inserted into the text.

In *Cursor Rally,* your child practices moving the cursor accurately and quickly. A story appears on the screen with targets in place of some letters and words. Your child moves the cursor up, down, right, and left to reach these targets. Whenever he or she hits a target, the missing words appear, and your child earns from 10 to 200 points. The goal is to see how high a score he or she can get in the shortest time.

In *Eagle-Eye Editor,* your child practices proofreading and using the word processor's editing features. With the help of on-screen clues, he or she makes four kinds of changes by using the editing commands Erase, Insert, Copy, and Move Text (letters, numbers, and spaces). A short story containing mistakes appears, and your child must correct the errors in the shortest time possible. Your child can select the Write screen, where he or she makes changes by typing in text, or the Edit screen, where your child uses the editing commands or requests a clue.

In *Word Processor,* your child produces text by using all the keyboarding and editing skills that he or she has practiced in the four preceding games.

Each of the four games has three segments: Instructions, Play Game, and Challenge Upgrade. Challenge Upgrade provides customizing features and record-keeping options. In *Keyboard Quest,* you can select the lesson to be covered (1–9), the speed of presentation (slow, medium, fast, and blazing), and the amount of time for play (1–5 minutes). In *Tiffy Text,* you can choose the story to be used, the level of the story (easy or hard), and whether the program offers examples. Each example defines a part of speech and supplies nine examples of that part of speech. In *Cursor Rally,* you can select the story to be used (1–12 or random); the difficulty level (easy or hard), which is defined by how long the flashing target box stays in one place; and the time available for play (1–9 minutes). In *Eagle-Eye Editor,* you can select the story to be used (1–12 or random) and whether the program offers help cues, which tell your child how to edit the mistakes. In all segments, you can turn the sound on or off and set the program to keep performance records for the 20 most recent games.

Think Quick!

7–14 years
Grades 2–9

The Learning Company, 1987, $49.95

Hardware
Apple II series, 64 KB
- ★ Essential: 3.5-inch or 5.25-inch disk drive
- ☆ Recommended: color monitor, joystick

IBM PC and compatibles, 128 KB
- ★ Essential: 3.5-inch or 5.25-inch disk drive, color graphics card
- ☆ Recommended: color monitor, joystick

Abilities Needed
Your child should be reading at the third-grade level in order to read the step-by-step instructions independently.

Curriculum Areas

The program teaches critical-thinking skills by having your child develop strategies to solve problems and make logical decisions. The program demonstrates that problem solving is a process of exploration requiring multiple approaches (exploring situations, stating and restating questions, devising and testing strategies over time) and risk taking.

Reasoning

- *Gathering information* — recalling relevant information
- *Analyzing information* — recognizing patterns
- *Developing hypotheses* — making inferences and deductions, eliminating alternatives
- *Planning strategies* — making decisions, selecting relevant information to create a plan of action, formulating solutions, managing resources

Arithmetic

- *Concepts* — understanding spatial concepts

The Program

(Tutor/Tutee). In this fast-paced interactive adventure game, your child overcomes obstacles and solves intricate maze puzzles while maneuvering through more than 100 rooms in the Castle of Mystikar.

The object of the game is to build a knight who can rid the castle of the evil dragon that guards it. Your child does this by moving through the castle, collecting clues and objects that help him or her acquire the necessary pieces. For example, your child opens locked doors, discovers clues in secret panels, and finds Magic Things and Passage Finders. After he or she has created the enchanted knight, the knight attacks the dragon and removes it, ending the game. On the way, your child learns to interpret maps, use logic to decipher codes and clues on secret panels, design strategies for avoiding the dragon and the slime worms that infest the castle, manage resources, and make decisions quickly. Your child must remember many directions and a great deal of information as the game progresses.

This versatile program has many attractive features, including six progressive game levels (two age levels, with three levels of difficulty in each) that offer increasingly challenging games. Your child earns more points as the level of difficulty increases.

An optional game timer allows your child to move at his or her own pace, while encouraging risk taking and spontaneous decision making. If your child prefers to play at a slower pace, he or she can escape to the Hideout, where he or she can take more time to study castle maps and plan the next move; if your child can play at a faster pace, he or she can earn more points. Castle Creator, the game editor, allows your child to design and build a new castle or to alter existing games by manipulating multiple variables.

Those Amazing Reading Machines I

8–11 years
Grades 3–6

Series
MECC, 1986, $59.00

Hardware
Apple II series, 64 KB
★ Essential: 3.5-inch or 5.25-inch disk drive
☆ Recommended: color monitor, printer

Abilities Needed
Your child should be reading at the third-grade level to use the program. He or she should also be able to understand complicated instructions, hold substantial amounts of information in memory, and visually process highly detailed graphics.

Curriculum Areas
The program reviews reading for detail and sequencing text. It also offers incidental practice in phonics, word building, and reading for comprehension.

Reading
- *Comprehension skills*—combining sentences, recalling details from stories, reading stories, identifying sequences of events, following complex directions, identifying main ideas, reading fictional texts

Writing

- *The process* — editing texts

The Program

(Tutor). This program offers your child the job of helping a company prepare its machinery catalog. The Editor asks for help in doing three jobs in three different rooms. Your child views wacky, cartoonlike machines in operation and then matches them with written descriptions.

In *Graphics Room,* your child matches a written description with the correct machine from a choice of three possible machines. For example, one description reads, "The teapot sits on a hot stove. Soon the water boils. The cork in the spout pops out and hits the ice cream cone. The ice cream cone falls off the shelf. The cone and ice cream land with a splat and hit the golf ball. The golf ball falls off the ledge and hits the spray-can button. Out comes a cloud of paint that nudges the cat food box. The box of cat food falls over. Food pours into the hungry kitty's bowl." Your child must analyze three complicated graphics and find the one that matches this detailed description.

In *Editing Room,* your child must identify and correct the mistakes in one of the lengthy paragraphs of a description so that it matches the picture of a machine.

In *Cut and Paste Room,* your child reorders the scrambled paragraphs of a machine description to match a particular machine.

Your child can access clues and help at any time during any activity. When he or she requests them, explicit instructions for completing the activity appear on the screen.

When your child completes an activity successfully, he or she is rewarded by seeing and hearing the machine function as outlined in the description.

Each of the three activities has from 1 to 6 levels of difficulty. (The number of components in the machines increases at each level.) You can vary the number of parts contained in each machine, the number of problems per activity, the mastery level for successful completion, and — in *Cut and Paste Room* — the difficulty of the paragraphs. The program allows you to save and print out your child's records to keep track of progress.

The series contains three additional programs, all offering the same kinds of activities.

THOSE AMAZING READING MACHINES II (1986, $59.00) is geared to children reading at the fourth-grade level.

THOSE AMAZING READING MACHINES III (1986, $59.00) is geared to children reading at the fifth-grade level.

THOSE AMAZING READING MACHINES IV (1986, $59.00) is geared to children reading at the sixth-grade level.

Tic Tac Show

5 years and older
Grades K and up

Advanced Ideas, 1982, $39.95

Hardware
Apple II series, 48 KB
Commodore 64/128, 64 KB
   ★ Essential: 5.25-inch disk drive
IBM PC and compatibles, 128 KB
   ★ Essential: 5.25-inch disk drive, color graphics card

Abilities Needed
If your child is a prereader, you will need to read the questions aloud to him or her.

This program is appropriate for the learning-disabled child, although a child who has significant problems in rote recall of information might have difficulty with it.

Curriculum Areas
The program fosters recall skills by having your child answer challenging questions on a broad array of topics.

Reading
■ *Comprehension skills* — recalling information on topics

Reasoning
■ *Gathering information* — recalling relevant information, seeking information in reference and available sources

The Program

(Tutor). An animated game show host asks questions in one of four formats: true/false, question/answer, fill-in-the-blank, and multiple choice. Using these formats introduces your child to important strategies used in school test taking. The game is played like Tic-Tac-Toe. Your child picks a box on the board, and a question appears. If he or she answers the questions correctly in three boxes in any row, he or she wins the game. Your child can compete against another player or against the computer.

You or your child can use the Change or Build a Subject Area option to create questions on subjects of your own choosing.

The basic game disk covers a wide range of topics, such as Myths, Math, Mother Goose, Sports Facts, Capitals, Body Systems, Presidents, and Children's Classics.

LEARNINGWARE SUBJECT DISKS are available ($19.95 each) to be used in conjunction with the basic program. Each disk contains 500 additional questions on a variety of topics.

Fun with Facts I (5–7 years, Grades K–2) and *Fun with Facts II* (6–9 years, Grades 1–4) contain math, language and social studies questions in 50 areas.

Young Explorers (5–8 years, Grades K–3) has hundreds of lessons to help your child explore the world around him or her.

History (9 years and older, Grades 4 and up) covers 36 areas, including such topics as explorers, composers, artists, and famous battles.

Sports Facts (11 years and older, Grades 6 and up) offers information about baseball stars, the Olympics, water sports, and other sports statistics, terms, and facts.

Foreign Languages: Question and Answer (11 years and older, Grades 6 and up) offers ready-to-use lessons in Spanish, French, and German.

Tip 'N Flip

9 years and older
Grades 4 and up

Sunburst Communications, 1986, $65.00

Hardware

Apple II series, 128 KB
 ★ Essential: 3.5-inch or 5.25-inch disk drive
IBM PC and compatibles, 128 KB
 ★ Essential: 5.25-inch disk drive, color graphics card

Curriculum Areas

The program teaches reasoning skills by having your child think through a series of moves to arrive at a pattern that matches a specified design.

Reasoning

- *Gathering information* — seeking information in available sources, taking notes
- *Analyzing information* — organizing details, recognizing patterns
- *Developing hypotheses* — eliminating alternatives
- *Planning strategies* — making decisions, selecting relevant information to create a plan of action

Arithmetic

- *Concepts* — understanding spatial concepts

The Program

(Tutor/Tool). The program shows your child a series of designs. Each design can be rotated in four ways: It can be turned 90 degrees to the right or 90 degrees to the left, and it can be flipped from one side to the other or from top to bottom. In the more complex problems, the design undergoes more than one rotation. The program offers two basic games.

In *Game 1,* your child sees the original design and two similar designs. He or she must recognize which of the two designs is the flipped version of the original.

In *Game 2,* your child sees a design and then a rotated version of it. He or she must figure out what rotations were used in changing the original design.

In both games, your child has access to the Scratch Pad, a help device with which he or she can try out various rotations before making a final decision. Your child can use the Scratch Pad a maximum of 12 times on any problem. The goal is to reach a solution with as few uses of the Scratch Pad as possible. He or she gets 10 points for each correct answer and a bonus of 2 points for giving the answer in the shortest number of moves. However, your child loses a point for each use of the Scratch Pad.

The teaching aspect of this program is strong. When your child makes an incorrect choice, the computer asks if he or she would like to see why the selection was wrong. It then tells what rotations were necessary and shows your child the effects of each rotation, so that he or she sees the process step by step.

The program offers wide variation that maintains interest and motivation. In each game, your child can select one of four levels of difficulty, choose which of three possible designs to work with, and specify the number of problems in the game.

This program lends itself to team play, with your child working with a partner.

Tonk in the Land of Buddy-Bots

4–8 years
Grades PreK–3

Mindscape Educational Software, 1984, $29.95

Hardware
Apple II series, 64 KB
IBM PC and compatibles, 128 KB
★ Essential: 5.25-inch disk drive
☆ Recommended: joystick, color monitor

Abilities Needed
Your child should be reading at the second-grade level to be able to play the game independently from the start. Otherwise, he or she will need your help to become familiar with the varied formats.

This program is appropriate for the learning-disabled child, although a child with significant organizational or timing problems might have difficulty with it.

Curriculum Areas

The program teaches reasoning skills by having your child analyze visual patterns on the basis of detail, sequence, and timing.

Reasoning

- *Gathering information*—recalling relevant information
- *Analyzing relevant information*—distinguishing relevant from nonrelevant cues, organizing and sequencing details, recognizing patterns
- *Developing hypotheses*—eliminating alternatives
- *Planning strategies*—making decisions

Arithmetic

- *Concepts*—understanding spatial concepts
- *Applications*—using visual representations

The Program

(Tutor). The program offers two main activities.

In *Adventure,* Buddy-Bot has fallen apart and your child guides Tonk around Buddy-Bot Land looking for Buddy-Bot parts so that he or she can put the creature together again. For example, your child can lead Tonk into caves, where Tonk can play a game. If Tonk is successful, the reward is one of the missing parts. The game has 4 difficulty levels: In the first level, 3 parts are missing; in the second level, 6 parts are missing, and Tonk encounters dangers during the search; in the third level, 12 parts are missing; and in the fourth level, 12 parts are missing, and there are more dangers in the search, such as Gork and Gork's Soldiers. If Tonk comes into contact with them, he loses one of the parts he has found. The manual provides a map that your child can use to plan the search through Buddy-Bot Land.

In *Games,* your child chooses one of six activities.

- In *Different/Alike,* your child sees six creatures and has to identify the one that is different or the two that are the same.
- In *Match the Shadow,* your child sees a creature and six outlines, or shadows. Your child has to identify the shadow that matches the creature.

- In *Minibot Shuffle,* a Minibot (a robotlike creature) hides in one of three boxes. Much as in the shell game, the program shuffles boxes around on the screen. When the shuffling stops, your child must identify the box that contains the Minibot.

- In *Remember Me,* a Buddy-Bot appears, and then vanishes. Your child then sees a range of parts, some of which are correct and some of which are not. He or she decides which parts to use in reconstructing a figure so that it is identical to the original Buddy-Bot.

- In *Buddy-Bot Puzzle,* once again, a Buddy-Bot appears, and then vanishes. A series of parts, all correct, then appears. Your child must place the parts in the same sequence as they appeared in the original picture.

- In *Minibot Factory,* your child sees an assembly line of Minibot parts. Your child gets a part from the assembly line by pressing a key. He or she then gradually creates his or her own minibot.

With the exception of *Minibot Factory,* each game offers four levels of difficulty. In *Different/Alike,* for example, the differences between the creatures become more subtle at each level, whereas in *Remember Me,* the game speeds up at each level, and your child must really concentrate in order to perform accurately. The levels allow for great variation, and even you are likely to be challenged by some of the games.

In most of the games, the program tells your child, after the first attempt, when he or she has made an incorrect choice.

The graphics and sound in this program are very attractive. The manual is clear but relatively extensive. Unless your child can read directions independently, you should plan to go over the manual thoroughly with him or her before he or she plays the games.

Type to Learn

7 years and older
Grades 2 and up

Sunburst Communications, 1986, $75.00

Hardware
Apple II series, 64 KB
- ★ Essential: 3.5-inch or 5.25-inch disk drive (two-disk set), color monitor
- ☆ Recommended: printer

IBM PC and compatibles, 128 KB
- ★ Essential: 5.25-inch disk drive (two-disk set), color graphics card, color monitor
- ☆ Recommended: printer

IBM PS/2 256 KB
- ★ Essential: 3.5-inch disk drive (two-disk set), color monitor
- ☆ Recommended: printer

Abilities Needed
Your child should be reading at the second-grade level to use this program independently. He or she should also have developed the manual dexterity necessary for keyboarding.

This program is appropriate for the learning-disabled child.

Curriculum Areas
The program teaches keyboarding using a language-based format that also teaches many written-language rules, such as spelling and punctuation.

Writing
- *The mechanics*—keyboarding, spelling single-syllable words, spelling multisyllable words, using elements of a word processing program, analyzing sentences for parts of speech, using punctuation

The Program
(Tool/Tutor). Qwerty, an animated asterisk, guides your child through the program, which teaches keyboarding techniques for letter, number, and punctuation keys in combination with language-arts skills. During

various keyboarding exercises, for instance, the program arranges words to show spelling patterns, which your child must reproduce. The main menu offers four choices.

In *Learn New Keys,* your child works through 23 lessons that systematically teach the keys on the keyboard. At the beginning of each lesson, the program tells your child which letters will be taught and displays a pair of on-screen "guide" hands poised above a keyboard. These hands demonstrate correct hand placement and finger reach. For example, Lesson 1 teaches the F key, the J key, and the Spacebar. The key to be learned flashes on the on-screen keyboard, and the corresponding finger on the guide hand changes color and demonstrates the reach for the new key. After the first lesson, each succeeding lesson teaches two new keys.

In *Games,* your child plays one of four different games that reinforce the typing skills he or she has learned up to that point and offer practice in language-arts skills, such as verb inflections. The keys used in each game mesh with the lesson your child is currently working on in *Learn New Keys.*

- In *Zap 'Em,* your child zaps letters, words, phrases, sentences, numerals, or punctuation marks by typing them as soon as they appear on the screen. He or she earns points for each correct keystroke in one minute of play.

- In *Take Me to the Top,* your child balances Qwerty on a board and tries to move it to the top of the screen by typing different words. The program presents words that require your child to type with only the right hand or only the left hand, so that he or she becomes familiar with the right and left parts of the keyboard.

- In *Know Your USA,* your child types postal service abbreviations of state names and uses the Shift key for capitals.

- In *How Many?* your child types in numerals that answer questions—for example, "How many colors in the rainbow?"

In *Scratch Pad,* your child uses a simplified word processor in which he or she can practice the typing skills he or she has learned up to that point.

In *Speed Up!,* a speed drill, your child types text, line by line, as shown on the screen. When the screen is full, the program highlights errors, and your child makes the corrections. He or she can print the work and ask the program to reveal the typing speed for that drill.

The program handles your child's mistake carefully. As soon as your child makes an error, the animated on-screen hands show him or her how to correct it, and he or she cannot continue until he or she strikes the correct key. In certain segments, such as *Learn New Keys,* a new practice session appears only after your child performs the keystrokes correctly.

The program offers your child several rewards when he or she is successful. In *Learn New Keys,* for example, whenever your child successfully completes the introductory exercise in a lesson, Qwerty reappears on-screen and spins. In *Games,* your child works for points and speed. Feedback on speed and accuracy is provided throughout all segments of the program.

This well-designed and versatile program can grow with your child's ability. You can vary the vocabulary level of the exercises. At the primary level, the exercises are at the second-grade reading level, and at the advanced level, they are at the fifth-grade reading level. You can also vary the text size (large, small, and mixed), set speed goals in words per minute (1–30 wpm), set accuracy goals of 50 to 99 percent, specify the frequency of lesson breaks (2–15 minutes), and turn the sound on or off. The program automatically keeps records for your child, which you can view or print out.

As with many programs that are designed for school as well as home use, the manual is extensive. It includes a special section with hints about how to use the program at home. The *Type to Learn Student Textbook* ($7.95) is a good additional resource. It helps develop keyboarding skills along with language arts skills involving vocabulary, grammar, and punctuation.

Where in the World Is Carmen SanDiego

9 years and older
Grades 4 and up

Series
Broderbund Software, 1985, $39.95

Hardware

Apple II series, 128 KB
- ★ Essential: 5.25-inch disk drive
- ☆ Recommended: color monitor

Apple IIGS, 512 KB ($44.95)
- ★ Essential: 3.5-inch disk drive (two drives or one drive and a hard disk)

Apple Macintosh, 512 KB ($44.95)
- ★ Essential: 3.5-inch disk drive
- ☆ Recommended: color monitor

Commodore 64, 64 KB ($34.95)
- ★ Essential: 5.25-inch disk drive

IBM PC and compatibles, 128 KB
- ★ Essential: 3.5-inch or 5.25-inch disk drive
- ☆ Recommended: color monitor

ALTERNATIVE VERSION

Where in the World Is Carmen SanDiego: Deluxe Edition
Broderbund Software, 1990, $79.97

Hardware
IBM PC and compatibles, 640 KB
- ★ Essential: hard-disk drive

Abilities Needed

Before using the program, it would be useful for you to show your child the value of the reference books included with the program and the importance of taking good notes.

Curriculum Areas

The program provides practice in the reasoning skills of organizing, analyzing, and researching information.

Reasoning

- *Gathering information* —recalling relevant information, seeking information in references and available sources, taking notes
- *Developing hypotheses* —making inferences and deductions, eliminating alternatives
- *Planning strategies* —making decisions, selecting relevant information to create a plan of action, managing resources

Reading

- *Comprehension skills* —recalling information on topics, following complex directions

The Program

(Tutee). This program motivates your child to learn facts of history, geography, economy, and culture while solving fascinating crimes. In an exciting game of pursuit, your child chases the notorious Carmen SanDiego and her gang of master thieves (the Villains' International League of Evil) all over the globe. The criminals are out to steal priceless national treasures and cultural icons—for example, the Statue of Liberty's torch or the gondolas of Venice. The Acme Detective Agency hires your child as a detective assigned to crack the cases. Your child must solve each case in a fixed amount of time, so planning and efficient use of information is vital. Solving cases leads to promotion from Rookie Detective to Sleuth and then to Ace Detective. At the start of a new case, the program assigns detectives of higher rank more challenging cases with more complex clues.

Your child starts out at the scene of the crime, questioning witnesses who offer clues. Then he or she must select one of four different tacks to continue the search. *See Connections* lists all possible destinations reached by connecting flights from the present location, *Depart by Plane* lets your child depart for the next destination, *Investigate* permits the unearthing of clues to help track down the criminal, and *Visit Interpol* narrows down the list of suspects and provides a warrant for the arrest of the suspect.

The program includes a reference book filled with facts and maps that your child can use to help decipher the clues. The clues, along with the reference information, lead him or her to the next destination. Your child can gain a considerable amount of basic knowledge if he or she takes the time to integrate the data on the computer with the material in the reference sources.

Your child can chase 10 suspects through 30 possible cities around the globe. Because each game features a new set of information, the program offers great variety. It teaches 1000 facts about the different countries, which are also available in the *World Almanac Book of Facts* provided with the program. Your child must interweave information from the program's Crime Computer and Police Dossiers as well as from the *Almanac,* to unravel clues and apprehend the crooks.

The DELUXE EDITION offers spectacular location graphics that look very much like photographs. The pictures, digitized slides from the National Geographic Society, form realistic backdrops for the animated Carmen.

There are three other programs in the series.

WHERE IN THE USA IS CARMEN SANDIEGO (1986, $44.95), for children 9 years and older (Grades 4 and up), is available for the Apple II (128 KB), the Apple IIGS (1 MB), the IBM PC and compatibles (512 KB), the Apple Macintosh (512 KB), and the Commodore 64 (64 KB). The program has your child travel through the United States learning about the history, geography, and economy of the 50 states and the District of Columbia. This package includes *Fodor's USA Travel Guide* and a map of the United States. The program involves 16 possible suspects and 1500 clues.

WHERE IN EUROPE IS CARMEN SANDIEGO (1988, $44.95), for children 9 years and older (Grades 4 and up), is available for the Apple II (128 KB), the Apple Macintosh (512 KB), the Commodore 64 (64 KB), and the IBM PC and compatibles (256 KB). The program has Carmen going after the treasures of Europe. In order to stop her, your child travels through all 34 European nations, tracking one of 16 possible suspects and using 1000 clues for each crime. The package includes the *Rand McNally Concise Atlas of Europe,* an online database containing additional facts on the countries, and a computerized Crimestopper's Notebook in which your child keeps track of clues to the suspected criminal's identity.

WHERE IN TIME IS CARMEN SANDIEGO (1989, $44.95), for children 11 years and older (Grades 6 and up), is available for the Apple II series (128 KB), the Apple Macintosh (1 MB), the Commodore 64 (64 KB), and the IBM PC and compatibles (512 KB). The program involves not only tracking suspects to different locations, but travelling in time from A.D. 400 to the present. Your child uses the Time Chronometer to travel through the centuries to 48 locations. In this complex program, it is essential for your child to keep notes as he or she gathers clues. The package includes the *New American Desk Encyclopedia*.

Wild West Math (Level 3)

8 years
Grade 3

Series
Micrograms Publishing, 1990, $49.95

Hardware
Apple II series, 48 KB
- ★ Essential: 5.25-inch disk drive (three-disk set)
- ☆ Recommended: color monitor, printer

Abilities Needed
This program is appropriate for the learning-disabled child.

Curriculum Areas
The program teaches arithmetic by offering practice in using math symbols such as greater than (>) and less than (<) and in completing number sequences with three- and four-digit numbers. The program covers basic math facts using the four operations. Your child also solves addition problems that involve carrying and subtraction problems that require borrowing.

Arithmetic

- *Numeration* — counting sequentially
- *Concepts* — recognizing terms and signs for mathematical operations, understanding relational concepts
- *Fundamental operations* — operating with addition, subtraction, multiplication, and division

The Program

(Tutor). The program's Wild West theme features animated characters such as Trailhand Dan, Marshal Dillon, and Bronco Buck and appropriate settings, such as the jailhouse, the corral, and the prairie. The program is on a set of three disks with two exercises on each, for a total of six activities.

In *Greater Than, Less Than* (Disk 1), your child compares two money bags showing different numbers. Your child reads the less-than (<) or greater-than (>) sign on the bank wall and compares the numbers displayed on the bags. For example, your child sees 1880 < 1763 and decides whether this is a true statement.

In *Completing a Number Sequence* (Disk 1), your child must determine the pattern in an ascending or descending number sequence. He or she then enters the missing three-digit number—for example, 158 163 168 __ or 117 __ 113 111.

In *Basic Math Facts* (Disk 2), your child, by solving basic addition, subtraction, multiplication, and division problems, uncovers one of 12 pictures of Wild West characters. Each picture is covered by 12 problems. When your child answers a problem correctly, a segment of the picture appears.

In *Addition and Subtraction* (Disk 2), your child solves addition problems that involve carrying and subtraction problems that involve borrowing. The program displays the problems on a poster outside Marshal Dillon's jailhouse.

In *Computational Corral* (Disk 3), your child practices basic math facts in addition and subtraction with two- and three-digit numbers. In this activity there is no animation, and larger numbers appear.

In *Wild West Test* (Disk 3), your child is tested on all the problems covered in preceding activities. This activity offers no motivational graphics, no aural or visual feedback to indicate right or wrong answers, and no tutorial help screens.

This program features appealing graphics and animation, excellent tutorial help screens, and a good monitoring system for tracking your child's progress. The rewards for correct answers are nicely tied into the Wild West theme.

A special strength of this series is the inclusion of interactive tutorial help screens that guide your child, step by step, through the specific problems with which he or she has difficulty. These screens are automatically triggered whenever he or she gives an incorrect answer twice. On the first incorrect answer, the program tells your child to "Try again." On the second incorrect attempt, the help screen appears. Your child can also request this help at any time during an activity. The help screens are available in all activities except *Wild West Test*. The program assists your child in solving the problem on the help screen before he or she returns to the activity proper.

The program allows you to tailor the activities to individual needs by selecting multiple levels of difficulty. In *Greater Than, Less Than,* you can vary the number of digits (3 or 4) in the comparison numbers and determine whether the program presents only one symbol at a time. In *Completing a Number Sequence,* you can vary whether the sequences are ascending, descending, or mixed; whether the sequences are incremented by 1's, 2's, 5's, or 10's; and whether the sequences are incremented by any single digit or by a multiple of 10. In *Basic Math Facts,* you can vary the operation presented (any of the four basic operations or a random array). In *Addition and Subtraction* and *Computational Corral,* you can select the type of problem to be worked on, such as addition problems with carrying, subtraction problems with borrowing, or mixed problems. You can also vary the number of digits in the numbers (two or three digits). In *Wild West Test,* you can use any of the options from the preceding activities.

The program offers a good monitoring system by keeping summary records for each activity as well as cumulative summaries for all activities. If a printer is available, you can print and save your child's performance records.

WILD WEST MATH (LEVEL 4) for 9-year-olds in Grade 4 and WILD WEST MATH (LEVEL 5) for 10-year-olds in Grade 5 are the two other programs in this series (1990, $49.95 each). Each program contains three disks, with six activities in a format similar to that of the Level 3 program.

In WILD WEST MATH (LEVEL 4), your child works on place values through billions and on rounding numbers to the nearest ten, hundred, and thousand. Your child also does timed drills on basic math operations with two-, three-, and four-digit numbers.

In WILD WEST MATH (LEVEL 5), your child determines factors of numbers, identifies prime and composite numbers, and reads different types of graphs for information. He or she also computes whole numbers and decimals using the four math operations, reduces fractions to their lowest terms, makes equivalent fractions, and adds and subtracts proper fractions with like denominators.

Word Attack Plus!

9 years and older
Grades 4 and up

Davidson, 1988, $49.95

Hardware
Apple II series, 128 KB
  ★ Essential: 3.5-inch or 5.25-inch disk drive
  ☆ Recommended: printer, mouse or joystick
IBM PC and compatibles, 512 KB
  ★ Essential: 3.5-inch or 5.25-inch disk drive, color graphics card
  ☆ Recommended: printer, mouse or joystick

Abilities Needed
This program is appropriate for the learning-disabled child, although a child with problems in rote memorization might have difficulty with it.

Curriculum Areas
The program helps build your child's receptive vocabulary (words that your child understands when he or she hears or reads them). Your child learns new words, their meanings, and the correct usage.

Reading
  ■ *Decoding skills*—enlarging vocabulary, defining words
  ■ *Comprehension skills*—recalling information on topics, playing word games

---

ALTERNATIVE VERSION

Word Attack
Davidson, 1983, $49.95

Hardware
Apple II series, 48 KB
Commodore 64/128, 64 KB ($29.95)
 ★ Essential: 5.25-inch disk drive
 ☆ Recommended: printer
Apple Macintosh, 128 KB
 ★ Essential: 3.5-inch disk drive
 ☆ Recommended: printer
IBM PC and compatibles, 128 KB
Tandy 1000, 256 KB
 ★ Essential: 3.5-inch or 5.25-inch disk drive, color graphics card
 ☆ Recommended: printer

The Program

(Tutor). The program teaches over 700 words and their meanings, grouping them into 10 levels of difficulty. These levels correspond to grade level.

All activities feature easy-to-use pull-down menus from which your child can select adjectives, nouns, or verbs to work on.

In *Word Display,* the program introduces your child to each word on the list, providing a synonym or brief definition and a sentence illustrating correct usage. An example is *"Aegis:* a shield, power, or protecting influence. At one time, Great Britain had many nations under its *aegis."*

In *Multiple Choice,* your child practices, through two activities, the words introduced in *Word Display*. In Choose Word, the program shows a definition with four word choices. For example, your child might see the definition "A forerunner, a herald." The four word choices might be *aegis, levity, avocation, harbinger.* The reverse activity is Choose Definition.

In *Sentence Completion,* your child completes sentences by typing in 1 of 12 words from a list, after first being given a synonym or definition. For example, he or she might see "very old; In __ times man lived in caves." This activity requires recall, correct usage, and spelling.

Your child can ask for help in this activity by calling up the list of 12 words whenever he or she chooses to do so.

In *Word Match,* your child plays a strategy game in which he or she must correctly match words and meanings.

In *Word Attacker Game,* your child plays an arcade-style game in which he or she practices matching list words and their definitions. Working against the clock, your child earns points by moving the Hattacker character directly under the word that matches the definition shown on the screen.

The program uses high-resolution color graphics, animation, and sound effects for positive rewards.

Your child has two tries to choose the correct answer; after that, the computer offers the right answer. After five correct answers, graphics and sound offer positive reinforcement.

This work-at-your-own-pace program features an Editor, which allows you or your child to add your own words in three additional languages (French, German, and Spanish); a FlashCard Maker, which allows you to make flash cards with words and meanings for study away from the computer; a Test Maker, which lets you print sentence-completion tests; and a Printer Option, which allows you to print flash cards and Certificates of Excellence (for scores of 100 percent in *Multiple Choice* and *Sentence Completion* activities). The program also has a record-keeping feature. You can view the records on-screen or print them out for ease of assessing your child's performance.

WORD ATTACK and WORD ATTACK PLUS! data disks ($19.95 each) are available for grades 2 through high school. A special SAT Prep disk and a Roots and Prefixes disk are also available. Each disk contains an additional 500 words keyed to a specific grade level. In addition, data disks are available for Beginning Spanish (Levels 1 and 2) and Beginning French (Levels 1 and 2). Workbooks are available for grades 2 through 4 ($4.95 each).

Word Munchers

6–9 years
Grades 1–4

MECC, 1985, $39.95

Hardware

Apple II series, 64 KB

IBM PC and compatibles, 512 KB ($49.95)

★ Essential: 3.5-inch or 5.25-inch disk drive

☆ Recommended: joystick

Apple Macintosh, 1 MB ($49.95)

★ Essential: 3.5-inch disk drive

Abilities Needed

Your child should have a foundation in vowel concepts before beginning this program.

This program is appropriate for the learning-disabled child, although a child who has significant visual-spatial or timing problems might have difficulty with it.

Curriculum Areas

The program teaches reading by offering practice in distinguishing vowel sounds.

Reading

■ *Decoding skills*—blending clusters of letters into
  sounds, analyzing words for their elements

The Program

(Tutor). In this Pac-Man–type arcade game the program presents a word at the top of the screen, and your child must move Word Muncher around a grid so that it can "eat" other words that have the same target vowel sound—for example, /oo/ as in *book* or /e/ as in *tree*. The program covers both long and short vowels and vowel groups. While matching vowel sounds, your child must also be on the alert for danger: He or she can lose Muncher by selecting the wrong word, or Muncher can be eaten by a Troggle.

If your child guides Muncher to eat an incorrect word, the game ends. When this happens, the program does offer a cue about the mistake. For instance, your child might see an explanation such as the following: "The word *grew* does not have the same vowel sound as the target word *book*."

Your child earns points for correct answers. The number of points determines whether he or she enters the Word Muncher Hall of Fame.

Two options allow you to adjust the program to your child's level of ability. You or your child can select the target vowel sounds, and you can control the difficulty of the words.

Although the game is timed, your child can select a Time Out feature that allows a pause in the action. However, your child loses points when he or she activates this option.

Writer Rabbit

7–10 years
Grades 2–5

The Learning Company, 1987, $49.95

Hardware
Apple II series, 64 KB

★ Essential: 3.5-inch or 5.25-inch disk drive

☆ Recommended: color monitor, printer

IBM PC and compatibles, 256 KB

★ Essential: 3.5-inch or 5.25-inch disk drive, color graphics card

☆ Recommended: color monitor, printer

Abilities Needed
Your child should be reading at the second-grade level to use this program independently.

This program is appropriate for the learning-disabled child, although a child who has significant language problems might have difficulty with it.

Curriculum Areas
The program teaches writing skills through focusing on the basic sentence parts and exploring how the parts fit together to form complete sentences.

Writing
- *The process*—completing fictional texts
- *The mechanics*—constructing phrases and sentences, analyzing sentences for grammar

The Program

(Tutor). In a series of six well-sequenced games, your child helps Writer Rabbit make refreshments for his lively parties, while learning parts of speech, sentence construction, and creative story construction.

In *Ice Cream Game,* your child identifies the kinds of information that different sentence parts provide. For example, the phrase *before dawn* appears on the screen, and your child determines which of the following questions that prepositional phrase answers: Who or What, Did What, When, Where, How, or Why?

In three *Cake Games,* your child identifies the sentence part that answers particular questions. For instance, in the sentence "Two strangers forgot everything behind the door," your child picks the part of the sentence that answers the question *Who?* Then your child combines sentence parts into complete, orderly sentences.

In *Juice Game,* your child decides whether a group of words is a complete sentence, selects phrases that can be added to sentences, and determines which of several sentences has its parts in the best order.

In *Silly Story Party,* your child writes phrases for inclusion in a nonsensical story.

The program introduces activities in a systematic manner and quite extensively teaches and reviews the construction and organization of sentences. This program's strengths include the use of imaginative graphics and immediate and appropriate feedback.

The program controls the number of errors your child can make and offers good explanations about incorrect choices. In some of the advanced levels of play, the explanations are even more substantial. In most of the games, your child can attempt each problem twice. If he or she makes a mistake, the program first explains, in writing, the function of the incorrect phrase. Then, if your child makes a second incorrect choice, the program offers the correct one. The program also offers a Sentence Hints option that defines the parts of speech.

Each time your child selects the correct answer, he or she makes carrot cakes, fills up glasses of carrot juice, or makes ice-cream cones.

He or she loses a point for each incorrect answer. Each time your child answers five questions correctly, Writer Rabbit dances a jig, and a scoreboard appears on the screen.

The foolish stories your child creates in *Silly Story Party* capitalize on the fun of turning the familiar world on its head. Your child can save and print these stories.

The games develop progressively, and special options allow you to customize the program to match your child's ability and reading level. You can vary the speed (three settings), the number of sentence parts (two to four parts), the reading level (the words cover three grade levels), and the types of sentence parts. You can also decide whether to include the more difficult concepts of *why* and *how*.

The program can keep track of your child's progress. For some games, it keeps scores on separate charts and displays scores by skill area. Your child can save and print these charts, which are handy for assessing strengths and weaknesses. Your child can also print out an Award Certificate for the work he or she has completed.

Zeroing In

8 years and older
Grades 3 and up

Sunburst Communications, 1990, $65.00

Hardware
Apple II series, 64 KB
  ★ Essential: 3.5-inch or 5.25-inch disk drive
  ☆ Recommended: color monitor
IBM PC and compatibles, 256 KB
  ★ Essential: 5.25-inch disk drive, color graphics card
  ☆ Recommended: color monitor
IBM P/S 2, 256 KB
  ★ Essential: 3.5-inch disk drive
  ☆ Recommended: color monitor

Abilities Needed
Your child should be reading at the third-grade level to use this program independently.

This program is appropriate for the learning-disabled child, although a child who has significant visual or organizational problems might have difficulty with it.

Curriculum Areas

The program teaches reasoning and arithmetic skills by having your child use strategies involving addition and subtraction to achieve a result of zero. It also encourages your child to try different problem-solving strategies.

Reasoning

- *Analyzing information* — distinguishing relevant from nonrelevant cues, organizing details
- *Planning strategies* — making decisions, formulating solutions

Arithmetic

- *Fundamental operations* — operating with addition, operating with subtraction, applying the operations to negative numbers

The Program

(Tutor/Tutee). This challenging game can be played either with a friend or with one of six computer-generated opponents.

The game is played on a 3-by-3 grid that is filled with numbers randomly generated by the computer. Your child, for example, might see the following:

2	–7	–9
9	1	6
–5	5	8

The program also gives each player three additional playing numbers to use during the game. For example, your child might have *1 5 7* and another player might have *2 9 8*. Using the operations of addition and subtraction, your child must go through a series of steps that ultimately change the grid numbers to zero. The first player to create four zeros is the winner.

In the grid above, for example, your child might begin by using the number *2* in the upper left cell. He or she might use addition to combine that number with the playing number *5* in order to create the number *7* in the first cell. On his or her next turn, your child can use the playing number 7 and subtract it from the number 7 now in the first cell, which results in *0*.

The program helps your child on each turn by highlighting the numbers that can be used on that turn. When your child has successfully created a zero, he or she sees a message such as "Zero! Good job!" In addition, a counter on the screen records each player's zeros.

The program offers three levels of play.

In the *Easy Level,* most of the grid numbers are one-digit numbers, and only one operation is generally needed to reach zero.

In the *Medium Level,* more two-digit numbers appear on the grid, and most numbers require two operations to result in zero.

At the *Difficult Level,* most of the numbers involve two digits, and your child must execute two to four operations in order to achieve a result of zero.

Besides the ability to select different levels of play, the computer offers your child six computer partners, each with unique playing strategies. For instance, Joe the Monkey can count only to 9 and is bad at planning ahead, whereas Professor McClure has a Ph.D. in ancient Tibetan rope making and is an expert player of ZEROING IN. The program manual explains the different strategies of each player. It is helpful for your child to observe how these opponents play in order to learn various game strategies.

This flexible program offers many options. Your child can select game boards with numbers limited to positive numbers or extended to include positive and negative numbers. He or she can also call a tie game, give up, play the same game again, go to a new game, choose a new opponent, change the difficulty level, or go back to the main menu. In addition, he or she can turn the sound on or off and specify whether the computer-generated opponents are represented by pictures or text.

As with many other programs that are designed for school as well as home use, the manual is extensive and includes suggestions for additional activities.

This is a challenging game for anyone who loves to play with numbers. The multiple-step strategies needed to win at the upper levels of play are captivating, even for adults.

5 SETTING UP A COMPUTER CENTER IN YOUR HOME

Children seem to have easy access to worlds unreachable to their elders; they casually use what adults must wrestle with. Today that world happens to be electronic.

—Edward Rothstein, writing in *The New York Times* about the "high-tech child"

You've probably been amazed and possibly a bit intimidated if you've had the chance to see children interacting with computers. Even preschoolers who can't read a word on the screen seem to possess a sixth sense that helps them glide through the programs. It's almost as if they had been waiting for the computer to appear so that they could express skills that had been holed up inside them.

Your own reactions are likely to follow a different course. If you're like many adults, your adaptation to the computer age has been slower than your child's. You probably have the insecurities of a novice, and your child has all the assurance of an expert—a reversal of the usual parent-child roles. Instead of your guiding your child, your child is likely to be guiding you. Nevertheless, you play a crucial role.

YOUR INPUT IS VITAL

Even if your child is a whiz with the technology, it's quite another matter to use that technology to plan and maintain an effective educational

375

program. That job—the essential task of helping your child use the software in a disciplined and organized manner—falls to you.

You need to supervise your child's use of educational software in much the way you supervise other aspects of his or her learning. You work with your child to set up schedules for activities such as art, music, and sports; you monitor progress; and sometimes you need to modify the activities or redirect your child's efforts. Now you must help him or her establish routines for working on the computer.

Some Suggestions to Get You Started

The following questions and answers offer some guidelines for setting up a computer-based educational program in your home. The questions are those that parents most frequently ask us. You will need to shape the answers to suit your particular situation. For example, setting up a schedule is important, but your family's routine will naturally govern the specific schedule you set up.

Space is a problem at our house. Where is the best place to put the computer so that my child will use it comfortably and get the most from it?

Most children like to be close to the main center of activity in the household. Your child will not be enthusiastic about using educational programs regularly if it means having to work in the attic or basement. He or she will only feel exiled when it is time to use the computer. Nor should you put the computer in a high-traffic area where there is lots of noise and activity. A quiet corner in or near the main part of your house or apartment is best. That way, your child will feel a part of things and will be able to come to you easily anytime he or she needs help. And you, in turn, can readily keep track of how your child is doing.

If your child has his or her own room, that can be a good place to put the computer. If two or more children must share the computer, however, it's generally not a good idea to locate it in one child's room. Put it in a shared common area to avoid battles about time and ownership.

If space is tight, you might want to put the computer on a dolly so that you and your child can easily move it into place when he or she wants to use it. The dolly should have shelves or adequate space for each of the components, including the keyboard and printer, so that your child has everything he or she needs in one place.

What kind of work-space arrangements will my child need?

You'll need to allocate a bit more space than the computer itself occupies. Aim at creating a workstation that functions like a small, well-designed office. It should have shelves to hold the software, reference books, paper, and other supplies your child will be using. It should also have some desk space. Some programs involve more than a single disk, and your child will need a nearby surface on which to place all the necessary disks so that he or she can easily use them. In addition, some programs require note taking, and your child will need a flat surface for writing.

The terminology seems so complicated, and new terms seem to appear all the time. How do I ensure that I buy the right software and peripherals for my computer?

The reviews in Chapter 4 are one important source of information. Consult the Hardware sections of the reviews to familiarize yourself with the equipment you'll need.

Establish regular contacts among knowledgeable salespeople in a local computer store, and take your questions to them. They can provide you with information about both hardware and software. Remember that *software must be compatible with your equipment,* so you should know the brand, model, and memory capacity of the equipment you have in your home. With that information, a salesperson can help you determine whether your machine can handle a particular program or whether you can modify your hardware so that it will run the program. Note that you can run software programs for the Apple II series on a Macintosh LC if you have the new-style Apple 5.25-inch floppy-disk drive and if you add an Apple II series emulation card. Some stores let you preview—either in the store or at home—the programs you're interested in.

Read the computer magazines that focus on educational software; you can find them at newsstands or in the public library. They are good sources of information on the newest developments in technology, and they will also help you become familiar with the vocabulary—which in itself will make you more comfortable.

Publishers of software programs are another great resource. If you have trouble running a program, or if you have questions about it, call the publisher. Appendix B at the end of this book lists the names, addresses, and phone numbers of the publishers of all the programs we review in Chapter 4.

How much care do the computer and the software need?

The major requirements have to do with simple but disciplined housekeeping routines. Establish a pattern of good use and help your child follow it.

Hardware is quite sturdy. With reasonable care, it is not easy to damage, with one important exception: Liquids and electronic equipment don't mix. Quite apart from safety concerns, the fastest way to damage a computer is to get it wet. Spilled beverages are the most common threat, so it's a good idea to simply establish a rule against having anything to drink while working at the computer.

Software is the component of your system that needs the most attention as far as your child is concerned. Touching any exposed portion of the disk can damage the data on it, as can storing the disk near a magnet, such as the telephone, or in an overheated location. Dust and moisture can also damage disks. Show your child how to handle the software carefully—how to put a disk into the computer and how to return it to its envelope when he or she has finished using it.

Having a backup—a copy—of each program is important. With a backup, your child still has a copy of the program even if the original disk is damaged. With most programs, either the publisher will supply a backup disk with the original program or the manual will tell you how to make one. You'll also need to make backups of some of the data files that you or your child create. For example, when your child has used a word processor for creating reports, he or she will want to have backup copies of the work. Similarly, some programs allow you to create materials geared specifically for your child. You'll want to make copies of these.

The Apple II family of computers offers some simple software to help you make the necessary backups; you need to know little about the operating system that allows the backups to be made. With other computers, you need to become more familiar with the operating system commands you'll need in order to make copies.

When you buy new software, fill out and mail the registration card. That way, you're covered by a warranty in case of problems, and the publisher will also be able to notify you about upgrades in the program.

You'll find many well-written books in your library or bookstore that cover the basic care of your equipment and disks. Some of these are listed in Appendix A at the end of this book.

What sort of routine should I set up for my child? How often should he or she use the educational programs?

One-shot learning is a rarity. Most learning requires time. For the programs to have an impact on his or her skills, your child should use the software three to four times a week. Each session should generally run 20 to 30 minutes—enough time for your child to work through one or two programs. Sessions for a preschool-age child should be somewhat shorter—about 10 to 15 minutes.

It's best to set a fairly regular schedule. All children, with the exception of the youngest preschoolers, appreciate knowing what the overall schedule will be. If your child is over 8 years old, you can talk it over and jointly determine the best plan. Decide, too, how the educational software should be used in combination with his or her homework routine. As a rule, it's best for your child to complete homework assignments first because that's the primary obligation he or she has to meet.

How many programs should my child have an opportunity to work with over the course of several months?

Over the course of 2 or 3 months, your child should be able to choose from among 10 to 15 programs. That number of programs provides the variety that will keep him or her from becoming bored. The range is also large enough so that you can allocate 3 to 5 programs each to the four major skill areas of reading, writing, arithmetic, and reasoning.

On the other hand, that number is small enough to allow your child to use each program regularly. An educational program can have an impact only if your child sustains his or her use of it over time.

Some programs seem to be teaching identical skills. How do I determine which program is the right one for my child?

Actually, it's a good idea to have three or four programs that appear, at least to the skilled adult, to be teaching the same thing. Each program will treat the same basic skill somewhat differently. Having several similar but different programs keeps your child's interest level high and gives him or her experience in using the skills in a range of contexts, which strengthens execution of the skills.

Of course, you need to use good judgment about when redundancy is useful. It is particularly helpful in both spelling and math drill. But in some areas—for example, drill and practice for keyboarding skills— your child doesn't need more than one well-designed program.

How can I keep track of what my child is doing?

You don't have to spend a lot of time monitoring your child's work with a particular program, but you do need to follow the progress he or she is making. As we've mentioned in the reviews, some programs have record-keeping capabilities that provide you with a good idea of how well your child is dealing with the program.

You should also keep a steady eye on what programs he or she is using. Your child, quite naturally, is likely to favor programs that call upon skills in which he or she is strong and avoid programs that touch on weaknesses. It's important to ensure that the selections are balanced. One way to oversee your child's pattern of use is to set up a simple chart that lists the programs your child has used each time he or she has worked with the computer. Figure 5-1 shows one possible format for this chart. You'll want to use at least an 8½-by-11 sheet of paper so that you have plenty of room to write. That size will probably allow you to keep track of your child's use over a period of 4 to 6 weeks.

If your child is in preschool or kindergarten, you'll need to choose the programs. By filling in the chart each time your child uses the computer, you can ensure that you're covering all the main areas on a regular basis.

When your child is older, he or she will probably want to select the programs for each session. You can still use a chart but in a different way. You might explain the purpose and design of the chart to your child and then enter the names of the programs he or she has available. (Enter only one program title opposite any single block in the Dates Used column.) Your child can do the rest. After every computer session, all he or she has to do is enter the date next to the program or programs used in that session. In this way, you'll accomplish two important goals: You'll keep track of the work your child does and you'll be using the grid to teach your child organizational skills.

RECORD OF PROGRAMS USED

PROGRAM

Dates Used	Reading	Writing	Arithmetic	Reasoning

Figure 5-1. *A chart helps you track your child's progress.*

How often should I change the programs my child uses?

You'll find it useful to review your child's programs about every 3 months so that you can evaluate which ones need to be changed. If your child is old enough, you can discuss your decisions with him or her.

You'll probably want to keep some software—especially tools, such as word processing and drawing programs—as "regulars" that your child can use over many months or even years. You might want to permanently remove others that involve skills your child has completely mastered and replace them with new ones that are fresh and challenging.

You might also want to put some programs away for awhile and reintroduce them later. Some arithmetic programs, for example, teach skills across a range of grades. After your child has fully mastered the segment for one grade, you might put the program aside and bring it back when your child encounters a new part of the curriculum for which the program again proves useful.

How much should I interact with my child at the computer? How much assistance should I offer?

A major attraction of good educational software is that it readily lends itself to independent work. As long as you select age-appropriate programs, you'll generally find that your child is willing and able to work with the software on his or her own.

If your child is under 5 or 6 years old, you naturally need to be more available than you would be for an older child. As we've indicated in the reviews, your presence is particularly important in your child's first few sessions with a program. After your child is familiar with the format, you're likely to find that even your preschooler is able to move ahead without your steady involvement.

Of course, your child doesn't have to work at the computer alone. Your child loves to have your attention, and you're likely to enjoy many of the programs. The great advantage of educational software is that you needn't feel pressured to work with your child on it—but if you want to participate, it affords a wonderful opportunity for interaction.

In sum, be available to help your child over difficulties when the need arises, and feel free to interact at the computer in a more involved way when the program is one you'll both enjoy.

You'll be better able to help and work with your child if you use the manuals that accompany most software. Well-designed manuals contain information and suggestions that enable you to plan and to manage the programs in the best way. You needn't be concerned with sections, such as suggestions for group activities, that are designed for classroom teachers. Use only the information that is right for your needs.

I tried to buy a program and was told it was no longer on the market. What can I do?

Software is changing as fast as the rest of the computer field. Companies are continually adding and withdrawing programs. When this book went to press, every program we reviewed was still available. Furthermore, most have been issued recently, and they're almost certain to be in the catalogs and stores for the next couple of years.

Nevertheless, if it seems that a program is no longer available, it needn't put a serious crimp in your plans. First double-check with the publisher. Often the program *is* still available but—because of a corporate merger—is published by a different division or by an affiliate of the company.

Of course, you might find that the program has indeed been withdrawn. In that case, it's likely that the publisher has issued a new program covering similar skills. Before going ahead with the purchase, it's best if you can review the new program to see if it is equivalent to the original. In addition, the software charts in Chapter 4 can help you identify a comparable program from a different company.

I would like to coordinate my child's use of the computer at home with what he or she is doing at school. How can I accomplish this?

Schools are increasingly interested in working with parents because they're learning that parents' participation is critical to the success they will have in teaching the children. But coordination of home computer learning with the school curriculum requires time and effort, and some schools are better equipped to assist parents than others. The only way to find out about your child's school is to initiate the contact and see what arrangements are possible.

The first step is to talk with your child's teacher and tell him or her about your interest. Ask whether the school has a printed version of its curriculum or a syllabus that you can have. That way, you can see what the goals for the year are and select software that complements classroom activity.

This sort of information is useful to you regardless of the computer services that your child's school offers. Unfortunately, some schools still have minimal facilities. If your child's school is one of those, his or her experience with the computer will come almost solely from out-of-school activities. You can still use the curriculum information your school gives you to guide your selection of programs.

On the other hand, many schools now have computers available, and your child's home experience with the computer will be reinforced by the school experience. Incidentally, the teachers are often as new to the software as you are. In these cases, they are likely to be interested in exchanging ideas and information with you.

Of course, some school systems have extensive computer departments run by trained specialists. These professionals can be an invaluable resource to you in learning more about both hardware and software and in developing a home course of education.

A FINAL NOTE

As you work to become a full-fledged citizen of the computer age, keep in mind that you needn't try to learn everything at once. Ivan Berger, a *New York Times* reporter, offered the following comforting and useful advice: "Park yourself in a chair and spend a few hours reading [the manuals and guides]....Be patient." He's right! Over time, you'll be surprised to find out how skilled you've become.

APPENDIX A
SUGGESTED READINGS

Below is an annotated list of books and resources that you might find helpful in supporting the work you do with your child. It includes not only books about computers and education but also guides to recommended books for children.

Computer Learning Foundation. *Parent Pack*. Palo Alto, Calif. This set of three books—*Family Activities Guide, Everything You Needed to Know (But Were Afraid to Ask Kids) about Computer Learning,* and *Preparing for a Career in the 21st Century*—is published by an organization whose goal is to help parents effectively use computers and software with their children. You can write for the book at P.O. Box 600007, Palo Alto, CA 94306.

Hearne, Betsy. *Choosing Books for Children: A Commonsense Guide,* revised edition. New York: Doubleday, 1990. This is an updated edition of a book that has served parents for nearly a decade as a rich source of help in selecting books for children. It offers informative discussions about literature curricula in the schools and includes criteria for selecting books as well as an annotated book list.

Hohmann, Charles. *Young Children and Computers*. Ypsilanti, Mich.: High-Scope Press, 1990. Designed primarily to help preschool teachers set up computer centers in their classrooms, this book also offers information that parents will find useful, such as how to purchase computers, how to use software to improve language and math skills, and how to interact with a child at the computer.

Kimmel, Margaret Mary, and Elizabeth Segel. *For Reading Out Loud!* New York: Dell Publishing, 1987. Many parents want to use educational software in combination with other materials. This guide to sharing books with children helps you broaden your child's mastery of reading skills. It offers an annotated bibliography of 140 books, for children from 5 to 15 years old, that lend themselves to being read aloud.

Loftus, Geoffrey R., and Elizabeth F. Loftus. *Mind At Play: The Psychology of Video Games.* New York: Basic Books, 1983. This is a useful book if you're interested in psychological interpretation of why the computer is such a powerful force for motivating your child. The discussion is somewhat academic, but if your curiosity extends into this realm, you'll find the material informative.

Naisbitt, John. *Megatrends: Ten New Directions Transforming Our Lives.* New York: Warner Books, 1982. This book provides insight into the powerful changes that people in the United States are experiencing. It pinpoints where our sophisticated technology is taking us and offers a glimpse of the skills your child will have to master in order to be a competent adult in the years to come.

Papert, Seymour. *Mindstorms: Children, Computers, and Powerful Ideas.* New York: Basic Books, 1982. This book, by the developer of Logo Math, is one of the pioneer works in the field of computer-based education. Concentrating on mathematics, Papert outlines methods of teaching that capitalize on children's curiosity and problem-solving abilities. It is not a how-to guide, but if you're interested in models of how children learn, it is an engaging book.

Stewart, Lynn, and Toni Michael. *Parent's Guide to Educational Software and Computers.* San Diego, Calif.: Computer Publishing Enterprises, 1989. This book focuses on helping parents understand how to use computers with their children. It does not cover specific software but rather provides information about purchasing a computer and setting it up at home. It also provides useful references and resources, such as a list of organizations for children with special needs and a list of books covering a wide range of computer-related activities.

Taylor, Robert, ed. *The Computer in the School: Tutor, Tutee, Tool.* New York: Teachers College Press, 1980. This book was not designed for parents, but it has played an influential role in the way educators view the use of computers in the academic setting. If you want to get a "behind-the-scenes" look at education, you'll find this book informative.

Trieschmann, Mary, ed. *Innotek Software Resource Guide.* Evanston, Ill.: National Lekotek Center, 1990. This is a guide for selecting software for children with special needs. It includes information appropriate for children with major disabilities, such as autistic disorders, behavioral disorders, and severe mental handicaps. You can write for the book at 2100 Ridge Avenue, Evanston, IL 60204.

Wresch, William. *Practical Guide to Computer Uses in the English–Language Arts Classroom.* Englewood Cliffs, N.J.: Prentice Hall, 1987.

Wilson, Mary Sweig. *Sequential Software for Language Intervention.* Winooski, Vt.: Laureate Learning Systems, 1991. This booklet provides a detailed description of a language hierarchy and explains how appropriate software can be used for intervention at each of seven stages of language development. You can write for the booklet at 110 E. Spring Street, Winooski, VT 05404.

If your child has special needs, you might also find it useful to contact the following organizations:

Center for Special Education Technology
1920 Association Drive
Reston, VA 22091
(800) 873-8255

National Lekotek Center
2100 Ridge Avenue
Evanston, IL 60204

**IBM National Support Center
for Persons with Disabilities**
P.O. Box 2150
Atlanta, GA 30055
(404) 238-3000
(800) 426-2133

APPENDIX B
PRODUCERS OF SOFTWARE

Listed below are the addresses and telephone numbers of the publishers whose programs are reviewed in this book.

Advanced Ideas
2902 San Pablo Avenue
Berkeley, CA 94702
(415) 526-9100

American School Publishers
151 North Wacker Drive
Chicago, IL 60680
(800) 843-8855

Baudville
5380 52nd Street S.E.
Grand Rapids, MI 49512
(800) 728-0888
(616) 698-0888

Britannica Software
345 4th Street
San Francisco, CA 94107
(800) 572-2272
(415) 546-1866

Broderbund Software, Inc.
17 Paul Drive
San Rafael, CA 94913-2947
(800) 521-6263

California Dreams/ Electronic Arts
780 Montague Expressway
Suite 403
San Jose, CA 95131
(800) 245-4525

CompuTeach Educational Software
78 Olive Street
New Haven, CT 06511
(800) 44-TEACH
(203) 777-7738

Data Command, Inc.
P.O. Box 548
Kankakee, IL 60901
(800) 528-7390
(815) 933-7735 (in Illinois)

Davidson & Associates, Inc.
3135 Kashiwa Street
Torrance, CA 90505
(800) 556-6141
(213) 534-2250

DLM Software
One DLM Park
Allen, TX 75002
(800) 527-4747
(800) 442-4711 (in Texas)

Electronic Arts
1820 Gateway Drive
San Mateo, CA 94404
(800) 245-4525

First Byte/Davidson
3135 Kashiwa Street
Torrance, CA 90505
(800) 556-6141
(213) 534-2250

**Fisher-Price/GameTek/
IJE, Inc.**
2999 N.E. 191st Street
Suite 800
North Miami Beach, FL 33180
(305) 935-3995

Hartley Courseware, Inc.
133 Bridge Street
P.O.Box 419
Dimondale, MI 48821-0419
(800) 247-1380
(517) 646-6458

Houghton Mifflin Company
One Memorial Drive
Cambridge, MA 02142
(800) 733-1712
(617) 252-3000

Lawrence Productions, Inc.
1800 South 35th Street
Galesburg, MI 49053-9687
(800) 421-4157

The Learning Company
6493 Kaiser Drive
Fremont, CA 94555
(800) 852-2255

MECC
Brookdale Corporate Center
6160 Summit Drive
Minneapolis, MN 55430-4003
(800) 685-6322

MetaComet Software
P.O. Box 231337
Hartford, CT 06123-1337
(203) 223-5911

Micrograms Publishing
1404 North Main Street
Rockford, IL 61103
(800) 338-4726

Microsoft Corporation
End Users Sales and Service
One Microsoft Way
Redmond, WA 98052
(800) 426-9400

Mindplay
Dept. C4, Unit 350
P.O. Box 36491
Tucson, AZ 85740
(800) 221-7911

**Mindscape Educational
Software**
Department D
1345 W. Diversey Parkway
Chicago, IL 60614
(800) 829-1900

Orange Cherry Software
P.O. Box 390
Westchester Avenue
Pound Ridge, NY 10576
(800) 672-6002
(914) 764-4104

Roger Wagner Publishing
1050 Pioneer Way
Suite P
El Cajon, CA 92020
(619) 442-0522

Scholastic Family Software
2931 East McCarty Street
P.O. Box 7502
Jefferson City, MO 65102
(800) 541-5513
(800) 392-2179 (in Missouri)

The Software Toolworks
60 Leveroni Court
Novato, CA 94949
(800) 231-3088
(415) 883-3000

South-Western Publishing Company
5101 Madison Road
Cincinnati, OH 45227
(800) 543-0487
(800) 543-7672 (in Ohio)

Spectrum Holobyte
2061 Challenger Drive
Alameda, CA 94501
(800) 695-GAME
(415) 522-0107

Spinnaker Educational Software
A Division of Queue, Inc.
338 Commerce Drive
Fairfield, CT 06430
(800) 232-2224
(203) 335-0908

Sunburst Communications
101 Castleton Street
Pleasantville, NY 10570-3498
(800) 628-8897
(914) 747-3310

Tom Snyder Productions
90 Sherman Street
Cambridge, MA 02140
(800) 342-0236
(617) 876-4433

Unicorn
6000 S. Eastern Avenue
Building 10, Suite I
Las Vegas, NV 89121
(702) 597-0818

Walt Disney Computer Software
500 S. Buena Vista Street
Burbank,CA 91521
(818) 841-3326

Weekly Reader Software/ Optimum Resource, Inc.
10 Station Place
Norfolk, CT 06058
(800) 327-1473
(203) 542-5553 (in Connecticut)

Wild Duck
979 Golf Course Drive
Suite 256
Rohnert Park, CA 94928
(707) 586-0728

WINGS for learning, Inc.
A Sunburst Company
1600 Green Hills Road
P.O. Box 66002
Scotts Valley, CA 95067-0002
(800) 321-7511
(408) 438-5502

INDEX

Page numbers in italic refer to tables.

The manuscript for this book was prepared and submitted to Microsoft Press in electronic form. Text files were processed and formatted using Microsoft Word.

Principal word processor: Debbie Kem
Principal proofreader: Shawn Peck
Principal typographer: Ruth Pettis
Interior text designer: Peggy Herman
Principal illustrator: Lisa Sandburg
Cover designer: Rebecca Geisler
Cover illustrator: Terry Furchgott
Cover color separator: Color Control

Text composition by Microsoft Press in New Century Schoolbook with display type in Avant Garde, using the Magna composition system and the Linotronic 300 laser imagesetter.

Printed on recycled paper stock.